POWER, POLITICS AND LAND:
EARLY MODERN SLIGO
1568–1688

Power, politics and land:
Early Modern Sligo
1568–1688

Mary O'Dowd

The Institute of Irish Studies
The Queen's University of Belfast

In memory of my father

Published by
The Institute of Irish Studies
The Queen's University of Belfast

© Mary O'Dowd 1991
Published 1991

ISBN 0 85389 404 3

Printed by W. & G. Baird Ltd at the Greystone Press, Antrim

CONTENTS

LIST OF ILLUSTRATIONS

ACKNOWLEDGEMENTS

A book which began as a thesis over fifteen years ago has incurred a great many debts. I have acknowledged some – although by no means all – in the end notes, but I would like to express particular gratitude to those who encouraged the project in its initial stages: my supervisor, Professor Francis John Byrne, who first suggested that I study Sligo; the late R. W. Dudley Edwards and the late T. D. Williams whose advice, conversation and guidance I will always value; and the external examiner of my thesis, Professor Aidan Clarke whose comments and questions I found very stimulating. I would also like to thank the members of the Sligo Field Club, who were generous with information and assistance. The Queen's University of Belfast has supported the research and writing of this book at several stages: first, while I was a research fellow at the Institute of Irish Studies, and later when the university funded a sabbatical year which enabled me to transform the thesis into a book. My colleagues in the Department of Modern History at Queen's have always provided a congenial atmosphere in which to pursue research. I owe a special debt to my mother and my late father for their encouragement and support. I would also like to record my appreciation of the assistance and guidance given to me by the staff in the following institutions: the Bodleian Library, Oxford, the British Library, the Genealogical Office, Dublin, Hatfield House, Lambeth Palace Library, Marsh's Library, Dublin, the National Archives, Dublin, the National Library of Ireland, the Public Record Office, London, the Public Record Office of Northern Ireland, the Main Library in Queen's University, Belfast, the Royal Irish Academy, Sheffield Central Library, Sligo County Library, the Manuscripts Room in Trinity College, Dublin, the Archives Department and the Library in University College, Dublin.

In the production of the book, I would like to thank Colm Croker for his very useful comments and excellent copy-editing, Gill and Ian Alexander and Dr Anne O'Dowd for drawing the maps and Dermot O'Hara for permission to reproduce the illustration on p.88 from *The Book of O'Hara*, ed., Lambert McKenna (Dublin, 1951). The illustrations on pp 49, 67 and 109 are reproduced from F. Grose, *Antiquities of Ireland* (2 vols, London, 1757), ii; p. 147 from W.G. Wood-Martin, *History of Sligo county and town* (3 vols, Dublin, 1882–92), ii, frontispiece; p. 135 from William Petty, *Hiberniae Delineatio* (London, 1685).

Physical map of the Sligo area.

THE SLIGO AREA: AN INTRODUCTION

Access to Sligo

In the days of pre-industrial travel one of the easiest ways to approach the Sligo area was by sea. The area forms part of the north-west coast of Ireland and lies in the centre of 'one of the largest bays' which an Elizabethan naval captain had ever seen 'between the headlands of Cape Teelin and the Stags of Killala'.[1] Access to the area by sea has been recognised since prehistoric times, and it is probable that many of its earliest settlers arrived there by boat. The coastline of the region lay along a popular sea route which brought travellers from Scotland southwestwards towards the north and north-west coast of Ireland. It was via this route, for instance, that the Fir Bolg were reputed to have returned to Ireland following their temporary exile to Scotland by the Tuatha Dé Danann, and archaeologists have suggested that the builders of many of the prehistoric monuments of Sligo may also have used this sea route. Similarly, the Viking fleet which raided the island of Inishmurray off the north coast of Sligo probably came from the Hebridean Isles, while the Scottish mercenary soldiers of the middle ages are recorded to have first landed in Ireland at Sligo, where several groups were still living in the sixteenth century. The sea route was often hazardous. The destruction of the Spanish Armada as it travelled this route in 1588 was not a unique event in the history of the sea between Scotland and Ireland. Later in the seventeenth century the sea connection with Scotland continued to be important as many more Scottish migrants came to live in the region.[2]

The sea also established wider contacts. Some of the megalithic builders who settled in Sligo may have originated in the Mediterranean, and the maritime links between the Sligo area and the south of Europe were revived in medieval times when Sligo appeared on the portolan maps of Italian navigators. The earliest portolans which included Sligo date to the middle of the fifteenth century when Mediterranean seamen began to explore the north-western parts of the Atlantic Ocean. The interests of the explorers in Sligo were not motivated simply by curiosity, and it is probably not a coincidence that the earliest references to the port of Sligo date also to the middle years of the fifteenth century.[3]

The development of the port is not well documented, but in the late sixteenth century Sligo merchants were trading with French and Spanish merchants, and with merchants from the port towns of western England, and this pattern continued into the seventeenth century. For a later period, W. B. Yeats recalled the foreign sailors with ear-rings who frequented Sligo port in his childhood; and the local sailors' stories made him feel the world was full of 'marvels and monsters'.[4]

The coastal position of Sligo also provided it with easy contact with southern Donegal, and there are several early accounts of boat journeys from Sligo to Donegal. It has been suggested, for example, that St Patrick visited Donegal by sea from Sligo, and in later times it was George Bingham's sea raid on the Donegal coast from Sligo which precipitated the taking of Sligo castle in 1595, thereby bringing the lords of Connacht into the rebellion of the chiefs of Ulster.[5]

Not all travellers to Sligo arrived with the peaceful intentions of trading or settling on unoccupied land. The sea connections of the area left it continually exposed to raiders from the sea. The Viking raid on Inishmurray has already been noted, and the continual fear of the inhabitants in the area of such attacks is dramatically illustrated by the wide variety of defence structures, ranging from prehistoric forts to nineteenth-century Martello towers, which stud the long sea coast from Killala Bay to Ballysadare. The Tudor administrators feared a continental invasion of Ireland via Sligo — a fear which perhaps was belatedly justified in the late eighteenth century when French forces landed near Killala.

Apart from being easily approached by sea, the Sligo area could, again in the days of pre-industrial travel, be approached without much difficulty by land. Before the invention of modern forms of transport the situation of roadways was closely related to natural phenomena: 'Such physical features as mountain ranges and rivers have in all countries direct influence on the course of roadways. The gaps in the hills and the possible crossing places on the rivers are the most likely positions for roads to run.'[6] G. A. Hayes-McCoy has pointed out that there were three accessible natural passes from Ulster into Connacht, one being via the Sligo area, which, as he documented, was of vital military importance.[7] Hayes-McCoy's studies on military tactics and warfare can be elaborated by a great deal of documentary evidence which reveals that the Sligo area contained a road network which linked Ulster with south and west Connacht. An examination of the names of places through which the roads passed indicates their overwhelming dependence on the natural features of the landscape.[8]

Beginning at Lifford, the main north–south road passed through the Barnesmore Gap (*Bearnas Mór*: big gap or mountain pass), Ballyshannon (*Béal Átha Seanaidh*: ford mouth of the hillside/sloping ground), Bundrowes (*Bun Drobhaoise*: mouth of (the river) Drobhaois) southward into the north Sligo region, where it ran along the coast, travelling between the peninsulas via sand *fearsaidí* (sandbanks). The road then entered Sligo, passing on the way such places as *Bealach Dúin Iarainn* (pass of iron fort) and Kintogher (*Ceann Tóchair*: head of (the) causeway). The road passed from Sligo to Bellanadrihid (*Béal an Droichid*: the mouth of (or approach to) the bridge), where a number of side routes broke away from the main north–south road, which continued southwards to the *Bealach Buidhe* (yellow pass) of the Curlew mountains. From Bellanadrihid, a road ran through a pass in the Ox mountains into the territory of the Luighne (later designated as as the barony of Leyny). It skirted the edge of the Ox mountains and passed into Mayo via Belclare. Another road crossed the famous strand of *Tráigh Eochaille* near Ballysadare and extended along the sea coast via such places as Buninna (*Bun Fhinne*: mouth of (the) Finn (river)), Bunowna (*Bun Abhna*: mouth of the river) and Enniscrone (*Eiscir Abhann*: esker of the river). It travelled down the east side of Killala Bay and crossed the Moy river into Belleek (*Beal Leice*: mouth of (the) flagstone i.e. 'the approach to a ford distinguished by the presence of a flagstone') in County Mayo. Another route connected Leitrim or O'Rourke's country with these roads, coming through Ballintogher (*Baile an Tóchair*: the townland of the causeway) into the pass south and west of *Sliabh Dá Éan.*[9]

The place-names reveal the reliance of the routes on natural features. Man made use of these natural features and facilitated 'Providence' as the description in the Books of Survey and Distribution put it, by building bridges, notably at Sligo, Bellanadrihid and Collooney.[10] The road networks also influenced the positioning of castles and forts in the area. Many of these structures were erected along the roads, some perhaps serving as stopping-points for travellers, others as military defence points. The roads of Sligo are characteristic of many early roads, i.e. they tend at times to skirt the edges of mountains rather than extending, as today, down through the plains. Such roads, according to J. H. Andrews, follow geological features such as eskers and 'other patches of free-draining soil' and avoid 'bogs and alluvial flats where possible'.[11] This phenomenon explains another feature of the castle distribution of the Sligo area. A number of castles or forts were built in what today are very remote mountainous areas; but when viewed in juxtaposition with the roads, these fortifications can be seen to have in fact overlooked the routes below.

There is a great deal of evidence for the use of these roads from the earliest times down to the present day. Henry Morris traced the journeys of St Patrick through Sligo and indicated the saint's travels along the Sligo roads. The factual basis of the biographies of the saint may be doubted, but one of the earliest biographers, Tírechán, was a native of north Mayo and would have been familiar with the roads of Sligo, at least as they existed in his own time.[12] Colm Ó Lochlainn has listed the journeys which occur in many early Irish texts. Among these journeys can be found several accounts of the Sligo roads being travelled by such men as Columba and Finnian.[13] In the middle ages the annals refer to the *gnáthsligid móir* which passed over the Curlews. The O'Donnells made frequent use of the Sligo routes in the late fifteenth and sixteenth centuries, and it is the annalistic accounts of their journeys which provide much of the descriptive material of the routes.[14] Sir Henry Sidney wrote the first official administrative account of the north–south road in 1566 when he travelled from Donegal down into Sligo and over the 'craggie' mountains of the Curlews. Both Sir Nicholas Malby and his successor as president of Connacht, Sir Richard Bingham, were very concerned about the journeys which the Scottish mercenary soldiers made along the Sligo roads on their way from Ulster into Mayo, where they were employed by the Burkes. Similarly, some of the Scottish settlers recorded as living in Sligo and Mayo in the seventeenth century probably originally came to Connacht via Ulster and the road network of Sligo.[15]

The inhabitants of the Sligo area must have been accustomed to providing food and lodgings to travellers on the roads. The Binghams, for instance, apprehended a number of Sligo people whom they suspected of having provided refreshments for the Scottish soldiers before their defeat at Ardnaree in 1586.[16] The depositions of the 1640s likewise record the assistance given to British families by native Sligo inhabitants as they fled from their homes in Mayo and Sligo along the Sligo roads, heading either northwards towards Ulster or southwards to Boyle.[17] Perhaps, too, some of the cattle raids on the area in the middle ages and in the sixteenth century can be interpreted simply as the actions of hungry travellers. For example, the member of the Burke family known as the 'Devil's Hook' raided a town in Leyny on his way home to Mayo in 1593.[18] Similar raids on the region by O'Rourke and by other Burkes might be seen in the same context.

Viewing these routes in the wider context of the map of Ireland, it is clear that the Sligo area acted as a crossroads for the north-west of Ireland. It provided access from Donegal, Fermanagh and Leitrim into south and west Connacht. As Sir Geoffrey Fenton put it in his argument in favour of the crown possessing Sligo castle:

Yf yor lordship behold the chart, you shall find that this castle (being countenunced with a meane garrison) is of farr more ymportance to answer service in several partys in the north than any other, fir yt is such a brydle in Orewkes mowth, as yf he styrr never so lytle owt of order, yt checketh him and stayeth him at pleashr. Yt curbeth the Burkes in Tyrawley and stoppeth their intellegence with the Scottes, which heretofore had been the onlie grounde of all the great alterations in Connought. Yt maistereth the McGlanaughes and all the other wylde people of those fast countries, even to McGwyers countrey and lastlie yt keepeth in awe all Tyreconnell, and in tyme maie be a meanes for Her Majesty to gett Bellashenon, which is the strayte by which the Scotts were wont to make their waie thorowe Ulster into Connought. The chart will disclose these places more sensibilie.[19]

Sir Richard Bingham summed up the position of Sligo in 1586 when he described it as 'the door and key to that part of the province'. As chapter 7 will explain, similar sentiments were voiced in the 1640s when Thomas Preston was informed that the taking of Sligo castle would 'give the lord nuntio more satisfaction . . . than all the inland forts of Connacht'.[20]

Although Sligo castle was strategically positioned on a strait overlooking the north-south route, it was not on the intersecting point of the crossroads. The centre of the crossroads was situated to the south of the castle in a valley within the Ox mountains. The crossroads nature of this district is vividly illustrated from natural and human forces. It is here that the rivers Owenbeg, Owenmore and Unshin emerge from the watershed and flow together into Ballysadare Bay. It is here too that the diocesan boundaries of Elphin, Achonry and Killala (which probably coincide with pre-Norman kingdoms) converge. As one later traveller put it: 'river, road and railways jostle each other in their passage from the Central Plain to Sligo Bay and Sligo town'.[21]

Again documentary evidence demonstrates the manner in which the crossroads area was utilised. It was at Ballysadare that Columba allegedly held a meeting where

all the prelates of the neighbouring regions, and vast numbers of holy men and women had come to meet him; and to say nothing of the rest of the multitude, which was almost beyond counting, a great many distinguished saints of the race of Cumne are recorded to have been present.[22]

Columba, like St Patrick before him, is described by his biographer as having crossed over the strand at Ballysadare into Tireragh.

The assembly of Columba was a friendly meeting. The annals, however, are full of accounts of this valley as the scene of battles which usually began with a chase along one of the Sligo roads. The prehistoric battle of Moyturra is recorded to have extended as far as the strand at Ballysadare. Likewise the region appears several times in the accounts of the conflict between the Norman and native settlers of Connacht. In fact one of the first annalistic references to a member of the O'Connor Sligo family occurs in an account of a battle which took place in Collooney. Similar confrontations are reported during the wars at the end of the sixteenth century and in later times.[23]

The essentially mobile character of Irish warfare, combined with the crossroads position of the Sligo area, meant that the latter was frequently the stage for battles which did not directly involve the inhabitants of Sligo but were concerned with the seizure of the area for its strategic value. In all the major conflicts of sixteenth- and seventeenth-century Ireland the capture of Sligo assumed an important military significance. In the early sixteenth century Sligo castle was passed frequently between the Burkes and O'Donnells. Similarly, in the wars of the 1590s, O'Donnell's seizure of Sligo castle in 1595 initiated Connacht's participation in the conflict and also led to numerous plans on the part of the English administration to retake the castle. Indeed, it was while in pursuit of this object that Sir Conyers Clifford, president of Connacht, was killed in 1599.[24] In the 1640s the possession of Sligo castle assumed a symbolic importance in the battle between the parliamentarians and the confederates, and the castle changed hands several times during the decade.[25] And in the Williamite wars at the end of the century the seizure of Sligo castle was of crucial significance for the outcome of the war in Connacht. Between 1689 and 1691 possession of the castle changed five times when it was competed for by the Jacobite and Williamite forces.[26]

It is clear, then, that the Sligo area was from the earliest time of man's involvement in the region frequently visited by travellers, some of whom came with peaceful intentions of trading or of passing through Sligo on their way to somewhere else, but some of whom had more warlike interests in the area. Whatever the purpose of individual travellers to the region, all of them would have been exposed to the same natural environment.

Environment

The natural environment of the Sligo area is unusual in that, as T. W. Freeman noted, it contains a 'variety of landscape and life and absence of any marked individuality'. Geologists and geographers have noted that the area forms part of several different geological regions, some of which are 'more impressively and continuously developed' in neighbouring districts.[27] Thus the region is part of the drumlin-drift belt which extends from Dundalk to Sligo Bay; and also part of the limestone plateau which includes the present counties of Sligo and Leitrim; as well as being part of the Connacht highlands or highland border which can be traced northwards from Westport through Sligo into Omagh.[28]

These variations in the geological formation of the area are important, as will be indicated below, for an analysis of landownership, but it is likely that the casual traveller through the region was more impressed by the obvious features of the landscape such as the mountains, rivers and lakes which formed part of the road network or which could be viewed in the distance along the road.

There are several mountain ranges in the area which serve as natural borders of the region but also provide passes through which the roads described above could run. The Ox mountains, 'those tremendous up-heavals of the earth's crust, those strange mighty walls and barriers interposing between Tireragh and Leyny',[29] are the most dominating range of mountains in the region, and a physical map illustrates the way in which they effectively divide it into two parts. They extended from Clew Bay in County Mayo to beyond Manorhamilton in County Leitrim. The western part consists of exposed grey granite and gneiss, but further to the east quartzite appears, forming the 'peculiar bare rocky knobby hills about Collooney . . . and then a high narrow wedge of gneiss continues, rising over the southern shores of Lough Gill and penetrating among the cliffy limestone hills'. These hills join up with the range of mountains which begins in the south-east of the Sligo area with the Braulieve mountains and extends beyond Benbulben – a range of mountains which effectively divides the present County Leitrim (formerly O'Rourke's country) from County Sligo (formerly O'Connor Sligo's country). In the south the 'dark heathery ridge' of the Curlew mountains, consisting of old red sandstone and Silurian rocks, are, even today, a formidable border between County Sligo and north Roscommon (formerly the territory of the MacDermots).[30]

The mountains acted not only as boundaries but also provided passes through which the roads travelled. The 'daungerous passes' of the Curlews were described by many travellers, while the Ox mountains contained a number of passes which were used by Sir Richard Bingham in 1586 in his famous pursuit of the Scottish mercenary soldiers. Similarly, the passes in the Leitrim/Sligo mountains were used by travellers as well as by native refugees fleeing from English administrators.[31]

This latter function of the mountains, i.e. as a place of refuge, was important for many travellers and inhabitants in Sligo. The peculiar characteristics of medieval Irish warfare, as described by Dr Katharine Simms, involved frequent flights of chiefs, together with their stock and followers, into the mountains.[32] The failure of the Tudor administration to curb the power of O'Rourke can largely be explained by his ability to hide out in the mountains in the north of his country which bordered on Sligo. The Sligo family of O'Hart and the sub-chiefs of O'Rourke, the MacClancys, also inhabited this mountainous region, and they too were a continuous source of trouble for the administration. In 1588, when Lord Deputy Fitzwilliam travelled to north-west Connacht to view the Armada wrecks, he found that all the inhabitants of the area had fled into the 'strong mountains and fastnesses of the woods'. Captain Cuellar, a refugee from the Armada, landed near Grange in north Carbury and made his way into the mountains; in the course of his account of his Irish adventure he described the flight of MacClancy with his villagers and cattle into the mountains on hearing that the English army was on its way to besiege them.[33]

Cuellar also wrote that 'the custom of these savages is to live as the brute beasts among the mountains, which are very rugged in that part of Ireland where we lost ourselves'.[34] Cuellar's comments raise another point concerning man's relationship with mountains. Did the inhabitants of the mountains have a different lifestyle to those who lived in the lowlands? In the sixteenth century the north Sligo area between Leitrim and Sligo as well as the Curlew mountains were considered dangerous areas to travel through because encounters with bands of armed men were thought likely. Cuellar certainly gave this impression of the north-west, home of the O'Harts and MacClancys, while attacks on travellers in the Curlews were also of frequent occurrence. Bingham wrote in 1588 of the 'passaige and recourse of the bad men which daly haunte the Corlewes'.[35]

Caricature of 'mountainy men' in Ireland was also common. Yeats's portrait of the 'knight of the sheep' who lived in the mountains north of Benbulben was kinder than the satire composed by Tadhg Dall Ó hUiginn on the O'Haras who lived in the Ox mountains:

The first that I saw, he was the best equipped of the band, a youth whose vest was not worth more than a groat; one whom feasting or gaming never impoverished.

The second man, as I found, coming in front of the company, was a miserable fellow whose marrow had gone from him, I shall not leave him out of the reckoning.

7

The munition of the third wretch was an old javelin and an untempered, gapped ax; he and his makings of an ax in an encounter, I pity such a battle-equipment.

The equipment of the fourth fellow who flux-smitten marched with them, four shafts, that never knocked a splinter out of a target, slung across his rump.[36]

The hills and mountains of the Sligo area with their multitude of prehistoric monuments were the subject of many legends and folk beliefs which no doubt contributed to the perceived strangeness of their inhabitants. As late as the early twentieth century a native of Sligo remembers being warned as a child that the 'mountainy men of Leyney would come and carry me off' if he did not behave.[37]

The rivers of Sligo, like the mountains, acted as boundary lines. The most formidable river boundary was the Moy, which separates County Sligo from County Mayo. The Moy tended to flood following heavy rain, and it was reported that St Patrick, Sir Henry Sidney and Sir Oliver Lambert all experienced similar difficulties crossing the Moy from Mayo into Sligo.

Three rivers, the Owenbeg, the Owenmore and the Unshin, join together in the gap in the Ox mountains to flow into the sea in unison at Ballysadare Bay and also served as territorial borders: the Owenmore divided Leyny from Corran, while the Unshin, formed part of the border between Corran and Tirerrill.

Both Sidney and Lambert lamented their lack of boats to cross the Moy – which thus suggests that the river was navigable.[38] The prehistoric canoes found in Lough Gara provide evidence of the continued use of small boats for moving around the rivers and lakes of Sligo. In 1618 William Crofton was granted a licence to operate a ferry on Templehouse Lake and the Owenmore river, with power to collect fees for men, horses, mares, cows, sheep, heifers and pigs carried on the ferry. The ferry, which may have formalised an existing system, could have been used to transport stock some of the way to the port of Sligo, just as in the early 1640s boats loaded with yarn travelled along the Garavogue river to a ship waiting in Sligo Bay.[39]

The Sligo area has a plentiful supply of lakes. It is perhaps best known for Lough Gill, but in the south there is Lough Arrow and the wide expanse of Lough Gara, while in the centre there is Templehouse Lake and further to the west in the midst of the Ox mountains lie Lough Easky and Lough Talt. A noticeable feature of the lakes is that they attracted settlers who established residences along the shores. In particular, several of the fifteenth-century tower-houses of the Sligo area were built along the shores of these lakes. Thus Ballindoon castle lay on the shores of Lough Arrow, while Templehouse castle was built on the edge of the lake which was later called by the same name as the castle. Similarly, there are several castle ruins on the eastern shores of Lough Gill, while the O'Garas built their castles on the shores of Lough Gara. The reason for building these castles or tower-houses near lakes was that, like the mountains, the lakes could be used as places of refuge in times of war. This tradition continued into the late seventeenth century when the tenants on the Templehouse estate carried their goods to the island of the lake on the outbreak of the Williamite wars.[40]

Quality of land

A survey of 1976 estimated that about half the county of Sligo (approximately one-quarter of a million acres) was good-quality farm land; about one-fifth was in need of drainage and reclamation; and the rest was suitable for rough grazing.[41] Obviously this picture may need to be modified for earlier times. Land reclamation, particularly of bogland south of the Ox mountains, has increased the amount of good farm land in the area, but seventeenth-century descriptions of the quality of the land in the county provide some corroboration of the fact that the agricultural potential of the soil has not changed substantially over the last three centuries. It was, for example, the areas described as containing good farm land by the 1976 survey which attracted the most attention from land-hungry Tudor and Stuart officials.

The best land in the county is situated in the vicinity and hinterland of Sligo town and extends westward along the coast towards Killala Bay. This is also the area noted in a survey of the 1630s as containing 'good arable land'.[42] South of the Ox mountains the quality of the land is more mixed. As an account written in the 1630s put it, there was

in every part or quarter of land, land for the most part arable, meadow, and pasture, in some parts heathy and in some parts woody with red bog in some part necessary for fireing; but in other parts too great abundance thereof altogether unprofitable.

Other land in the same region was good for

all sorts of graine especially wheat beare and oate the usuall corne in that country; as alsoe for all sortes of cattle, consisting for the most part of small hills each hill being compassed about with low valley meadow ground, in some places, and in other places with turfe boggs, and small little loghs and through the middle of these low valleyes run small streames in deep narrow channels.[43]

A third of County Sligo consists of mountain and lowland bog which cannot be cultivated. Valuation of land is, of course relative, depending on the use to which it is put. As later chapters will indicate, many of the landlords – new and old – in early modern Sligo used their lands for grazing sheep and cattle. For this purpose even the resources of the poor mountainous lands of the area could be exploited. The Books of Survey and Distribution noted, for example, that the Ox mountains had a 'great store of mountain pasture', and the 1635 survey of the county also noted the pasture value of each quarter of land and commented that much of it was 'good for sheep'. In addition, the survey claimed that County Sligo had some of 'the best turf in Ireland'. Turf was a valuable resource for heating and cooking which could be marketed in Sligo town.

Another profitable natural resource in early modern Sligo was its woods. Up until the 1630s Sligo had a plentiful supply of woodland, mainly situated in areas which today would be considered boggy and unprofitable. The most valuable timber in the area lay in the woods of Coillte Luighne, which extended along the southern slopes of the Ox mountains, eastwards as far as Lough Gill, where they joined the woods of Slish and Killery and stretched southwards towards the slopes of the Braulieve mountains. There were also extensive woods along Lough Gara and Lough Arrow and on the southern slopes of the Curlew mountains. In the northern part of the Sligo area the Dartry mountains were also wooded.[44]

In medieval times the timber of these woods would have been used in the construction of boats, castles, houses, as well as for heating fuel, but it was not until the early seventeenth century that the exploitation of the woods of the Sligo area began on a large scale. The late Eileen McCracken wrote of the 'sort of industrial revolution' which took place in Ireland in the early seventeenth century – the product involved in this revolution was timber. Before this time the most important exports from Ireland were fish and salted hides, while iron was a major import. In the seventeenth century, however, the manufacture of staves for export became a prime industry, while pig and bar iron was made in sufficient quantities for home use.[45]

The new landlords of sixteenth- and seventeenth-century Sligo were interested in the woodlands of the county, and there is evidence of a trade in timber through Sligo town. The trade seems to have reached its peak in the first half of the seventeenth century, as the survey of 1635 reported that some of the woods of the area had disappeared or were in the process of disappearing, being 'dayley wasted by sale to Sligo'. The survey also notes the existence throughout the county of wood which could be used as 'firewood'.[46] There is little evidence for the establishment of iron or charcoal-burning works in the area at this time, although later in the seventeenth century a number of Sligo ironworks functioned for a short time.[47]

Fish was another valuable natural resource in the area. The salmon fishery of the Garavogue river in Sligo was alleged to have been blessed by St Patrick and consequently has had a plentiful supply of fish ever since. There is no record of St Patrick blessing the river Moy – perhaps because Tírechán reports that he was nearly drowned trying to cross it – but it too has a very valuable salmon fishery which has been exploited by men for centuries. In the fifteenth century Giolla Íosa Mac Firbisigh referred to the Ballysadare river as the 'beauteous stream of salmon', although it was not until the nineteenth century that the river was fully exploited for its salmon resources. The rivers Owenbeg, Owenmore and Unshin had, according to a mid-seventeenth century description, 'no comodity of fishing except some few eeles of noe great moment', although the 1635 survey indicates that eel and trout weirs were quite common on these rivers. The lakes of Sligo were also plentiful in fish, particularly trout, and Yeats's 'slumbering trout' of Glencar can also be found in Lough Talt in the Ox mountains as well as in Lough Gara.[48]

Conclusion

The Sligo area is situated in the centre of a natural passway which connects Ulster with Connacht. The presence of the roadway had a profound effect on the history of the area, as this study will seek to show. Physically, there is a wide variety of geological and geographical features in the Sligo area, with no one feature predominating. In general terms, the area is not over-rich in natural resources, but neither can it be classified as a poor area. There is some very good farmland in the district, and a large amount of reasonable pasture land which was used extensively in the seventeenth century. Even the boglands yielded turf in useful quantities. Up until the 1630s the area contained extensive woodlands, while its rivers and lakes were rich in salmon and trout. As T. W. Freeman pointed out, the Sligo region has many of the rich qualities of the central lowlands of Ireland, but it also has some of the characteristics of the very poor lands of the west of Ireland. Freeman compared Sligo with County Clare, which has a similar mixture of natural resources.[49] Despite the various geographical and geological divisions into which the district is divided, man had by the early modern period shaped it into a single political and administrative unit known as County Sligo. It is this process which is described in the next chapter.

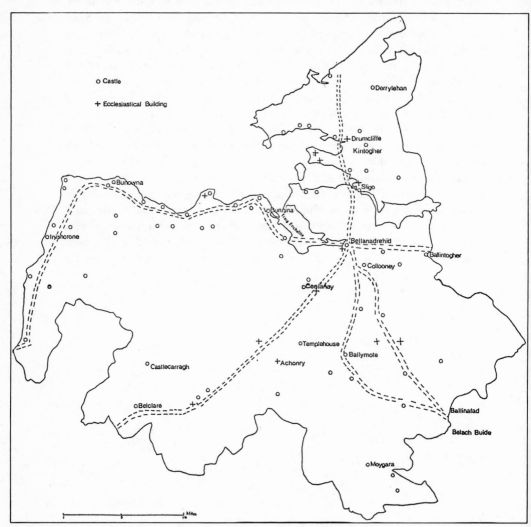

Routes and castles of the Sligo area.

THE MEDIEVAL LORDSHIPS
OF LOWER CONNACHT

As the previous chapter has indicated, the Sligo area did not form a natural physical unit. The major physical features of the region such as the Ox mountains, the Moy and other rivers divided the area rather than united it. The natural passway which crossed through the area did, however, give the area a coherence, and, not surprisingly, the roadway also dominated the political history of the region. The route which provided access between Connacht and Ulster meant that Sligo was strategically important and that political control of it was highly desirable. Indeed, in many ways, the history of the highway connecting the Erne with the Curlews or Ulster with Connacht is also the history of the domination of the Sligo area. At the same time, however, the presence of the roadway made it an easy target for attack from outside, and it was, therefore never a simple task to control the region. For these reasons, Sligo's evolution as a political unit was a slow process which was not complete until the later middle ages.

The Norman lordship

In pre-Norman times the Sligo area formed the junction point at which a number of kingdoms met – Uí Fiachrach Muaide, Luigne and Uí Briúin Bréifne – a fact still preserved in the three ecclesiastical boundaries which meet in the area. The initial Norman sub-infeudation continued the political division of the region. Following his royal grant of the province of Connacht in 1227, Richard de Burgo divided up his western territory among his vassals. He gave Hugh de Lacy the five 'cantreds' of Corran, Carbury–Drumcliff, Tireragh on the Moy, Leyny and Sliabh Lugha in 1235. This grant included much of the later county of Sligo, as well as the northern part of County Mayo, but excluded the western part of the county: the area which was designated as part of the king's cantreds and was reserved for crown use, along with other lands in and around Athlone. De Lacy, whose main interest was in Ulster, subdivided his grant between five other Norman lords: Maurice Fitzgerald (Carbury and the northern part of

Leyny), Jordan de Exeter (the southern part of Leyny), Piers de Bermingham (Tireragh), Miles de Nangle (Sliabh Lugha), and Gerard de Prendergast (Corran).[1]

Despite these subdivisions by the earliest Norman settlers, the beginning of the Sligo region as a political unit can in fact be attributed to the Normans. Maurice Fitzgerald and his son began the process by acquiring from other Norman grantees large holdings in north Connacht and Ulster, including parts of Leyny and Corran from Jordan de Exeter and the Prendergasts. This meant that in the Sligo region Leyny, Corran and Carbury were now united in what became known as the Fitzgerald manor of Sligo, and this was the estate subsequently inherited by Maurice's nephew, John FitzThomas, later the first earl of Kildare. There were still, however, four separate territorial units in the region: Sligo manor, the king's cantred of Tirerrill, and the cantreds of Tireragh and Sliabh Lugha.

The Fitzgeralds further contributed to the unity of the area by building Sligo castle in 1245, which was followed in 1253 by the foundation nearby of a Dominican abbey. The castle and abbey were situated at a key strategic point on the river Garavogue and thus played an important military role, particularly in hindering the O'Donnells' incursions into north Connacht from Tyrconnell. The O'Donnells had some claims over Carbury and clearly resented the Norman intrusion into the Sligo region. The building of Sligo castle established a more definite border between Connacht and Ulster and thus divided the two provinces more effectively than ever before. It also focused new attention on the Sligo region.[2] Sligo castle became the most important military site along the passway between the two provinces and, as such, was the target for attack and seizure. The long series of attempts to win control of the castle was one of the most continuous themes of the subsequent history of the area.

The establishment of the castle and abbey also formed the nucleus of a town which reinforced the coherence of the region. For the first time the Sligo area was developing into a recognisable unit in its own right. The Fitzgerald presence and that of the other Norman lords in the area was temporary, but their creation of Sligo town and its surrounding manor was to survive and expand in subsequent generations.

In the late 1290s a dispute arose between John FitzThomas and Richard de Burgo, first earl of Ulster (Richard de Burgo's heir), concerning the ownership of the lands in Connacht. Technically FitzThomas was a tenant of de Burgo's, but he tried unsuccessfully to hold his Connacht lands directly of the king. The dispute was settled in de Burgo's favour, and FitzThomas agreed to give all his Connacht lands to de Burgo. Sligo manor was thus absorbed into the much larger unit of the earldom of Ulster. In 1300, probably in order to emphasise his position as the major feudal lord in the region, de Burgo built the large and impressive Ballymote castle in the centre of his Sligo manor. But the de Burgos had a difficult struggle in maintaining their Connacht property. By 1338 the annals report that

Turlough O'Connor had established his ascendancy over Connacht and that the new settlers had been driven from Leyny and Corran.[3] The so-called Gaelic revival had begun.

The Gaelic revival

In north Connacht the Gaelic revival took several forms. First, the pre-Norman ruling dynasties, the O'Dowds, the O'Haras and the O'Garas, recovered some of their former territory. It is likely that they always remained in occupation on these lands, but they were submerged by Norman control in the thirteenth century. The revival of the former ruling dynasties was not spectacular, and none of them recovered the status or territorial control which they had enjoyed in pre-Norman Ireland. The O'Dowds (kings of Ui Fiachrach Muaide) were confined to a small portion of their former territory in Tireragh; the O'Haras of Luigne remained excluded from the southern part of old Luigne; while the O'Garas were reduced from being kings of Sliabh Lugha to being lords of Coolavin, a much smaller territory. All of these families lost territory permanently to Norman settlers who remained in Connacht despite the general decline in Norman control in the province. This gave rise to a second marked feature of the Gaelic revival in the area: the beginning of the gaelicisation of Norman families such as the Burkes, the Barretts, the Costelloes, Exeters and Fitzmorrises who settled to the west and south of the Sligo region. No prominent Norman family remained in the region itself, but the settlement by the Costelloes, Burkes and Barretts in the Mayo area effectively set the boundary limits to the land recovered by the older ruling families. Where Norman settlers remained, they retained control of the land.[4]

Not all pre-Norman rulers recovered their territory – even in a limited way. Some disappeared altogether. This was the case with the Ó Dobhailens of Corran, who were replaced not by a Norman family but by the Irish family of MacDonagh, a new dynastic power. The rise of new lordships was a third aspect of the Gaelic recovery in the area. The power of the older ruling families was never fully restored, but as the Norman control declined, newly founded Irish dynasties appeared to fill the political vacuum. The two most important new families to emerge in north Connacht were the O'Connors of Sligo and the MacDonaghs. Both these families make their first appearance in the annals in the late thirteenth century, and their emergence as significant political powers in the region coincides with the Norman decline and also, of course, with the weakening of their former superiors, the main branch of the O'Connors.

The O'Connor lordship

The Sligo O'Connors were a minor branch of the royal family, associated with the extreme northern part of Connacht bordering on O'Donnell's country of Tyrconnell. They first appear in the annals in 1291 as supporters of one of the two contending O'Connor septs for the kingship of Connacht.

They were given the title of *tánaiste*, possibly in recognition of their support for the ruling family. They quickly, however, benefited from the chaos in Connacht in the early fourteenth century to establish themselves as a significant political force in their own right. One member of the family, Cathal, managed to seize the kingship of Connacht for a short period, although he was later deposed by one of the more southerly O'Connor septs. However, in the developing circumstances of medieval Ireland failure to retain the provincial kingship was not important. The real power now lay in the growing number of autonomous lordships which were appearing in the province. The days of the provincial kingship were over: those of the lordships were just beginning. The O'Connors of north Connacht flourished in this new political world.[5]

The titles given to the leaders of the O'Connors in the annals reflect the growth in importance of the family. In 1307 Domhnall O'Connor died lord from the Curlews to Belleek, but by 1395 his descendant, another Domhnall, died lord of Sligo and Lower Connacht. Thus in the course of the fourteenth century the O'Connors expanded from their north Connacht base southwards as far as the Curlews and included Sligo castle among their acquisitions. The first reference to O'Connor occupation of Sligo is in 1362, when a member of the family died there; this suggests that they had probably seized the castle some time in the middle years of the fourteenth century. From this time on the castle became the main centre for the family, and by 1395 control of Sligo was an important part of their lordship.[6]

The O'Connors Sligo had taken over the Fitzgerald establishment at Sligo and also their lands in Carbury, but whether they immediately became lords of the whole of the former Sligo manor is not clear. As indicated above, by 1395 O'Connor was not just lord of Sligo but was also recognised as lord of Lower Connacht. This term is later taken to mean the territory of the O'Connors, the MacDonaghs, the O'Haras, the O'Garas and the O'Dowds, and would therefore have included all the manor land. The MacDonaghs from their first appearance in the annals (also in the late thirteenth century) are usually supportive of and, probably, subordinate to the O'Connors, despite the fact that they were a breakaway branch of the MacDermots and might have been expected to give allegiance to them. The MacDonaghs had in the course of the late thirteenth and early fourteenth centuries moved northwards, away from the MacDermot base south of the Curlews, into Tirerrill (formerly part of the king's cantreds). Their support and following of the O'Connors may have been an attempt to establish their independence of the MacDermots.[7] They seem to have recognised Domhnall O'Connor's title of lord from the Curlews to Belleek which would have included the O'Connor territory of Carbury as well as the MacDonagh lordship of Tirerrill.

In the course of the fourteenth century the O'Connors were also able to extend their overlordship westwards and southwards to include all the former Sligo manor lands of Leyny and Corran as well as Tireragh. The

Gaelic families in the latter areas had been weakened by the Norman presence and were not in a position to resist a strong overlord. By 1386 members of the MacDonagh, O'Hara and O'Dowd families were serving in Domhnall O'Connor's army, and, as military service was one of the main demands of Irish lordship, this does suggest that by that stage O'Connor was exerting the right of overlord over these families.[8] Domhnall O'Connor therefore seems to have deserved the title of lord of Sligo and of Lower Connacht which the annals gave him in 1395.

The political organisation in the region at the beginning of the fifteenth century was thus one of the dominance of the O'Connors of Carbury and Sligo over the less powerful families of the MacDonaghs, O'Haras and O'Dowds.[9] Each of these families, although subordinate to the overlordship of O'Connor, nevertheless controlled a territory known as a lordship: the O'Haras were lords of Leyny; the MacDonaghs were lords of Tirerrill and later also of Corran; the O'Dowds were lords in Tireragh. The O'Connors also had their own lordship of Carbury. There were thus two different levels of lordship operating in fifteenth-century Sligo: the overlordship of O'Connor and the more direct lordship of the sublords. Later the O'Donnells were to add a third type of lordship.

The O'Connors of Lower Connacht reached the zenith of their power in the early fifteenth century. During this time they successfully resisted aggressive attacks from O'Donnell and also played a prominent role in the wider world of Connacht politics. Their strength was due to a number of factors essential to strong lordship: internal family unity and fraternal co-operation and a strong military backing. The head of the family in the early fourteenth century, Brian, had a firm control over the O'Connor lordship of Carbury. He ruled from 1403 to 1440, an impressively lengthy period, and during those years there is little evidence of faction-fighting among the O'Connors. Rather Brian's brothers are documented fighting alongside him or separately on his behalf. No other member of the family was ever to achieve such family solidarity.[10]

Brian's military support was derived from a number of sources. First, members of the other lordly families served in O'Connor's army. In 1419, for example, Brian and 'the whole of north Connacht' made a great hosting against Tirhugh; and in 1420 MacDonaghs, O'Connors and O'Dowds were in the army which mounted a patrol into Ballyshannon under the leadership of Brian's sons. The military support of the sublords was reciprocated by the O'Connors through the protection which they offered to the less powerful lords, as for instance in 1416 and 1420 when the O'Connors came to the assistance of the O'Haras. Protection in return for submission was a common characteristic of lordship in medieval Ireland and elsewhere. The relationship between the O'Connor ruling family and the sublords was also strengthened through marriage alliances, of which there are several examples in the annals.[11]

Military power also came through the erection and warding of castles or, more precisely, tower-houses. Not all the tower-houses of Sligo can be dated, but there are several references in the annals to castles being built in the fifteenth century, and others can also be dated to this time.[12] Many of the castles were built for strategic reasons, being situated, as the last chapter indicated, in key military positions. A good example is Bundrowes, built in 1420 by Brian O'Connor – clearly in an attempt to state the territorial limits of his lordship and to prevent O'Donnell from encroaching into north Conacht. O'Donnell retaliated in a similar fashion three years later by building a castle nearby at Ballyshannon.[13] Castle-building and the warding of castles was an important aspect of lordship in the fifteenth century. In the sixteenth century O'Connor Sligo's strategic network included not only castles in the O'Connor lordship of Carbury but also castles and land in each of the other lordships. It is not known when the family acquired this property, but it may have been during the first half of the fifteenth century when their power in the region was at its height.

Apart from strategically based castles and the military support of his own family and other lordly families, O'Connor also made use of Scottish mercenaries. The latter first appeared in the services of northern Irish lords in the thirteenth century, but quickly moved southwards; several branches of them, notably the MacSweeneys and the MacDonnells, settled in north Connacht, particularly along the sea coast of Tireragh. They seem to have provided military service in return for being allowed to settle on land in the area.[14] O'Connor also had the services of a native military family, the O'Harts, who are described as the cavalry of the O'Connors.[15] O'Connor therefore had professional military assistance (the O'Harts and MacSweeneys virtually constituted a standing army) as well as the military services of the aristocracy of Lower Connacht.

Control of a large military establishment needs to be based on economic strength. Little is known about the financial expenditure or income of Gaelic lords at this time, but the growth of Sligo town in the fifteenth century and O'Connor's share in its customs must have contributed substantially to his financial ability to maintain a large military following.[16] Tribute collections from other lords would also have enhanced his economic position.

The chief of the O'Connors exercised an overlordship over the other lordships which was basically a military supremacy. It was not based on landownership – apart from the castles referred to above – and may not have asked for much more than the right to summon military assistance when it was needed. It was thus not a very demanding form of lordship, and the sublords enjoyed a considerable amount of autonomy.

Sublords: lords of land and people

These small lords had little political power outside their own territory, but they did have significant powers within it. In their own lordships they were lords of the land, taking decisions relating to war and peace and administering the law, as well as being patrons of poets and of ecclesiastical benefices. Individual sublords had independent military resources. The MacDonaghs, the O'Dowds and probably also the O'Haras employed their own Scottish mercenary soldiers.[17] The sublords may also have levied a tribute within their own territories. An early seventeenth-century survey listed the services due by tenants to local landlords in Sligo. These included a mixture of agricultural produce, labour service and other services such as a *cuid oidhche* at Christmas.[18] These may represent the remnants of the tributes and services which the sublords demanded of their followers and tenants in medieval times. At this level, however, it is difficult to decide whether the lords were being paid rent for land or a more 'lordly' form of tribute. Indeed, in most cases there is no clear dividing-line, because the lord was often both landlord and lord of the lordship and what may have begun as tribute was transformed into rent in the course of the late middle ages.

None of the sublords posed a military theat to the O'Connors, largely because most of them were weakened by internal division. A noticeable feature of the late fourteenth and early fifteenth centuries is the extent to which permanent divisions took place among nearly all the lordly families of Lower Connacht. The MacDonaghs divided into two separate lordships: Tirerrill and Corran; the O'Haras divided into the O'Hara Reagh and O'Hara Boy, while the O'Dowds were also weakened by internal division, and the territory of Carbury was divided among four branches of the O'Connors.[19] These divisions undoubtedly weakened the military power of the sublords, but paradoxically they also created a much more stable political situation in Lower Connacht, with sub-branches of each ruling family beginning to possess clearly defined territories and retaining the same lands over centuries. The building and occupation of tower-houses by all the lordly families also contributed to an impression of permanence and stability. The tower-house where the lord and his family resided became the permanent centre of the lordship. This development also helped to strengthen the lord's position as lord of land as well as of people.

Apart from their rights as lords of the land, the sublords also had the right to administer justice within the lordship and serve as patrons of church benefices and literature in their lordships. The MacDonaghs and O'Haras had a particularly strong hold over the church within their territories. The O'Haras had a monopoly over the offices associated with the diocese of Achonry, while the MacDonaghs controlled benefices within their lordship, as well as providing a large number of the abbots for Boyle abbey in the MacDermot lordship of Moylurg.[20] Two of the most important literary compilations of medieval Ireland were written in the north Connacht area and were patronised by two lordly families: the Book of Lecan was patronised by the O'Dowds, and the Book of Ballymote was dedicated to a MacDonagh. These compilations also, of course, provided the new ruling families like the MacDonaghs with respectable pedigrees and titles and thus legitimised their right to rule.[21]

Evidence of administrative organisation in the lordships or the existence of lords' officials is scarce. Constables for supervising the mercenaries and looking after the wards of castles probably existed in all the lordships. The O'Haras, MacDonaghs and O'Dowds also had bardic and legal families living in their lordships. Among the records associated with the Blake family there are several documents attested with seals of the O'Dowds, MacDonaghs and O'Connors – the latter were also attested with the seal of the Dominicans at Sligo abbey. This does suggest some sophistication in administration and also the involvement of local clerics (who were often relatives of the lords) in the official business of the lordship.[22]

The Blake documents also indicate possible sources of income for the sublords. As with the O'Connors, lordly income was a mixture of tribute or rent from land (with labour service providing a cheap means of building and maintaining the lords' residences) as well as some commercial income. The MacDonaghs, like the O'Connors, had a share in the customs of Sligo, and other lords no doubt contributed to the hide and fish exports from the town.

Although not significant politically, these families were nevertheless important in their own areas, and there is little evidence of the O'Connors of Sligo exercising an autocratic form of lordship which constantly interfered in the internal affairs of the sublordships. The semi-autonomous position of the sublords made it, indeed, difficult for O'Connor to weld the region into a very strong unified lordship. O'Connor's overlordship did not demand total control of a territory. Submission and readiness to follow the lord when summoned was sufficient. For O'Connor the fact that he could call on his sublords for military assistance was the most important aspect of his overlordship. This relatively mild form of lordship gave way to a more demanding one in the late fifteenth century.

The O'Donnell lordship

O'Connor control in the Sligo region was always inhibited by an important factor: the strategic attraction of the region for stronger outside lords. The threat of outside attack was always present, and the O'Donnells, in particular, sporadically tried to exert authority in the area in the early middle ages. The attraction of the area for outsiders became particularly strong in the second half of the fifteenth century, when O'Donnell, the Lower MacWilliam and Clanricard Burke struggled for control of north Connacht and ultimately for control of the whole western province. The fight for dominance in north Connacht was indicative of a more general phenomenon of the late fifteenth century, i.e. the attempts by some of the stronger lords to expand outside their own lordships and move towards control of the province. As Katharine Simms has documented, the O'Neills virtually achieved this in Ulster.[23] The conflict in Connacht was compounded by the absence of any powerful lord, and so it became a three-cornered struggle between the O'Donnells and the two Burke families. In the contest the Sligo area was important because control of it (and particularly of the strategically placed Sligo castle and the by then profitable town) was seen as crucial for military control of the whole province. The conflict between O'Donnell and the Burkes devastated the Sligo region as each ruler tried to exercise his authority. The local inhabitants mainly played the role of passive supporters of the military rivalry between the two outside powers. The conflict had a particularly detrimental effect on the O'Connor unity which had been developed by Brian O'Connor in the first half of the century. Both the Burkes and O'Donnell saw the wisdom of having local support, and so each magnate supported a different branch of the O'Connor family. Sligo castle was passed backwards and forwards between the O'Connors as the Burkes or O'Donnell gained control of it. At one stage in 1476 the whole Lower Connacht area was actually divided in two between O'Donnell and Burke.[24]

By the early sixteenth century, however, it was clear that O'Donnell was emerging as the superior power, and he was soon making annual visits to Lower Connacht to collect tribute and impose his rule. O'Donnell's overlordship was a demanding and ruthless one which seems to have been very different in style to the earlier rule of O'Connor. In 1568 O'Donnell listed the exactions which he claimed he was entitled to annually from the area. It included military service (32 horsemen from the O'Connors of Carbury, and 30 from each of the other lordly families: a total of 152 horsemen); victuals and wages for 320 galloglass for four months in the year from August to November (80 galloglass with the O'Connors, 60 with each of the other lords); as well as 360 marks sterling and the king's cocket in the port of Sligo and in two other minor coastal ports (which was specified as amounting to one mark for every last of hide).[25]

Apart from these annual demands, which must have imposed a considerable economic burden on the region. O'Donnell claimed that he had the right to destroy and burn the crops and land of any lord who refused to deliver his tribute. And there is plenty of evidence in the annals to indicate that he did just that. On numerous occasions in the late fifteenth and early sixteenth centuries O'Donnell inflicted severe punishments on local inhabitants who resisted his demands. He also occupied and warded castles in the area and stayed in several of them during his journies through Lower Connacht. In 1512, for example, he was in Bricklieve, described in the annals as 'his own stronghold'. In 1516 he took the castles of Collooney, Castleloghdargan and Dún na móna[26]. O'Donnell's agreement in 1539 with Tadhg O'Connor to whom he entrused Sligo castle (having regained it after losing it in 1536), indicates the sort of terms which he made with a ward of a castle. Under the terms of the agreement, O'Donnell recognised Tadhg as a reliable ward of the castle who would act as his agent in Sligo. Tadhg was instructed to surrender the keys of the castle to O'Donnell whenever he requested it (even if it was for the purpose of destroying the castle). Tadhg was also obliged to accompany O'Donnell's stewards and marshals on their journeys through Connacht and arrange for the levying of their bonaght in

21

the localities. He was also to collect and send to O'Donnell the cocket of Sligo port. Tadhg and possibly other wards were thus O'Donnell's representatives in the area.[27]

By the late 1520s O'Donnell's control over the Lower Connacht area was so complete that he was able to use it as a base to enforce his authority on the MacDermots in the area south of the Curlews, and he was even making incursions further south.[28] Overall the annals give the impression of a ruthless, autocratic rule which was more demanding than the earlier overlordship of O'Connor. It seems to have asked for more than military service and support. The occupation of castles and the annual visits imposing O'Donnell's rule and punishing opposition imply a much more vigorous type of overlordship. It was still, however, a lordship without land – and this was a crucial weakness. In order to maintain his control, O'Donnell needed to make annual visits to the area to collect his tribute and deal with opposition.

Even with O'Donnell's regular itineraries through the area, opposition could be effective. Several attempts were made to weaken O'Donnell's hold on the region by outsiders as well as by local inhabitants. In 1522 O'Neill's assistance was availed of, and later the earl of Kildare joined in an attack on O'Donnell, though with no great success.[29] The interest of O'Neill and Kildare in the conflict is another reflection of the changing nature of Irish politics in the late fifteenth century as it became focused around a number of provincial and national groupings and factions.

The O'Connors also tried to resist O'Donnell's demands in the area by use of their own initiative. In 1533 the leading members of the family joined together to resist O'Donnell and succeeeded in seizing Sligo castle. And recalling the family unity of the mid-fifteenth century, Tadhg O'Connor launched an attack on O'Donnell with the help of the other main branch of the family (for many years a rival of Tadhg's sept). As if to indicate the beginning of a new era, Tadhg adopted a new title, that of Ó Conchobhair. Hitherto, according to the annals, the O'Connors of Lower Connacht had been known as 'Mac Domnaill meic Muircheartaigh' (i.e. descendants of Domhnall who died in 1395). Tadhg took the new title 'to ennoble his line and to excel the kings who had preceded him'. Tadhg also made a number of journeys to other parts of Connacht, probably in an attempt to gather support against O'Donnell and also to try to establish his own position as lord of Lower Connacht. He collected tribute and refused to yield to O'Donnell.[30] But the O'Connor revival was only temporary. By 1539 O'Donnell was firmly back in control. The revival of the O'Connors can in fact be explained by the failing strength of Hugh O'Donnell, who died in 1537. His son and successor, Manus, almost immediately retrieved the losses of his father in north Connacht.[31]

The Burke/O'Donnell conflict, followed by O'Donnell's rule of the region, undermined the overlordship of the O'Connors, despite the flurry of activity in the 1530s. In the following twenty years their power was further eroded by encroachment from MacDermot expanding northwards over the Curlews – a reflection of O'Connor weakness rather than MacDermot strength.[32] The O'Connors had risen to prominence in north Connacht when the larger overlords were weakened by the Norman settlement in the province, and their decline coincided with attempts to revive provincial lordships. They were never in a position to fully establish their own autonomy and were therefore never in a position to play a serious role in the provincial battles of the late fifteenth and early sixteenth centuries. Their weakness may have lain in the loose control which they exercised over their sublords, but their task was not made any easier by the continual threat from outside. The strategic position of the region – which had been strengthened and emphasised by the Norman foundation of Sligo castle and town made the area too attractive to large outside lords attempting to control a much wider territory than O'Connor's lordship, and consequently it was difficult to use it as a base from which to expand. Political unity and control were always fragile.

In the late middle ages the area experienced several different types of lordship. The Norman lordship began the recognition of the area as an important unit, but the newcomers were ousted from their largely superficial lordship by the expanding O'Connor lordship. The latter consisted of a mild form of overlordship which essentially demanded military service from the sublords. The sublords had an impressive amount of autonomy and were the real lords of the land, acting as both military lords and landlords as well as literary and ecclesiastical patrons. Towards the end of the fifteenth century a new and more demanding form of overlordship appeared, with O'Donnell ruthlessly exploiting the area for tribute and military service. In the sixteenth century the O'Donnell lordship was replaced by yet another type of lordship: that of the Tudors.

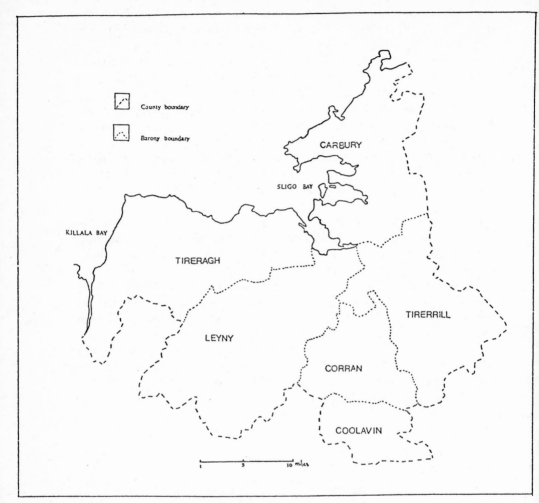

County boundary

Barony boundary

CARBURY

SLIGO BAY

KILLALA BAY

TIRERAGH

TIRERRILL

LEYNY

CORRAN

COOLAVIN

1   5   10 miles

Baronies of County Sligo.

3

THE LORDSHIP OF THE TUDORS

Initial Tudor contact

Clearly by the early sixteenth century O'Donnell control of Lower Connacht was the dominant factor in the political structure of the region; and, not surprisingly, it was O'Donnell interest in north Connacht that first attracted the attention of the Tudor administration. Manus O'Donnell was among the lords with whom Lord Deputy Anthony St Leger negotiated his famous 'surrender and regrant' agreements in the early 1540s. The agreements were an attempt by the government to win by peaceful methods the support and loyalty of Gaelic chiefs throughout Ireland. Part of the agreement which St Leger made with O'Donnell involved the surrendering by the lord of his Irish title or name and the granting to him of an English peerage. In exchange for the title of the O'Donnell, Manus O'Donnell asked to be created 'Erle of Tyrconnell or Slygogh'. The Clanricard Burke also made an agreement with the crown, and he requested the title of earl of Connacht.[1]

The requests of the Clanricard Burke and of O'Donnell reflect the rivalry between them for control of north Connacht. Manus O'Donnell was concerned to have his claim to Sligo officially recognised by the Tudor government. In 1541, in addition to petitioning for the earldom of Sligo, he also asked that his chaplain, one Connaught Ó Siaghail, be appointed to the see of Elphin. This was a subtle request because the bishop's house was in Sligo town; thus Ó Siaghail could serve as O'Donnell's representative there. In 1542 O'Donnell renewed his request for the earldom of Sligo, claiming with some exaggeration that his ancestors had held the castle and the surrounding territory for over a thousand years. He continued his petition for recognition of his Sligo claims in the following year when he asked St Leger for the moiety of the cocket of all ships coming to Sligo to trade and agreed to share the profit of the cocket with the king. Clanricard made similar requests for the 'cocket of Sligo'.[2]

Although neither the O'Donnell nor the Clanricard requests concerning Sligo were granted, the Tudor administration reluctantly recognised that the O'Donnells had some sort of claim to north Connacht. And throughout the Tudor period, as will become clear below, the government's policy towards north Connacht was largely determined by its attitude to O'Donnell.

Domhnall O'Connor Sligo and the lordship of the Tudors

Tudor plans for Manus O'Donnell and his son, Calvagh centred on efforts to support and bolster the O'Donnells as a focus of resistance in Ulster against O'Neill's hostility to the Dublin government. The surrender and regrant agreement between St Leger and Conn O'Neill had not created the peaceful scenario in Ulster envisaged by the government. The agreement had in fact engendered considerable hostility towards Dublin among the O'Neill septs, most of whom refused to accept Conn's recognised heir, Matthew, as their chief. Instead the O'Neills declared their support for another son of Conn's, Shane, who continued his predecessors' attempts to exercise control over the whole of Ulster.

Government support for the O'Donnells was made manifest in 1564 when Calvagh O'Donnell went to London and made a formal submission to the queen. Two years later Calvagh was formally reinstated in Tyrconnell by the new lord deputy, Sir Henry Sidney. While he was in the north-west Sidney also made individual agreements with all the lords of the area over whom O'Donnell claimed the rights of an overlord.[3] In the agreements the lords acknowledged the queen as their liege lord as well as recognising O'Donnell's claims in their lordships. Most importantly from a government point of view, they also agreed to help O'Donnell against O'Neill. Among the lords who made an agreement with Sidney was Domhnall O'Connor Sligo. The phrasing of O'Connor Sligo's agreement was slightly different to that of the other lords. While O'Connor Sligo acknowledged the queen as his liege lord, he did not, without qualification, acknowledge O'Donnell's overlordship in Lower Connacht. The agreement recognised that the queen, the earl of Clanricard and O'Donnell had claims to rent from the area but was unclear about the respective merits of these claims. It was agreed that O'Connor Sligo, having already paid a half-year's rent to O'Donnell, should pay rent for another half-year, i.e. until May of the following year, and should also tender aid to O'Donnell against O'Neill for the same period. In the meantime the lord deputy agreed to investigate the matter.[4]

The terms of the agreements reveal the main concern of the government: to create a strong O'Donnell lordship to undermine O'Neill's control over Ulster. Nonetheless, the agreements were also advantageous to O'Donnell and to O'Connor Sligo and were easily accommodated within the Gaelic polity. In return for his acknowledgement of the queen as his overlord, O'Donnell received crown military protection and royal recognition of his rights over his sublords. In other words, the queen accepted the hierarchy of the Gaelic political world. From O'Connor Sligo's point of view, the agreement with the crown was also beneficial. The O'Donnell overlordship in Sligo was no longer unhesitatingly accepted by the government, and the agreement also raised the possibility of Tudor lordship being substituted for

the O'Donnell lordship of Lower Connacht. In the course of the negotiations, O'Connor Sligo discussed this possibility with Sidney. O'Connor
acknowledged that he should pay rent to someone for his lands, but indicated his preference for holding them 'only of Her Majesty and be defended
from the rest'.[5] The words are important because in recognising the queen
as his lord, O'Connor desired protection in return, as he might legitimately
expect from any strong overlord. He had seen for himself the protection
which Sidney had offered O'Donnell, and no doubt admired the impression
of military strength which the lord deputy and his entourage in the north-
west conveyed.

O'Connor Sligo followed up his initial contact with the chief governor by
attending a ceremony at Galway where O'Donnell was formally presented
with his letters patent. Once again O'Connor Sligo expressed his desire to
hold his lands directly of the queen and also his willingness to go to England
'to receave not onelie his countrie but as he termeth it regeneracon at Your
Majestie's hand'.[6] The expression 'regeneracon' suggests that O'Connor
was thinking in terms of a new type of lordship.

When Sidney returned to England in the autumn of 1567, O'Connor
Sligo accompanied him, and on 20 January 1568 he went to Hampton
Court. There on his knees and with the help of an interpreter he made his
submission to the queen. He acknowledged the queen as his liege lord and
surrendered and resigned the office of 'captain of O'Connor Sligo'.
O'Connor asked that he henceforth be reputed an Englishman and, accordingly, be exempt from subjection and servitude and from all other
burdens to be exacted by O'Donnell and others. It was also agreed that,
following a survey by the lord deputy of the extent of his territory, the queen
would grant him letters patent for his lands at an annual rent not exceeding
£100. Finally O'Connor agreed to be bound to the queen for the sum of
£10,000. The queen, for her part, acknowledged O'Connor Sligo's refusal
to join with Shane O'Neill, received him to her grace and protection, and
granted him a knighthood.[7]

The queen's agreement with O'Connor followed the general formula of
other 'surrender and regrant' agreements which, from the government
point of view, contributed to the process of anglicising Gaelic lordships.
The issuing of letters patent would, in theory, bring O'Connor under the
jurisdiction of English common law. But it is important to appreciate that
the agreement was also acceptable within the Gaelic political structure and,
seen from the Gaelic lord's point of view, was very attractive. O'Connor
offered allegiance and rent (at a lower and more regular rate than the
arbitrary exactions of O'Donnell) to the queen in return for her protection
from O'Donnell. Henceforth he was to be an Englishmen or, in Irish terms,
a follower of the queen or lord of England rather than a man of Tyrconnell
or subject of O'Donnell. He had, indeed, received his 'regeneracon'. It
required no cultural or political adjustment on O'Connor's part to accept
his royal indenture. It made sense in the Gaelic world. The agreement

involved no diminution of his own internal lordship over the other Sligo lords; and the royal recognition of him as the head of the O'Connors Sligo strengthened his control over the other branches of the family.

From the time the indenture was made, O'Connor made it clear that he did indeed expect protection from the queen and her representatives. He returned to Ireland as Sir Domhnall O'Connor Sligo, armed with royal letters instructing the lords justices to take action to relieve his complaints, not only relating to O'Donnell but also concerning the border encroachments on his territory by O'Rourke and the Burkes.[8] In the spring and summer of 1568 a triangular correspondence took place between O'Connor Sligo, O'Donnell and the lords justices (who were temporarily in charge of the Dublin government during the absence of the lord deputy). O'Connor demanded defence and protection against O'Donnell's threats and claims to tribute from his territory, while O'Donnell insisted on his right to jurisdiction over Sligo and produced a historical defence of his claim, itemising his tribute from each lordship. The lords justices tried, rather feebly, to defend O'Connor by writing to O'Donnell and reprimanding him for threatening to interfere in O'Connor's territory. They sugggested that he report any matter of injustice in O'Connor's territory to them rather than dealing directly with it himself. By September, however, O'Donnell still refused to abandon his claims to Sligo, and so the lords justices in despair decided to refer the matter to arbitrators chosen by the two opposing sides, with the proviso that if Lord Deputy Sidney returned from England before the arbitrators met, then he would deal with the matter. This seems to have been what happened as nothing more is heard of the arbitration. But Sidney's return did not resolve the issue; and the letters patent, allowed for in O'Connor's agreement with the queen, were never issued.[9]

The correspondence of the lords justices, their ineffective reprimanding of O'Donnell and their gesture of despair in referring the matter to arbitration revealed the crucial weakness of O'Connor Sligo's hopes and plans for crown defence of his lordship. The early Tudor government in Connacht did not have the military resources, or indeed the motivation, to provide O'Connor with effective protection against O'Donnell. O'Connor Sligo may have been misled by the support given to Calvagh O'Donnell. This support had been offered as part of the central aim of the Dublin government to undermine the O'Neill hegemony in the north. O'Connor Sligo's differences with O'Donnell did not merit the same attention. Indeed, the crown assistance given to O'Donnell against O'Neill made it difficult for the government to risk alienating him by insisting that he abandon his claims to Sligo.

Sir Henry Sidney's settlement of the north-west formed part of his wider reform programme for Ireland. A central part of the programme was the introduction of provincial government to the country. By 1570 two presidential councils had been set up in Munster and in Connacht. The establishment of the provincial administration offered new prospects to O'Connor that the government might now be in a position to offer him the protection which he sought. However, the first president of Connacht, Sir Edward Fitton, became so embroiled in conflict with the earl of Clanricard and his sons that he had little time to concern himself with the northern part of his provincial charge.[10] His successor, Sir Nicholas Malby (1579-84), was more interested in County Sligo (as the territory of O'Connor Sligo and of O'Rourke was now denominated), but far from solving O'Connor's problem, Malby did much to make it more complex. To begin with, much of Malby's presidency was taken up with efforts to make new agreements with all the chief lords of Connacht, similar in many ways to the earlier surrender and regrant agreements of St Leger's government but with more emphasis on revenue and military support.[11] The agreement that O'Connor Sligo had concluded with the queen in 1568 was an obstacle to Malby's plans to arrange new terms with the Connacht chiefs. Malby found O'Connor Sligo's ten-year-old indenture unsatisfactory for a number of reasons. First, the indenture was supposed to have been followed by a survey of O'Connor's lands and the issuing of letters patent. This had not been done. Secondly, when an inquisition was held, on Malby's instructions, it was discovered that O'Connor's territory extended over a very large area, which should have paid a far higher rent than the maximum £100 Irish laid down in the indenture. O'Connor Sligo was accused of deceiving the queen concerning the true extent of his territory. And finally, Malby claimed that the indenture agreed to grant to O'Connor only the lands of the O'Connors of Carbury. It was not, he alleged, intended that the crown would acknowledge O'Connor's claims over the other lords in Lower Connacht. Malby was given instructions to make separate agreements with the other Sligo lords to hold their lands of the queen and not of O'Connor Sligo.[12]

Malby's criticisms of the O'Connor indenture reflected the new emphasis of the government in the late 1570s and early 1580s. The aim in relation to Connacht was to curb the power of the lords over subordinate territories, to have all landlords hold their lands directly of the crown, and to increase the financial contribution of the lords towards the maintenance of the crown forces in the province. In the agreements made with O'Donnell and the other lords of the north-west in the 1560s the Sligo region was only of marginal interest to the central authorities. When O'Connor Sligo made his agreement in 1568, there were no provincial forces to be maintained, and the main concern of the government was to win the support and allegiance of the lords without seriously interfering with their internal jurisdiction or demanding large financial contributions from them. O'Connor Sligo's indenture did not refer specifically to his supremacy over the other lords, but his overlordship was recognised in the royal letters which defended his claims to Ardnaree, Ballintogher and Bundrowes, only one of which was in the O'Connor territory of Carbury. It was unfair to accuse him ten years later of deceiving the queen. The real problem was that by the late 1570s government priorities had changed. For the first time serious government attention was focused on the Connacht lords and plans were implemented to undermine their lordly powers. In this context, O'Connor's indenture of 1568 was out of date, and Malby wanted to replace it with an agreement which reflected the government's new interests.

Sir Domhnall O'Connor Sligo, however, was determined in his refusal to change the terms of the agreement, as he interpreted them, until the problem of O'Donnell was resolved. As Malby reported, O'Connor Sligo claimed that the agreement meant that her majesty was 'bound to defend him' against O'Donnell, and he made impressive attempts to try to have his point of view enforced. He pleaded several times with Malby about the matter and, on request, showed Malby his written agreement with the queen (the counterpart having been mislaid in London, Malby wanted to take a copy). O'Connor also travelled to Dublin twice to discuss the problem. He presented an attractively rational argument against paying an increased rent to the crown until O'Donnell's rights in Connacht were terminated. O'Connnor argued that he was expected to pay tribute to O'Donnell and to the queen (which, incidentally, he had never actually paid). If, he suggested, the payment of tribute to O'Donnell ceased, then he would, naturally, be in a position to increase his payment to the queen. O'Connor was not refusing to pay rent, but he was refusing to pay rent to the queen for protection which she did not provide. It made sense in an Irish, if not an English, context.[13]

The continuing dilemma for O'Connor Sligo, and indeed for Malby, was that the government could not afford to alienate O'Donnell by strenuously resisting what he saw as his rights in north Connacht. The perennial Tudor problem of the O'Neill hegemony in Ulster remained, despite the death of Shane O'Neill in 1567. Government relations with O'Donnell fluctuated, but efforts continued to be made to keep O'Donnell detached from O'Neill and on friendly terms with the government. Thus in 1578 he was officially given possession of Bundrowes, which until then had belonged to the O'Connors (as the queen had in fact acknowledged in 1568); and in 1581 and again in 1582 government troops assisted O'Donnell in Tyrconnell. O'Connor Sligo, on the other hand, was advised to buy the goodwill of O'Donnell in 1580, i.e. by paying his tribute, and in 1581 Secretary Fenton wrote of deferring settlement of the dispute until 'a better time'.[14]

Government relations with O'Donnell, and ultimately with O'Neill, in fact made it impossible to satisfy O'Connor Sligo. The administration was more dependent on supporting O'Donnell against O'Neill than it was on the friendship or loyalty of O'Connor Sligo. It was only when dependence on O'Donnell was abandoned and his claims to Connacht staunchly resisted that the overlordship of O'Donnell could be firmly dealt with. The Tudor administration's attitude to O'Connor Sligo raises the more general problem of the difficulty of making agreements with small lords which rejected the great lords' claims, without providing the necessary military support to defend the agreements. In Irish and English terms, O'Connor Sligo might justifiably feel that he had not been treated fairly by the Tudor lordship.

Domhnall O'Connor Sligo consistently refused Malby's requests to make a new agreement with the crown, but within less than a year of Malby's death in 1584 he had done precisely that and, in addition, had gone to Dublin to receive letters patent for his lands. The main reason why O'Connor Sligo made his new agreement was the arrival – and, more particularly, the manner of the arrival – of Malby's successor as president, Sir Richard Bingham. Bingham came to Connacht in the spring of 1584 amid rumours that a Scottish invasion of Ulster and Connacht was imminent. While Lord Deputy Sir John Perrot marched to Ulster, Bingham dealt with the northern borders of Connacht, or, to be more exact, with County Sligo. He seized O'Rourke's son as a pledge for his father's good behaviour and also, following a siege, took possession of Ballymote castle in the centre of O'Connor Sligo's part of County Sligo. Bingham evicted the MacDonagh residents of the castle and claimed it for the crown, allegedly because it had formerly belonged to the earl of Ulster, but mainly because, as the largest castle in County Sligo, he considered it ideal to defend north Connacht from the encroachments of the Scots. Bingham, much more than his predecessors, recognised and stressed throughout his career in Connacht, the strategic importance of the Sligo region.[15]

O'Connor Sligo was, not surprisingly, upset by the seizure of Ballymote and also by the style of the new president, who was strongly critical of his lordship over the other lords in the Sligo area. Instead of dealing directly with Bingham, however, O'Connor Sligo resolved to bypass him and communicate directly with his superiors. He sent his brother to the London authorities while he himself went to talk with the lord deputy in Dublin. Even Bingham was forced to acknowledge O'Connor's determination to defend his authority in Connacht.

The outcome of the Dublin visit was that O'Connor Sligo finally agreed to a new arrangement with the crown and received letters patent for his lands on 22 December 1584. He surrendered his estates and received a regrant of them by crown grant. In addition to the £100 Irish rent, Sir Domhnall and the other inhabitants agreed to pay an extra £50 per year and 100 beeves yearly (after three years this was increased to 130 beeves) and provide military service in lieu of any cess, i.e. demands for provisions for crown soldiers, thereafter to be imposed. O'Connor Sligo's authority in County Sligo was recognised: all freeholders were to hold their land of O'Connor by knight's service; he was to have a share in all goods confiscated through attainder; and he was given permission to levy the royal rent from the inhabitants of the area. Finally, the agreement was to be doubly secured by an act of parliament. Ballymote was excluded from the letters patent. It was reserved for the crown along with twelve quarters of land, which was, however, considerably less than the whole barony of Corran which Bingham had asked to be reserved for crown use. Provision was also made in the letters patent for the O'Connor Sligo estate to be inherited by the male descendants of Domhnall – a provision which was thought necessary because he had no living sons. This latter clause might also explain why O'Connor agreed to the new arrangement. He was ageing and wanted to secure his estate for his heirs. Malby's investigation had revealed that despite the provision made for letters patent in the agreement of 1568, none had in fact been issued to O'Connor, and Bingham's seizure of Ballymote exposed his vulnerable title under English law.[16]

The terms of the 1584 letters patent were certainly more onerous than the agreement of 1568, but in the circumstances of the time O'Connor Sligo still emerged with considerable advantages. First, his position as over-lord in Sligo was recognised. In the agreements which Malby had made with other Connacht lords, efforts were made to curb such authority, and it was Malby's wish to do the same in County Sligo. Bingham was even more anxious to limit O'Connor's power, so in this respect the 1584 agreement was a considerable triumph for O'Connor. Secondly, the rent which O'Connor agreed to pay was still less than most of the other Connacht lords. The distinction made between the land rent and money and beeves to be paid instead of cess might also be seen as a successful attempt to guard against any further demands by the Bingham presidency in the region.

However, O'Connor Sligo was not able to secure himself completely against the new president's activities, and in the autumn of the following year, 1585, the lords of County Sligo – now separated from O'Rourke's country which was renamed as County Leitrim – were brought more fully under the jurisdiction of the Connacht presidency when they participated in and agreed to the famous composition of Connacht. The composition was in effect a formalisation and elaboration of Malby's negotiations with the lords of Connacht. It had arisen partly out of concern to finance the Connacht administration, and partly out of the discovery that Malby had not only employed Irish and Scottish mercenaries but had also levied them and his English troops on the local inhabitants in a manner similar to any Irish lord. The composition agreements arranged for the army and admin-istration to be paid in a more satisfactory and regular manner.[17]

The first part of the agreements which were made with all the chief lords of Connacht arranged for each inhabited quarter of land in the province to pay 10s annual tax, or 'composition money', as it was called, for the main-tenance of soldiers to serve the president and for the expenses of local government. This payment was to be made instead of all forms of cessing or levying soldiers on the local inhabitants. The composition money could be paid in cash or cattle, and if it was not paid by the stipulated time, the local administrators were permitted to seize goods for it instead.

The second provision in the agreements arranged for each former lord-ship to provide a certain number of horsemen and footmen to assist the provincial and central governments when requested. This was followed by clauses stating that the lesser lords would give up their chiefly titles and traditional customs of electing chiefs and dividing land. The principal lords would be issued with letters patent for the land which they held at the time of the agreement, and these were from henceforth to be inherited according to English common law. In County Sligo the indenture also carefully outlined the 'rent-charge' which O'Connor Sligo was to have from each lordship (each of which was now redesignated as a barony). The 'rent-charge' was to replace the lordly exactions which he had formerly claimed from the sublords. The indentures also noted the lands which were to be free of the composition tax. They included all of O'Connor Sligo's lands in Carbury and a castle and small portion of land belonging to the other sublords, as well as property found to belong to the church.

The immediate aims of the composition were fiscal and military. The government of Connacht was given a regular annual income as well as a local militia which could be summoned free of charge by the administration. But the indentures in the long term aimed, rather optimistically, to transform economic and social relations in the province. The lords were to hold letters patent for their land, abandon their Gaelic customary rights, and observe English common law. In Sligo the only acknowledgement given to the former Gaelic system was the rent-charge which O'Connor Sligo was entitled to collect. None of the other lords in Sligo were given a similar concession. If implemented, the full programme of the composition agreements would have resulted in a radical change in the lifestyle of the area .

From O'Connor Sligo's point of view, the indenture for County Sligo gave little cause for alarm. His own lands were discharged from payment of any new tax, and he had been given further official acknowledgement of his rights over the other Sligo lords, in spite of Bingham's strong objections. O'Connor's rent-charge, which amounted to £420, was considerably higher than that allowed to any other Connacht lord with the exception of O'Rourke. In other lordships the rent-charge was divided among a number of prominent men, but in Sligo it was all reserved for O'Connor Sligo.

The composition indenture upset the 1584 agreement in one important respect: the amount of money to be collected by the provincial administration in lieu of cess (10s per quarter, amounting to £345) was considerably higher than the £50 and 100 beeves agreed in the earlier arrangement. O'Connor's lands were free from payment, with the result that the new burden fell on the sublords and other inhabitants of the new county. From the other sublords' point of view, therefore, the implications of the composition indenture were not so fortunate as for O'Connor. Not only were they to pay a new tax on their land, but their lordly status was not recognised beyond the fact that they were allowed to keep for themselves and their heirs the land which they then held as lords, and they were granted a small portion of land free from composition. Their economic outgoings were in fact substantially increased as a result of the composition indenture. In addition to the composition rent they had also to pay a rent-charge to O'Connor Sligo. Some of the landlords were also paying land rent to the increasing number of English and Irish officials who had received grants of monastic land in their territories.[18]

It is impossible to assess how much of these new economic burdens were passed on by the lords to the tenants living on the taxed lands, but it seems likely that much of it was. Later reports indicate that the composition rent was usually paid by the tenant or lessee of the land. It should be noted, however, that the process envisaged in the composition indentures was never completed. Although the composition money was regularly collected from 1585 onwards, the letters patent promised to the lords were never issued. Thus the chiefs of Connacht never benefited in the way initially intended from the composition agreements – a fact which had serious repercussions in the seventeenth century, as the next chapter will indicate. The major impact of the indentures was, therefore, the introduction of a new tax which the inhabitants were obliged to pay to the administration and, in theory at least, the removal of all forms of arbitrary payment for the army and administration.

The composition of Connacht made no reference to O'Donnell's claims in north Connacht. Coinciding with the composition of Connacht, a similar reform programme was launched in Ulster by the lord deputy, Sir John Perrot. Composition agreements were made with the Ulster lords, and Hugh Roe O'Donnell was imprisoned in Dublin castle as a hostage for his father's good behaviour. These actions, combined with the tough military policy of Bingham may well have suggested that the claims of O'Donnell on Sligo were at an end. At long last the government looked as if it was prepared effectively to prevent O'Donnell demanding tribute or exactions from north Connacht.[19]

Indeed, the government's new attitude to O'Donnell, O'Connor's indenture of 1584 and his 1585 composition indenture gave Sir Domhnall O'Connor Sligo much cause for satisfaction as he approached the end of his life. For nearly twenty years he had negotiated with the government to win the sort of defence and protection which he asked for or expected from his initial contacts with the crown; and three years before his death in 1588, he seemed to have achieved it.

The lordship of the Binghams, 1588–95

Sir Domhnall O'Connor Sligo died in 1588 believing that his estate would pass intact to his nephew, Donogh, son of his brother Cathal, and that his wife would be maintained during her lifetime with her widow's third, but the Bingham regime had other ideas. Following O'Connor Sligo's death, a post mortem inquisition summoned by George Bingham, who was temporarily in charge of the province during the absence of his brother in the Low Countries, found that Donogh was illegitimate, and accordingly his Sligo estate was forfeited to the crown. A second inquiry summoned by the Dublin administration recorded that Donogh was the legitimate heir, but a third office, summoned by Sir Richard Bingham on his return to the province, agreed with the findings of the first.[20] The appearance of the Spanish Armada off the north-west coast in the late summer of 1588 fortified Bingham's case for retaining the estate, and he was given authority from London to do so. In despair Donogh O'Connor Sligo went to London to plead his case. But by that stage Bingham had convinced the government of the strategic value of Sligo, and Donogh's claims were quietly ignored. He was detained in London, and the Sligo estate remained in crown hands until the summer of 1595, when it was taken by O'Donnell.[21]

George Bingham was given custody of the castle and lands of Sligo in 1588. As custodian, Bingham was entitled to collect the rent of the O'Connor Sligo estate and also the rent-charge which had been reserved to O'Connor Sligo in the composition book of Connacht. George Bingham warded Sligo castle with a constable and garrison but his main residence was Ballymote castle, which he used as his administrative base in the county. He built a jail and gallows in the vicinity of Ballymote and leased out its demesne lands.[22]

George Bingham also served as sheriff in County Sligo for a number of years and was clearly the most important official in the county from 1588 to 1595. He not only took over all the old rights of the O'Connor Sligo lordship, but he was also in charge of the collection of the composition money. Bailiff errants were appointed to collect the money in different baronies, and the evidence suggests that every effort was made to collect it on a regular basis. If payment was not made on time, the authorities were given permission under the terms of the composition indentures to enter the defaulting lands and seize cattle in lieu of payment. This seems to have been a clause of which the Bingham administration made much use.

Apart from O'Connor Sligo's rent, the rent-charges and the composition money, members of the new administration were also entitled to payment of rent due on former monastic lands for which they held a lease or custodium. Sir Richard Bingham had the custody of Boyle abbey, which was found by inquisition to have extensive property in County Sligo. Sir Richard Bingham was, therefore, the landlord of this property, much of which lay in the northern part of the county. Richard's brother George acted as rent-collector for these lands also. Other resident English officials in Roscommon had leases of other monasteries with lands in County Sligo.[23]

There was, therefore, after 1585, and particularly after the seizure of Sligo castle in 1588, a remarkable increase in the number of payments which local inhabitants were obliged to make on an annual basis to the adminis-tration. The O'Hart family, for example, who lived at Grange, north of Sligo town, made three different annual payments to George Bingham: compo-sition money, the rent-charge due to O'Connor Sligo, and land rent because Grange was part of the lands of Boyle abbey.[24] At a lower social level, the tenants on the lands attached to Ballymote castle experienced a substantial increase in their rent during the years that George Bingham was their landlord: in some instances there was a fourfold increase. In addition to their land rent, all the inhabitants of Corran paid what was called a chief rent-charge due to the castle of Ballymote. This was probably a financial conversion of the tribute which the MacDonagh of Corran was entitled to – another instance of the new administration appropriating the rights of the old lordships.[25] Apart from the regular annual charges, there were also exceptional payments to be funded. The payment of a knight's fee, i.e. money towards the expenses of the member of parliament for the county in 1585, was one such payment. Fines for issuing of documents such as pardons and letters patent were others.[26]

The exactions of O'Donnell and O'Connor Sligo had come to an end, but their replacement can not have been much better and, in many cases, was probably worse for Sligo inhabitants. A system of English local government was in the process of being established in County Sligo. Sheriffs, sub-sheriffs, bailiff errants and constables were appointed, a jail house was built, and sessions were occasionally held. But the style of the new government must have looked familiar. The seizure of cattle for unpaid rent was common; lodging of military men and officials on local inhabitants continued despite the terms of the composition agreement banning this practice; and provision of foodstuffs, for the households and maintenance of the wards in Ballymote and Sligo, was also demanded. Sheriffs, like lords of old, travelled with large entourages and demanded payments and food for provisions and night lodgings. Later allegations suggested that they accepted bribes to stay away from certain areas, the English equivalent of the 'black rent' which in Gaelic society was paid by local inhabitants to strong military lords. [27]

Despite the economic demands of the new regime, the assumption by the Binghams of the role of O'Connor Sligo provoked little immediate hostility in Sligo. No rival O'Connor emerged to contest Bingham's rule; nor, initially, did the other lords display any strong resistance or protest against the new administration. This was in marked contrast with their neighbours in Mayo where Bingham's refusal to recognise a replacement for the MacWilliam who died in 1586 aroused considerable hostility, culminating in the summons to Mayo of thousands of Scottish mercenaries to resist Bingham interference. The pursuit by Sir Richard Bingham of the mercenaries took place largely on Sligo soil, but apart from the effects of two large armies travelling through the county and allegations that some Sligo inhabitants provided relief for the mercenaries, there is little evidence of support for the Burke resistance in Sligo.[28] With the removal of O'Connor Sligo, the natural leader of the area had gone. Other lords were quietly trying to accommodate themselves to the new establishment. David O'Dowd, the lord of the O'Dowds, for example, appears to have been particularly encouraged and supported by the Binghams. George Bingham described him as more civilised than the other lords, and Richard Bingham was sympathetic to O'Dowd's complaints against O'Connor's overlordship. Evidence suggests that the O'Hara Boy, Cormac was also anglicising his lifestyle.[29]

The spring of 1589 witnessed another outbreak of resistance led by the Burkes in Mayo and this time they were joined by a number of Sligo inhabitants as well as by the O'Rourkes and others in Leitrim. The rebellion of 1589 had its immediate origins in the wrecking of the Spanish Armada off the north-west coast in the autumn of 1588 as the defeated fleet tried to make its way back to Spain via the north and west coasts of Ireland. The event had a destabilising effect on the province for a number of reasons. First, it created fear and anxiety – amounting at times to hysteria – among local and central officials that the Spanish survivors of the wrecks would combine with the Irish lords of the north and launch an attack on the western province. It was not a very realistic fear, but it led to a strengthening of defence measures in the province and, among other things, as already indicated, provided an irrefutable argument for the retention of Sligo castle in crown hands. The provincial militia, agreed under the terms of the composition agreements of 1585, was summoned, and a proclamation was issued ordering the immediate surrender of all Spaniards to government officials and warning of the penalties for disobedience. It is not clear how many lords responded to the summons and the proclamation, but the president was clearly dissatisfied with the support which he received from County Mayo, where a number of Burkes were suspected of succouring Spanish survivors. They had also ignored the government call for military help.[30]

The second destabilising effect of the Armada centred on the scramble for the salvageable goods and property of the ships and their occupants. Local government officials and representatives from the Dublin and London administrations as well as local inhabitants were involved in the search for items of value. In most cases, to the great annoyance of the administrators, the local people were usually the first to arrive at the site of the wreck. By the time the officials appeared there was nothing left of value. This undoubtedly heightened the tension and hostility between the inhabitants and the administrators. George Bingham was particularly incensed at being deprived of goods which were washed up on the O'Hart lands at Grange, where he and his brother were acting as landlords. Later there were allegations that he imprisoned and tortured men whom he suspected of hoarding gold chains and coins found on Spanish soldiers. At least five ships had been wrecked off the Mayo coast, and so the sense of frustration on the part of local officials was greater there than it was in Sligo. The resentment over the misappropriation of salvaged goods, combined with the suspected harbouring of the survivors and the refusal of most of the gentlemen of Mayo to provide military assistance for the provincial government, led eventually, at the beginning of 1589, to Bingham issuing the sheriff of the county, John Browne, with a commission to prosecute the Burkes through the exercise of martial law.[31]

The commission issued to Browne exacerbated an already difficult situation in Mayo. Family feuding and faction-fighting were rife among the Burkes. There is also some evidence that the Mayo area was suffering from serious economic problems. There are a number of references to the poverty of the Burkes at this time. The new fiscal demands of the government and its supporters may have had a particularly detrimental effect on the lords of Mayo, none of whom had a large or prosperous territory at his disposal. The tactless grant of most of the relatively rich lands attached to the position of MacWilliam to a young and politically unimportant heir of a former MacWilliam in 1586 and the acquisition of Castlebar (formerly the central base for one of the main branches of the family) by John Bingham, younger brother of Richard and George, must have been particularly galling, given the poverty stricken background of the lords of Mayo.

More generally, the spring of 1589 seems to have been a time of dearth and economic crisis in the north-west which was partly due to the disruption caused by the Armada and the ensuing military campaigns of Bingham. In addition, late spring was a traditional time of food shortage and also the time when half the composition money (or cattle) was due.[32]

One of the main rebellious acts of the rebels was the seizure of cattle, often from the relatively prosperous eastern part of County Sligo. One contemporary commentator believed that the rebellion was the result of the poverty of the disaffected lords. Another observer suggested that O'Rourke's raid on Sligo in April 1589 was motivated by hunger: 'his people had starved if he had not'. A mutiny of English soldiers in the province at about the same time might be interpreted as further evidence of a subsistence crisis.[33] The suggestion that the rebellion was partly motivated by economic factors also explains the large numbers involved in it. The rebellion of the Burkes against the Bingham regime and the attempt to introduce martial law by John Browne spread quickly throughout Mayo and into the neighbouring counties of Sligo and Leitrim. The political instability created by the Armada obviously fueled an existing discontent due to the economic problems and also to the resentment created by insensitive officials collecting composition and other crown dues.

The rebellion was considered serious enough for the Dublin government to agree to an inquiry into the Bingham administration in the summer of 1589 which culminated in sessions being held in each county in the province in August 1589, to which local inhabitants were invited to bring their grievances. The result was the compilation of a large number of complaints against the Bingham administration. Although the commissioners involved in the inquiry were instructed to suppress complaints against Lord President Bingham himself, they nonetheless collected an impressive amount of evidence concerning his subordinates, and especially concerning the activities of his brother George as sheriff of Sligo and his sub-sheriff, William Taaffe.[34]

The main complainants in Sligo were David O'Dowd, chief of the O'Dowds, and Ambrose Carew, a former bailiff errant employed by George Bingham. Both complainants had co-operated with the Bingham administration but had obviously fallen into disagreement with it. O'Dowd's remonstrance was a mixture of complaints relating to the economic demands of the local administration and his sense of grievance that the new regime did not respect his co-operation with them. O'Dowd complained that Bingham and Taaffe released, on payment of bribes, prisoners whom he had sent to them for punishment. He also alleged that Taaffe had seized the land of local inhabitants while they were held in prison. Taaffe and Bingham, both before and after the composition agreement of 1585, had taken items of food, clothing, money and cattle from local inhabitants, allegedly for the provision of the wards in Sligo and Ballymote castles. They continually travelled around the county in the company of large bands of men who were billetted on local people.

O'Dowd's fellow-complainant, Ambrose Carew, also protested about the misbehaviour of local government officials. For example, he instanced numerous cases of men being imprisoned by George Bingham in Ballymote and subsequently released on payment of ransom. Prominent among these were the O'Harts, imprisoned on suspicion that they had Spanish gold or knew where it could be found.

The complaints of O'Dowd and Carew provide corroborating evidence that support for the rebellion in Sligo was provoked by the destabilising effect of the Armada; economic problems and by the insensitive behaviour of local officials. Carew explained Oilill O'Gara's resistance in terms of the great poverty to which he had been reduced by Taaffe and Bingham. He had been imprisoned by Bingham for sixteen weeks in Ballymote at the time of the Armada. During this time Taaffe, who had land adjacent to O'Gara's territory, enticed O'Gara's tenants to his lands. To secure his release from prison O'Gara paid Bingham eighty cows. The result was that he was left without tenants or stock and was thus in a state of great poverty and hence, according to Carew, he joined the rebels.

George Bingham did not deny the truth of many of the allegations, but explained that most of the exactions which he and his officials made were legitimate collections of composition money or rent belonging to the O'Connor Sligo estate or necessary household maintenance for Ballymote and Sligo. He may have been correct, but the sheer number of the financial demands of the new administration and the manner in which they were collected were not likely to win the local government many admirers. The composition agreements were clearly not working as intended. The whole process involved in collecting the money was alienating people from the English administration rather than attracting them to serve and obey it.

The complaints seemed to be a convincing indictment of the Bingham presidency, and the Dublin government arranged to bring Sir Richard Bingham himself to trial to answer the criticisms. But the attempt to indict and then dismiss Bingham failed because Bingham's supporters in London, led by Sir Francis Walsingham, secured for him a royal defence of his activities in Connacht, and in December 1589 Bingham was officially acquitted and returned to Connacht. The fear which the Spanish Armada created in the minds of the queen and her advisers provided the context in which Bingham's actions in the west were given tacit approval by London.[35]

The acquittal of Bingham marked an important stage in his presidency. He now had, despite the disapproval of Dublin, full royal backing for his martial activities, and between 1590 and 1593 he was given total freedom to impose a firm military rule in Connacht. In the course of these three years he waged an almost relentless campaign against the Burkes in Mayo, straining them, as one official put it, 'beyond the limits of government'.[36] He also dealt with O'Rourke and tried to arrange for the division of County Leitrim.[37]

In County Sligo Bingham's policy after 1589 emphasised the military and strategic importance of the county's location to the virtual exclusion of all other considerations. In 1590 he built a new fort in the Curlews, at Ballinafad on the borders between Counties Sligo and Roscommon. Shortly afterwards he seized Bundrowes for the crown and placed a ward there.[38] Thus, with Boyle, Ballymote and Sligo already occupied with crown forces, there was a line of defence along the main north–south route through the county. There were also other soldiers occupying castles in the western part of the county. In the early 1590s Bingham tried to increase the military fortification for the county by encouraging his old friend Ralph Lane, the newly appointed muster-master, in a suit for a grant of Sligo, Bundrowes and Belleek castles. Lane was a fortifications expert and must have seemed the ideal resident for these northern castles, which were of such vital military importance.[39]

In the period after 1589 Bingham not only consolidated his military control of the province but did so in a very personal and family way. During this period there is much evidence of relatives and friends of the Bingham family holding many of the most important military positions in the province, especially in County Sligo. It seems to have been a calculated policy from 1590 onwards. Ralph Lane, an old friend of Bingham's, is one example of such a trend. George Bingham's son Henry and his nephew Nicholas Martin (George Bingham married a Martin) served as constables in Ballymote Castle, and Nicholas was also subsequently constable and sheriff in Sligo; while John Bingham, the younger brother of Richard and George, played a prominent part in the campaign against O'Rourke and took up residence in Castlebar.[40] Captain George Bingham – a cousin of Richard and George – served in the military campaigns in the early 1590s and was living in Sligo castle in 1595 when it was taken by supporters of O'Donnell. On his death it was requested that his brother Higham Bingham be permitted to take over the military charge of his dead brother. When George Bingham was killed in Sligo castle, several other members of the Martin family, in addition to Nicholas, were reported to have been there with him.[41] Sir Richard Bingham's loyalty to his extended family had an almost Gaelic ring to it. By the beginning of 1595 it looked as if there really was a Bingham lordship in County Sligo. However, the events of the summer of 1595 were to change all that.

The lordship of O'Donnell, 1595–1602

Bingham's policy in the north-west after 1589 dovetailed with that of the central authorities in Dublin under the supervision of Sir William Fitzwilliam, who became lord deputy in 1588. Fitzwilliam embarked on yet another reform plan for Ulster. In 1589 he arranged a new land settlement in Monaghan after the execution of the chief of the MacMahons, Hugh Roe. In addition, English sheriffs were appointed for the counties of Monaghan, Fermanagh and Donegal. Thus Bingham's attempt to settle Ralph Lane on the borders of Donegal would have considerably assisted Fitzwilliam's plans in the north.[42]

Not surprisingly, this attempt to extend English administration into the north-west provoked opposition, particularly from the lords of Fermanagh and Donegal, Hugh Maguire and Hugh Roe O'Donnell. Hugh Roe had escaped from Dublin castle in 1591 and shortly after was inaugurated as the O'Donnell following his father's resignation. One of his first actions on his return from Dublin was to attack the English sheriff of County Donegal and drive him out. Hugh Maguire also made his hostility to the government clear in 1593 when he attacked government troops. Lord President Bingham assisted Fitzwilliam in the retaliatory attack. Thereafter Maguire and O'Donnell united in their hostility to the government.[43]

In the summer of 1595 Sligo became directly involved in the conflict when Ulick Burke, a servant of Captain George Bingham then resident in Sligo castle, turned on his master and stabbed him to death. Burke seized possession of Sligo castle and subsequently handed it over to O'Donnell. Following O'Donnell's acquisition of the castle, he very quickly consolidated his support in Connacht. In the course of one month, according to the annals, most of the province rallied to his cause. The reaction of the Sligo inhabitants to O'Donnell is difficult to determine, but there is no evidence of strong resistance. On the contrary, the Sligo inhabitants seem to have almost immediately accepted the commanding presence of O'Donnell in their country. The Bingham lordship came to an abrupt end.[44]

The rapidity with which O'Donnell won control and the fact that he was invited into the province by a Connacht man, who had served the constable of Sligo castle faithfully for a number of years, suggest that the atmosphere in Sligo in the period before June 1595 had changed and become more hostile to the government. The activities of O'Donnell and O'Rourke in 1592–4 may have encouraged resistance, but it is also likely that Sligo suffered badly during these years. Bingham's emphasis on military garrisons, fed and maintained by local produce, and his campaigns against O'Rourke and Maguire would have meant that the area witnessed much military activity and its inhabitants would have been obliged to feed and lodge large numbers of soldiers. One hint at increased hostility between English officials and local inhabitants was the murder of David O'Dowd by a member of the local administration in October 1594.[45] The cause is unknown, but it does suggest continued hostility in the area after 1589. The acquittal of Bingham in 1589, crown support for his tough martial rule and the dismissal of the inhabitants' complaints against him and his regime could not have helped relations between the governors and the governed in the province.

Of course, the support which O'Donnell received in Sligo was also due to the fear which he imposed on the inhabitants. As one commentator put it, they were 'awed by O'Donnell' and 'dare not but stoop under his rule'.[46] O'Donnell's activities in Sligo were, above all, motivated by military consid-erations. His attitude to the region combined a recognition of its strategic value with a determination to keep it out of English control. For this reason he destroyed Sligo castle and Ballinafad in the autumn of 1595; and in the following year, hearing reports of the return from London of Donogh O'Connor Sligo with government support, he destroyed three of O'Connor's castles in Carbury to prevent him from using them as a base from which he could rebuild Sligo. O'Donnell also consolidated his support in Connacht in late 1595 by nominating his candidates as lords of the MacWilliams, O'Dowds and other Connacht families. O'Donnell was also reported to have exacted a charge on the inhabitants of Sligo for the maintenance of his men.[47]

In short, many of O'Donnell's activities in Sligo at this time were very similar to those of his predecessors: imposing his rule, supporting loyal supporters as sublords, and collecting tribute. Again in the traditional fashion, Sligo became the main bone of contention between the two con-flicting sides. In the negotiations which O'Donnell and Tyrone conducted with the government in 1596 O'Donnell claimed Sligo castle as his possession. Tongue in cheek, he refused to acknowledge his offence in seizing and destroying it, since, he argued, the castle belonged to him, and so the loss was his, and there was thus no offence against the crown. At the same time he demanded his ancestors' rights in Connacht. While the government refused to grant his claim directly, it did concede that O'Donnell's claims to Sligo would be considered and, if found valid, would be recognised.[48] Sir Domhnall O'Connor Sligo would have found the argument familiar.

Donogh O'Connor Sligo's return to Sligo in 1596 formed part of a wider attempt by Sir Robert Cecil to counter O'Donnell's commonwealth with one of his own. O'Connor's brother-in-law, Theobald Burke, was also sup-ported by the administration against O'Donnell's candidate as MacWilliam, and O'Connor Sligo's marriage to the countess of Desmond was undoubtedly arranged by Cecil. The countess's son was also sent back to Munster from London by Cecil as the earl of Desmond. Later the baron of Dunkellin, son of the earl of Clanricard, was appointed military commander in Connacht. One experienced English official in Connacht cynically referred to these developments as the dissolution of English government in the province. In the case of O'Connor Sligo the policy was a disaster. He did not succeed in winning back the Sligo lords nor in reality could he have been expected to. The old problem remained. The O'Connors never could resist the strength of O'Donnell. Sir Domhnall O'Connor had realised this, and that is why he wanted crown support. To reverse the policy and expect O'Connor to win support for the crown was impossible. O'Connor Sligo's only real contribution to the war was to be the indirect cause of the death of Bingham's successor as president of Connacht, Sir Conyers Clifford. Clifford was attacked and killed in the Curlews in 1599 as he was on his way to rescue O'Connor Sligo from O'Donnell.[49]

For the next three years O'Connor Sligo and the Sligo region were firmly under O'Donnell's control. O'Donnell used Sligo as a base and refuge as the war became more serious in Ulster. The strategic importance of the area was always of more importance to O'Donnell than the support of its inhabitants, while they, in turn, had little choice but to accept his rule for the duration of the war. It was not until the end of the war in March 1602 that Sir Oliver Lambert reclaimed the county for the English crown.[50]

Conclusion

Sir Domhnall O'Connor Sligo's negotiations and agreements with the crown are revealing for a number of reasons. First, he did not make just one agreement with the crown. He made several, and the terms of each need to be studied in the context of its time. Each reflected the particular concerns of the government at the time, and examined together they indicate the manner in which Tudor policy in Connacht changed during O'Connor's lifetime. Initially the main concern was to encourage as much support for O'Donnell as possible, but in the 1570s and early 1580s more detailed attention was given to governing Connacht and limiting the local authority of the lords of the province. In 1585 the landholding customs of the Gaelic lords were also brought under government supervision. The change in policy was not, however, openly acknowledged by administrators, who stressed a consistency in government policy throughout the period. Thus in 1579 O'Connor was accused of having deceived the government in 1568 in relation to the extent of his territories. The reality was that no one had investigated O'Connor's landed possessions in the 1560s. It was not relevant to the purpose of the agreement, which was essentially about curbing the O'Neill hegemony in Ulster. The phraseology and concessions granted in the agreements are important because they reveal that both parties had much to gain. In particular, O'Connor's agreement of 1568 was quite acceptable in a Gaelic political world, and may indeed have been constructed in such a way that it would be so. Understanding the agreement from the Gaelic lord's point of view can do much towards explaining why he agreed to it and why he may have felt betrayed when it failed to live up to his expectations.

Secondly, the agreement of 1568 was not forced on O'Connor. He wanted defence and protection from a strong lord and eagerly sought this from Queen Elizabeth. O'Connor's quest for a strong lord was similar to that of other Gaelic lords, although not all chose Queen Elizabeth. In neighbouring Mayo an Old English administrator, Sir Theobald Dillon, offered his services as a defender to the Costelloes and was accepted.

The failure of the Tudors to provide adequate protection for O'Connor Sligo revolved around their failure to undermine O'Neill power in Ulster. The position of O'Connor Sligo vis-á-vis the O'Donnnells was not unlike that of the O'Reillys' relationship with O'Neill, as documented by Ciarán Brady.[51] It was probably not a coincidence that Sidney brought both O'Connor Sligo and O'Reilly to London in 1568.

Despite the stranglehold of the north, the Tudor government took some measures to reform the government of Connacht. The composition was an impressive attempt to transform collectively the economic and social relations of the lords. The lords appeared to have welcomed the opportunity to acquire letters patent for their lands and wrote several times in the years after 1585 to the central government asking that their letters patent be issued. But the post-1585 period also revealed how difficult it was to make the composition effective. For many inhabitants of the province the composition cannot have meant much more than the imposition of a biannual tax. Regular collection of a public tax was a very novel experience in Connacht and, not surprisingly, it caused considerable resentment. Arrangements for collection were haphazard, and force was often used. The old independent lordship of O'Connor Sligo was destroyed, but the English military rule which replaced it took on many of the characteristics of Gaelic lordship. The Binghams claimed the chiefry charges of the O'Connor Sligo, and their officers collected land rent and composition money in the manner of Gaelic lords collecting lordly tribute.

The years 1586–9 were crucial for the failure of the society envisaged by the composition indentures to be made a reality – and, indeed, crucial for the eventual collapse of Tudor government in Connacht. The crisis provoked by the Armada contributed to the hostility caused by the Bingham administration's collection of the composition money and other rents and crown revenues. The resulting rebellion in the spring of 1589 in which men from Mayo and Sligo participated marked the end of any possible accommodation between the local lords and the Bingham regime. Thereafter Bingham conducted what in effect amounted to a war campaign in the province as he subdued Mayo and headed northwards to the very borders of the province. His military policy was partly a response to the activities of the northern lords, but it also in turn provoked and encouraged hostility to the government on the part of O'Donnell and Maguire, who felt threatened by Bingham's activity in the north-west.

With the taking of Sligo castle in 1595, Sligo became a war zone, with the inhabitants in the familiar role of spectators. O'Donnell renewed the old lordship of his ancestors in the region and the century ended, as it had begun, with the O'Donnells in control.

THE COUNTY OF SLIGO

The peace settlement which followed the ending of the war resulted in the first sustained period of peace in Ireland for over a century. With the exception of the rebellion of Sir Cahir O'Doherty in 1608, the years from 1603 to 1641 were remarkable for the absence of any form of military conflict. It was during these years of peace that considerable progress was made in the establishment of English administration and justice in all parts of the country. The experience of Sligo was typical of this development, as this chapter will explain.

The county of Sligo was formally created in the 1560s. During the lifetime of Sir Domhnall O'Connor Sligo English administrative officials began to appear in the county, but, as the preceding chapter has indicated, their style of government had much in common with that of the Gaelic lordships which they replaced. In the years after 1603, however, English law and administration were sufficiently established for county government to function with some degree of effectiveness and regularity.

The structure of government which developed in early modern County Sligo was a complex one in which five different levels can be discerned. At the highest level were the central administrations of London and Dublin; below these there were the provincial government of the president and council, the county administration and, after 1612, Sligo town corporation. The role of the army as an instrument of government was also important. Outside of these structures, but still at times powerful and capable of commanding loyalty, were the remnants of the older forms of rule by Gaelic lordship.

The London administration

In the sixteenth century the queen and her advisers in London took a direct interest in the activities of the presidency of Connacht. They issued instructions to the president and supervised his execution of them. The presidents, for their part, communicated directly with London and, at times, behaved as if the Dublin government had no authority over their affairs. Sir Richard Bingham tried, usually successfully, to adopt this attitude to Dublin officials. In London Bingham had the patronage of Sir Francis Walsingham, a powerful weapon against a disapproving Dublin government. This was clear in 1589 when the Dublin officials tried to prosecute Bingham for alleged misgovernment of Connacht. Earlier Bingham had successfully persuaded London to uphold his seizure of Sligo castle, despite the opposition of Dublin.[1] In the early seventeenth century this situation changed. London continued to defend the president of Connacht, but the defence was of a more personal nature than in the previous century. The first president of the seventeenth century was the earl of Clanricard, a catholic with close associations with the royal court. The London authorities were anxious to protect Clanricard from prosecution as a catholic, but they no longer took such a direct interest in the affairs of Connacht as a whole. And this trend was continued with Clanricard's successors, Sir Charles Wilmot (1616–30) and Roger Jones, Viscount Ranelagh (1630–44), who never exercised the same autonomy in relation to the Dublin government as Bingham had done.[2] In the seventeenth century London normally delegated the supervision of provincial business to Dublin.

The Dublin administration

While in the sixteenth century the Dublin administration tended to leave control of the province to the president and his council, the early seventeenth century witnessed a greater centralisation of government, with the result that the Dublin government gradually increased its influence and authority in Connacht. It did this in a number of ways, but principally through the introduction of the assize judges, through the appointment of special commissions to implement or inquire into certain matters in the province, and through an increase in the number of taxes and subsidies demanded in the localities.

In the sixteenth century the jurisdiction of the judges in the Dublin courts only occasionally impinged on Connacht. There were no regular legal visitations of the province, and most legal matters appear to have been dealt with by the chief justice of the Connacht council or by the county sheriffs. In 1604–5, however, the Connacht circuit was established and Dublin judges began to travel to the province to hold assizes at regular intervals. From 1606 the vice-treasurer's accounts in London indicate that an assize was held in the province twice a year, in the spring and in the summer. Two Dublin judges attended and spent between forty and fifty days in the province on each assize, which, allowing time for travel, meant that they spent about a week in each county. In Sligo the assizes were held in Sligo town, where a new jail was built for offenders.[3]

No detailed account of the activities of the judges of the assize in Connacht at this time is known to have survived. However, Sir John Davies composed a report of his experience as judge of the assize for Munster in 1606, and it may be assumed that the Connacht assize was very similar.[4] Davies's report suggests that the interests of the judges were varied and by no means confined to the hearing of common law cases. The normal procedure for the judges seems to have been to deal firstly with the prisoners in the county jail: awarding punishments, arranging for pardons to be issued, and finding masters or lords for 'masterless' men (an increasing problem during peacetime). Then the judges dealt with abnormal matters such as catholic landowners or officials who had refused to take the oath of allegiance recognising James I as head of the church in Ireland, land disputes, notorious 'rebels' in the county, controversies between local gentlemen, and other problems which disturbed the peace of the county. Increasingly in the 1620s the assize judges had responsibility for administering the oath of supremacy to all office-holders. In the first years of James I's reign the assize judges also supervised the implementation of the general pardon proclaimed at the end of the war and the execution of other government proclamations.[5] In a more general way they provided the central government with information and descriptions of the state of affairs in the localities. They advised on the selection of local officials; and with their biannual visits, which totalled about three months in the year, they were a powerful force for the centralisation of government.

The non-judicial functions of the judges of the assize were not peculiar to Ireland. In Tudor and Stuart England the judges of the assize were 'the voices, the ears, the eyes and the arms of the council in the counties'.[6] In Stuart Ireland also the judges served as the overseers of local government for the council in Dublin and ultimately, of course, for the council in London.

One of the by-products of the annual court circuit was that it brought local people into contact with Dublin judges and also with Dublin courts. Cases which could not be resolved by the judges were often referred to Dublin, and as the seventeenth century progressed more and more cases from Connacht were heard in the central courts. For example, references to cases relating to County Sligo appear in the surviving Dublin chancery archives and repertories and calendars of the exchequer records (the originals were destroyed in 1922). The majority of these cases date to the seventeenth century, with a notable increase as the century progressed. Most of the surviving cases concern titles to land and include disputes between locally born landlords as well as disputes between new and old landlords or, in some cases, former landlords. All appeared to accept the authority and jurisdiction of the court.[7]

William Taaffe's dispute over land on the borders of Counties Sligo and Leitrim illustrates how complex and long-drawn-out a legal dispute could be. The case involved a number of different courts in Connacht and in Dublin. Surviving chancery pleadings for other areas suggest that litigants sometimes chose to have their cases heard in Dublin rather than in the localities, where the county jury might not have been sympathetic.[8]

The Dublin exchequer and chancery also had the authority to issue commissions to hold inquisitions into the ownership of property in any part of Ireland. Inquisitions were held in County Sligo in the sixteenth century, beginning in 1584 with the finding of Ballymote castle for the crown, but the number of inquisitions recorded for the county increased dramatically after 1603.[9] Although inquisitions were in theory held on the death of every landlord, those which survived in the Dublin archives were recorded there for two main reasons: (i) to find land for the crown where the owner had died in rebellion or without heirs or where the land belonged to a dissolved monastery. A large number of such inquisitions were held after the wars of the 1590s and were usually followed by a grant of the land in question to a servant of the crown. (ii) to find ownership of land where the heir was a minor. Such inquisitions were usually followed by a grant of wardship and were therefore a means used by the government to transfer the ownership of land from catholic to protestant possession. If the heir was found to be of full age, he could be penalised for entering the estate without permission.[10]

Other inquisitions were held to find concealed lands for the crown: in cases, for example, where territory had been omitted from a grant of monastic property and was subsequently found to have belonged to the monastery; or if an inquisition did not, for some reason, record all the land of an owner, a second or even a third inquiry might be held. In other words, inquisitions were used to assert central administrative control over land-ownership and to increase the pool of crown land in the form of property forfeited from attainted rebels or monastic land for distribution to suitable grantees.

Another Dublin court which occasionally took an interest in the affairs of the province was the court of castle chamber, where serious charges of recusancy or refusal to take the oath of supremacy were heard. It is not clear how often this was used for inhabitants of Sligo, but in 1617 increased anti-recusancy activity on the part of the Dublin government led to five members of a County Sligo grand jury being prosecuted in the castle chamber for refusing to indict recusants.[11] The court of wards, revived and updated in the early seventeenth century, also had jurisdiction in Connacht, granting wardships and prosecuting landlords who did not sue out their liveries, i.e. pay a fine to the crown when they inherited their estates. In common with many other areas, there is a notable increase in Sligo landlords paying such fines in the late 1620s and early 1630s, when a new oath was introduced which made it easier for catholics to agree with the terms of the court. Under the new oath allegiance was sworn to the crown, but there was no reference to the king's position as head of the church.[12]

The evidence is meagre and scattered, but it is clear that there was a steady increase in the contact between Sligo inhabitants and the Dublin courts in the early seventeenth century. By the mid-1630s many landlords were making use of and were familiar with legal procedures in the Dublin courts.

Apart from the courts and assize judges, another means by which the Dublin government exercised its authority in the localities was through the

18th century engraving of Ballinafad Castle which was built in 1590 to protect the passes of the Curlews. The castle was destroyed at the end of the sixteenth century but was rebuilt and garrisoned throughout the seventeenth century.

issuing of extraordinary commissions to inquire into specific problems or to implement an administrative programme. The commission for the composition of Connacht had been one such instrument in the sixteenth century, but the number of commissions increased in the seventeenth century, and government by commission became a normal mode of administration in Stuart Ireland. Some of the commissions were concerned with land: ascertaining tenures and later investigating the possibility of a plantation. Others inquired into the collection of government revenues: the composition money and later the subsidy money agreed by parliament.

Among the most significant commissions issued by the early Stuart government were the commissions for the surrenders and defective titles, which enabled landowners with defective land titles, or who held their land only by Irish law, to surrender their estates and receive letters patent for them from the crown.[13] These commissions were issued in 1605, but their operation was suspended in Connacht because it was feared that implementation might endanger the composition of 1585. There was concern that landlords who surrendered their estates would claim as part of their possessions chiefry rents and other lordly exactions which had been abolished by the composition indentures. It was a justifiable fear, for there is evidence to suggest that landowners were attempting to do precisely that. The earl of Clanricard, for example, was rumoured to be claiming a rent-charge which would have bound all the subjects of Connacht to him; and indeed, at an inquisition held to investigate Clanricard's claim to a chiefry rent in County Sligo, evidence was produced of the rents which he claimed the lords of Lower Connacht should give him. Not surprisingly, the local Sligo jury was sceptical about the nature of the evidence. Other Sligo landlords also insisted on chiefry rights, and some were successful in having such rights included in their letters patent.[14] There was in fact considerable confusion among Dublin administrators in the early seventeenth century as to the nature of the composition rent. There was uncertainty as to what lands were liable to payment, and general concern that the payments of the composition tax had declined since the sixteenth century. This confusion made it easier for landlords to ignore the terms of the composition indentures.[15]

The problem of reconciling the composition agreements with the new commissions and the general awareness that the amount collected was considerably less than in 1585 led to Sir George Carew including the matter in his general inquiry into Irish revenues in 1612. Carew's investigations revealed that one of the reasons why the composition revenues had fallen was the large number of landlords who claimed exemptions or freedom from the composition tax. As a result of Carew's inquiry, the administration had a better understanding of the composition agreements and a clearer idea of which landlords were entitled to exemptions.[16] By 1620 the composition revenue had dramatically increased. In 1608 the yearly income from the composition was £114 18s 4d; in 1609 it was £200 16s 8d; but in 1620 £217 16s 2d was recorded as the half-year income from the composition.[17]

The administration of Lord Deputy Wentworth (1633–40) carried out its own investigation into the nature of the composition agreements and maintained the high collection rates: in the 1630s £420 10s was collected, which was actually an increase on the original figure collected in 1585, a result of Wentworth's investigation into the problem of exemptions which led to a considerable reduction in the amount of land exempt from the composition tax.[18]

The composition agreements had arisen out of the need to finance and provide for the army and government in the province. In the early seventeenth century the composition revenues continued to finance the presidential administration. After the parliament of 1615, however, the composition money was not the only form of tax paid by the inhabitants of Connacht to the administration. The parliament agreed that the country as a whole should pay a subsidy to to the crown which would be collected on a county basis. Collectors of the subsidy were appointed, and although the details of the method of collection are unknown, it clearly was collected but not necessarily in cash. [19]

The beginning of the Anglo-Spanish war in 1625 led to an increase in the number of soldiers serving in the Irish army and a need for more money to pay for them. As a result, a three-year subsidy was agreed by the representatives of the Old English in return for concessions concerning the role of catholics in Irish society. In 1627 County Sligo's contribution to the subsidy was assessed at £600 sterling; but with the easing of international tension, the subsidy was reduced and each county was to pay £220 4s for army maintenance. The appointment of Thomas Wentworth as lord deputy led to these figures being revised, and at the end of the 1634–5 parliament new subsidies were announced: Sligo was to contribute £900.[20]

Thus by the 1630s landlords in County Sligo were contributing almost £1,300 annually in government subsidies and composition money to the central government. In addition, many paid rents to the crown which again were recorded and collected more efficiently as the century progressed. Other financial payments to the government included fines for entering estates and for selling land, as indicated above. Thus increased centralisation meant in effect increased taxes and subsidies.

Another financial outlay on the part of the Connacht landlords was in connection with another special commission. As already noted, the implementation of the commissions for surrenders and defective titles was suspended in Connacht because of fears that the composition indentures would be upset. However, following Carew's inquiry into the matter, selected landlords were permitted to make use of the commissions to acquire letters patent for their estates.[21] But it was not until the issuing of another special commission in 1615 that all the landowners in Connacht were given permission to surrender estates and receive regrants. In July 1615 Lord Deputy Chichester was instructed by the king to accept surrenders from every freeholder in Connacht and to make grants of letters patent for their lands.

The composition rent was to be reserved, and the grantees were to pay a fine for any alienations or sales of land carried out without official permission. The commission was seen as completing the unfinished process begun in 1585.[22]

Despite the reference to the past, the commission was in reality a direct outcome of the commissions for surrenders and defective titles of 1605 and was very typical of the methods of government used by the early Stuart regime to tidy up land titles in the country as a whole. As Bernadette Cunningham has shown, the 1615 commission was not completing the process envisaged by the composition indentures of 1585, since the original composition was never intended to deal with all landlords but only with the large ones.[23] The misconception is indicative of the confusion concerning the nature of the composition in the Dublin administration in the early seventeenth century, but it also illustrates the way in which Tudor and Stuart governments attempted to emphasise a consistency and continuity in government policy which did not in fact exist. Just as in the sixteenth century the agreements with O'Connor Sligo were all seen mistakenly as pursuing the same purpose, so too in the seventeenth century earlier agreements were reinterpreted to suit the new demands of the government. The emphasis in the seventeenth century on all landlords holding legitimate titles to land led to the earlier composition agreement being reinterpreted according to the present interests of the central administration. Archival mismanagement and loss of documents was of considerable assistance in arguing consistency in government policy over a long period of time. In the 1570s Malby could not locate a copy of O'Connor's agreement with the government, while in the seventeenth century the original documents concerning the composition were mislaid and thus not available for consultation.

A total of £8,559 was estimated to have been collected in fines from the freeholders in Connacht in connection with the 1615 commission, but, as with the early 1585 agreements, the letters patent were never issued, nor was the reason for this failure ever made clear.[24] It was attributed to clerical error, but it may also have been due to other developments. Shortly after the 1615 inquiry suggestions were made that the whole province of Connacht should be the subject of a plantation, possibly similar to that undertaken in County Leitrim, where one-fourth of the land was forfeited to the crown for use in the plantation. The main beneficiaries of the Leitrim plantation were new English officials in Connacht who purchased grants of Leitrim land from English grantees unwilling to come to live in Ireland. Some of these officials, such as Charles Coote and Maurice Griffith, also served on the 1615 commission. It was Coote and his allies who also advocated a wider plantation in Connacht, and presumably they were hopeful of benefiting in a similar fashion. To have secured land titles in Connacht through the issuing of letters patent might have created difficulties if the plantation scheme was implemented.[25]

However, nothing came of the plantation suggestion before the arrival of Lord Deputy Wentworth in the 1630s. He revived the plan with enthusiasm, and with characteristic efficiency carried out his own investigation into the whole history of the ownership of land in Connacht, the composition of 1585 and the surrenders of 1615. He located the original composition documentation and was thus in a position to make a more accurate analysis of the 1585 agreement. As a result of this investigation, Wentworth concluded that the surrenders and regrants of 1615 were illegal. He pointed out that the commission of 1615 was based on a false premise, i.e. that the commission was merely completing the work initiated in the 1585 indentures. Wentworth rightly pointed out that the composition of 1585 had not been commissioned for the purpose of regulating the landholdings of all the inhabitants of Connacht. There was, he asserted,

no promise that the inferior Freeholders should have any patents nor the chieftaines neither, but only some few of them, and they only of such lands wherein they were to have freedoms by the Indentures of the Compositions.[26]

The instructions of James I in 1615 which ordered the Dublin government to supervise the surrender and regrant of land in Connacht were, therefore, based on 'untrue suggestions and misinformations'. Wentworth was better informed than his predecessors, but he was as guilty as they were in interpreting the composition for his own purposes. Contrary to what he asserted, the composition agreements did propose to grant letters patent to the main chiefs. But from Wentworth's point of view, his reinterpretation suited the political aims of his administration. His analysis of the composition agreements, combined with a belated revival of the Stuarts' claim to all the land of Connacht, as heirs of the earl of Ulster, provided him with an acceptable legal argument on which to base the proposed plantation. Thus his interpretation of previous agreements served his political purpose in the 1630s.

The plantation of Connacht was never implemented, but the plans for it were seriously pursued from the summer of 1635, when inquisitions were held in all the counties in the province, until 1642, when it was formally abandoned by the king.[27] The plantation project clearly created a great deal of fear and unease among all landlords in Connacht. The close connections between townsmen in Sligo and Galway, where the king's title to Connacht was vigorously resisted, must have made Sligo landlords aware of the political opposition to Wentworth's proposals. In addition, the Sligo landlords were presented with a more direct indication of Wentworth's plans for their county. In 1635, when the commissioners for the plantation were meeting in Sligo, Sir Philip Perceval arranged to purchase most of the O'Connor Sligo estate in return for paying off all the mortgages and encumbrances due on the heavily morgaged lands. It was later revealed that Perceval was acting on behalf of the lord deputy and Sir George Radcliffe, who thus became owners of a large estate in County Sligo which included the valuable property of Sligo town. Subsequent allegations claimed that Perceval succeeded in acquiring the land from O'Connor by arguing that it was in reality the property of the king and thus O'Connor was likely to be dispossessed as a result of the plantation. As chapter 7 will show, the involvement of Wentworth and Radcliffe in the Sligo estate aroused considerable local hostility and contributed to the participation of local dignitaries in the rebellion in 1641.[28]

Much emphasis has been placed by historians on the way in which Wentworth outraged Old English sensitivities in his treatment of the earl of Clanricard; it has, however, been insufficiently stressed that Wentworth also had little respect for the titles of the New English landowners in Connacht, the more prominent of whom like Sir Charles Coote expected immunity from the plantation. Wentworth quickly informed Coote and others (including new landlords in County Sligo) that all landowners in the province were to be treated in the same way.[29]

In summary, the increased interest of the Dublin government in affairs in Connacht resulted mainly in increased taxation and, in the 1630s, in increased insecurity of land tenures as the plantation threatened all landlords. This, ironically, occurred despite the various commissions issued by the administration for the specific purpose of making land titles more secure.

President and council

As chapter 3 makes clear, in the sixteenth century the provincial president and council exercised a tight control over English government in the province which few lord deputies managed to influence. Nevertheless, the administrative functions of the president and council in the sixteenth century were limited. As the preceding chapter indicated, justice was implemented crudely and the main emphasis was on the military conquest of the province. The peace after 1603 opened up the possibility of a more civilian type of administration evolving. No records survive of the presidency during this time, so assessing its operation is difficult. Scant references in the records of the central government suggest that the presidential court functioned on a regular basis, and it seems likely that the legal function of the presidential council was the most important aspect of its administrative duties in the early seventeenth century. But the increased centralisation of government in same period placed the president and council of Connacht in a rather ambiguous role. The problem was eased by the frequent absences of the first Stuart president, the earl of Clanricard, in England. Clanricard left the administrative work in the province to his vice-presidents and members of the council and eventually resigned as president in 1616.[30] Thereafter the position was occupied by English-born office-holders, Sir Charles Wilmot and Roger Jones, Viscount Ranelagh.

Although Edward White, who had served on the Elizabethan provincial council, and Sir Oliver St John, vice-president in 1610, both complained of the reduction in their legal fees as a result of the referral of legal cases to Dublin, the presidency of Wilmot in the 1620s seems not to have aroused the same resentment.[31] This may have been because there was a general increase in the number of law cases heard in all courts, including that of the president, in the 1620s and 1630s. Wilmot may also have been careful to have had his legal powers defined more precisely. The renewal of his provincial commissions at the beginning of Charles I's reign spelt out the president's powers in a precise fashion: Wilmot and his council were granted a special commission for jail delivery, and for hearing and determining all treasons, murders, illegal assemblies, felonies, robberies, crimes and other offences in the four counties in their jurisdiction. Thus the presidential court retained its importance despite the growth in the business of the Dublin courts. The surviving chancery pleadings indicate that many of the cases which were heard in the Dublin chancery originated in the president's court. Cases might first be referred by visiting assize judges to the presidential court before transfer to Dublin. Other cases suggest that a conflict could arise among litigants, one of whom might prefer to have the case heard in the provincial court, where the local landlords might be more sympathetic to his cause.[32]

Wilmot's appointment may also have resulted in a closer association between the Dublin and the provincial governments. Wilmot was an important figure in Dublin administrative circles before his appointment as president. There is little evidence of the sort of hostility between him and the Dublin administration which had existed during Clanricard's presidency. Another close connection between the provincial council and the Dublin administration was Geoffrey Osbaldeston, chief justice in Connacht, 1607–16. Before his transfer to Connacht Osbaldeston had served as justice on the king's bench in Dublin.[33]

In England and elsewhere in Ireland the county judicial system depended on the holding of quarter sessions which were attended by the commission of the peace for the county and which in turn referred cases to the biannual assize. The justices appointed to the commission were chosen from the landlords in the county. Although the findings of the 1615 commission provided the government with a list of suitable landlords in County Sligo, there is very little evidence for the existence of quarter sessions in the county before the 1620s. The earliest reference to a quarter sessions being held in County Sligo dates to 1622.[34] In the chancery pleadings there are no references to cases being considered in the quarter sessions in Sligo but there are references, as noted already, to cases being referred from the provincial court. It may well be that the latter initially served the function of the quarter sessions in the counties of Connacht, and that separate quarter sessions were only gradually introduced.

Thus the president and his council continued to play an important part in the legal process in the province despite the increased centralisation of the administration of justice. The dominating control of the presidential council in the sixteenth century was, however, gone for ever. Its main function in the seventeenth century was legal, not political. The closer connections between members of the provincial council and the Dublin administration meant that this reduction in power did not arouse undue hostility on the part of the provincial officials.

County government

In looking at the operation of local government at county level, there is a serious problem of lack of evidence. There are no surviving descriptions of county government anywhere in Connacht before 1641. All that survives for County Sligo are a list of sheriffs; occasional references to sheriffs and other county officials in what remains of Dublin government archives; a list of potential justices of the peace for the county dating to the 1620s; and some miscellaneous information indicating the names of the M.P.s in the county and other county officials such as subsidy collectors, and the names of jurors who sat on inquisitions which were enrolled in the chancery in Dublin. Nonetheless, despite the scanty nature of the evidence, some interesting trends in county government can be detected.

The most important official at local level was the county sheriff. The list of Sligo sheriffs indicates that sheriffs were appointed annually from the 1570s onwards.[35] An examination of the names of the sheriffs reveals some notable developments which may be an indication of wider changes in the local administration. In the sixteenth century the first president to appoint sheriffs was Sir Nicholas Malby, who chose men belonging to disaffected branches of local ruling families. Malby's hope was that such men could be exploited and supported as counterbalances to the ruling lords. For example, in 1581 Brian O'Rourke was selected as sheriff in County Sligo in a deliberate attempt to undermine the control of the ruling O'Rourke (whose territory at the time was part of County Sligo). He was succeeded by William Burke, whom Malby supported in the vain hope that he could act as a rival to the ruling MacWilliam. It is unlikely that either of these men performed any serious administrative duties.[36]

During the regime of Sir Richard Bingham the president's brother George held the position of sheriff for at least three years, and some of the Bingham family's friends and supporters held the position after him, including Henry Bingham (George's son) and William Taaffe, who had previously served as sub-sheriff to George Bingham. As noted already, the activities of these late sixteenth-century sheriffs were the subject of many complaints. The main function of the sheriffs seems to have been the collection of crown rents and provisions for wards in Sligo and Ballymote castles and the maintaining of law and order in a very crude fashion. They made use of the jail built by George Bingham at Ballymote to imprison offenders, but court sessions or assizes were rare events. In 1589 Sir Richard Bingham noted that only two sessions had been held in County Mayo during his presidency.[37] The situation in County Sligo was unlikely to have been much better. The military role of the sheriffs was probably their most important value in the eyes of Lord President Bingham.

During the war years, 1595–1602, no sheriff was appointed, but from 1603 they were once again selected on an annual basis. The establishment of the Connacht assizes, with the biannual visits of the Dublin-based judges and the general improvement in the efficiency of the central government, expanded the administrative function of the sheriff. He was the local officer responsible for bringing offenders before the assize, serving writs, empan-elling jurors, and arranging the lodgings for the judges. He acted as the 'executive officer of the assize'.[38] He was also in charge of the local jail and had the responsibility of ensuring that the punishments imposed by the court were carried out. In addition, he was responsible for executing the orders of other courts, local and central, and for collecting the crown revenues in the county. Thus in the seventeenth century the duties of the sheriff changed from being mainly military to being primarily concerned with administrative matters. He became more like his English counterpart and less like the all-purpose military/administrative figure of the sixteenth century.

It is impossible to assess the extent to which the sheriffs in County Sligo fulfilled all their duties, but the surviving exchequer records in Dublin do contain references to sheriffs from the county returning crown revenues to the court. It should also be added, however, that the records also include names of Sligo sheriffs who had failed to come to Dublin with their rev-enues.[39] It was, therefore, only slowly that the new administrative functions were effectively carried out.

In the years immediately following the war locally born landlords such as Tadhg O'Hara served as sheriff, and one resident new landlord William Taaffe, reappeared on the sheriff list for the county. Both these men were catholics. After 1608, however, in the aftermath of the security crisis caused by the flight of the northern earls, the position of sheriff began to be monopolised by local New English protestant landlords. Roger Jones, an ex-soldier (not to be confused with Roger Jones, Viscount Ranelagh, president of Connacht), held the position four times in the years 1603–41, and four members of the Crofton family held it for a total of seven years during the same period. A revealing aspect of the lists of sheriffs is the number of appointees who were not landowners in the county. Nine times in these years the sheriff selected owned no land in County Sligo. This trend is particularly noticeable in the years 1616–19, when for four years in succes-sion the sheriff was not a landlord in the county. The years are significant because they coincided with a renewed anti-catholic campaign in the country as a whole, and this may have led the government to take particular care to select loyal protestant sheriffs. The sheriffs who are not identified as landlords in County Sligo can nearly all be identified as landlords elsewhere in Connacht, particularly in the counties of Roscommon and Mayo. Walter Harrison, for example, was sheriff in County Sligo in 1616 and had an estate in County Roscommon, as had George Nugent, sheriff in County Sligo in 1614, and Josias Lambert, sheriff in 1609 and again in 1610. Another sheriff with close associations with Roscommon was Captain John St Barbe. During St Barbe's year of office in 1612 William Harrison of Drum, County Roscommon, served as his sub-sheriff. The Croftons were also large landlords in County Roscommon. Similarly, there were also close connections with County Mayo among some of the Sligo sheriffs. Sir Robert Cressey, an important landlord in Mayo, was sheriff in 1626. John Nolan, who was sheriff in Sligo in 1623, was also a landlord in Mayo, where his brother George served as sheriff.[40]

The impression is, therefore, of a small group of New English landlords from Counties Roscommon, Mayo and Sligo dominating the position of sheriff in the period after 1608. A significant change occurred in the middle years of the 1620s when William Taaffe's son John (also a catholic) was selected as sheriff. It was probably no coincidence that in the same year (1624) the first catholic sheriff for twenty four years was selected in County Galway.[41] In the years 1627–30 the county sheriffs in Sligo were also catholics (Jasper Brett and Andrew Crean), and again it was probably not incidental that these years witnessed the zenith of Old English influence in Ireland. It is also significant that in the years 1640 and 1641 the Sligo sheriffs were also catholics; both men, James French (1640) and Andrew Crean (1641), played a leading role in the rebellion and organisation of the catholic forces in the county.[42]

The catholics who held the position of sheriff were predominantly Old English in background: Taaffe, Brett, French. The Creans, the native merchant family from Sligo town, also had close connections with the Old English network.

From 1603 to 1641 only four landlords from a Gaelic background held the position of sheriff of County Sligo: Tadhg O'Hara (1603, 1607, 1608); Owen MacDermot (1620); Tadhg O'Higgin (1634); and Kean O'Hara, son of Tadhg (1639). Tadhg O'Hara, despite his Gaelic ancestry, probably identified with the Old English position. He served as M.P. for the county in 1613–15 and signed the Old English petition protesting against the manner in which protestant M.P.s were elected to the parliament. His son Kean had been brought up as a protestant and was probably the most anglicised local landlord in the county.[43] Owen MacDermot was unusual in that he was one of a small number of Gaelic landlords who was in a position to buy and receive in mortgage lands of impoverished landlords in the locality. His main property was in County Roscommon, but he was active in Sligo, buying land from impoverished landlords in the 1620s and 1630s. His political outlook is unknown, but he later supported the 1641 rising and may have identified with the Old English position.[44] Tadhg O'Higgin was among the ten largest native landlords in County Sligo. His landed wealth in the 1630s reflected the careful way in which he and his father, the poet Tadhg Dall, had protected the family interests. His political outlook is also unknown. In the 1640s he was chosen as a delegate to the confederate assembly at Kilkenny, which is probably evidence of his political conservatism as much as of his catholicism.[45] With the exception of what appear, therefore, to be four conservative-minded and wealthy Gaelic landlords (one of whom was protestant), the majority of the Irish-born sheriffs of County Sligo were associated with the Old English political world.

The names of justices of the peace for the county confirm the trends perceptible in the sheriff list. The list of potential justices, dating to the 1620s or possibly earlier, is headed by Roger Jones, who also held the position of *custos rotulorum*.[46] Captain John St Barbe and two members of the Crofton family are also included. But the list also includes Owen MacDermot, Tadhg O'Higgin, Andrew Crean and Brian MacDonagh. The latter, a son-in-law of John Taaffe, had Old English connections. By 1641 the Old English influence among the J.P.s was even stronger. In that year Andrew Crean was sheriff and James French, John Crean (Andrew's son) and another Old English landlord in the county, Patrick Plunkett, were all serving as justices of the peace in the county.[47] This confirms the trend, suggested by the list of sheriffs, that by 1640 a group of resident catholic landlords with Old English sympathies were beginning to appear more prominent in county affairs and the county administration. A similar development is perceptible in the position of collector of subsidies: in 1617 William Harrison, the Roscommon landlord, held the position for County Sligo, but in 1637 James French of Sligo town was the subsidy collector for the county.[48] Likewise in the town corporation and the court of the statute staple the Old English group were more prominent by the late 1630s than they had been earlier in the century.[49]

The growing prosperity of Sligo town in which the Creans and the Frenches had played an active role; the development of the political awareness and organisation of the Old English at national level; and probably also the growth of local institutions such as the assize court and quarter sessions – all helped to strengthen the leading role among the catholics in Sligo which these men began to assume. Incorporated into this Old English group were some of the leading Gaelic landowning families in the county. Brian MacDonagh, for example, was married to a daughter of John Taaffe, and Tadhg O'Higgin's selection as sheriff in 1634 probably owed much to the support of the same Old English group. Donogh O'Connor Sligo also became linked to this group through his marriage to Lady Sarah MacDonnell, daughter of the earl of Antrim, who also identified with the Old English position.[50] It was not so much a county community but a catholic Old English community which was developing in Sligo in the decades before 1641.

Parliament

The political and social status of the Gaelic families connected with the Old English group emerges in the names of the parliamentary representatives of the county. The parliamentary list reveals the importance of the Taaffes, the wealthiest of the Old English families. In 1613 the county was

59

represented by Tadhg O'Hara, who signed the recusant petition, and by John Taaffe's son-in-law, Brian MacDonagh. In 1634 Tadhg O'Connor Sligo and another son-in-law of Taaffe's, Fergal O'Gara, represented the county, and in 1640 Taaffe's son Theobald held a county seat. By that time, however, the Radcliffe purchase of the Sligo estate also gave parliamentary representation to George Radcliffe. The borough of Sligo by 1640 was also represented by a Radcliffe. Other borough M.P.s were Tadhg O'Hara's son Kean and Roger Jones. Thus the catholic Old English community of Sligo had a strong control over the parliamentary representation of the county, but their control of the borough was more restricted. Their parliamentary influence was clearly directly threatened by the Wentworth/Radcliffe purchase of the O'Connor Sligo estate in 1637, a development which contributed to the growing hostility to Wentworth's government in the late 1630s. The activities of the parliament and contests for representation in it were therefore important at both local and national level. Parliamentary membership could act as a link between the Old English of the east coast and their supporters in the provinces.[51]

The army

In the sixteenth century the army played an important part in the government of County Sligo. It was during the administration of the second president of Connacht, Sir Nicholas Malby, that a garrison was first placed in Sligo in an attempt to stop Scottish troops travelling to Mayo via Sligo. Malby's garrison was not permanent and was withdrawn as soon as the danger had passed. During Bingham's term of office the military presence in the county became more permanent. From 1584 there was a small garrison at Ballymote, and by 1588 Sligo castle was garrisoned and soldiers were stationed in other parts of the county. There was also a large garrison at Boyle under the president's command, and in 1590 the castle in the Curlews was built. In addition, in the mid-1590s there were plans to garrison Bundrowes and Belleek.[52]

All of these garrisons vanished after 1595 when O'Donnell took control of affairs in the region. After the war, as indicated already, a civil administration functioned in the county and the role of the army diminished. It was nonetheless important, particularly after the flight of the northern earls in 1607 and in the climate of fear engendered in Dublin administrative circles after the rebellion of Cahir O'Doherty in 1608. A garrison was stationed at Sligo, and a new fort was built at Ballinafad with Captain John St Barbe in charge of the garrison of ten men. A similar type of fort was built at Drumrusk, County Roscommon, where Captain Mark Griffith was in command. There were also small garrisons maintained at Burrishoole, Bundrowes and Boyle. Thus the north-west was surrounded by a ring of forts, two of which had been newly built for the purpose in the first decade of the seventeenth century.[53]

The army was also important for fostering links between men and, of course, for introducing them to areas where they might later settle. Among the Elizabethan soldiers who 'stayed on' in Sligo were Captain John Baxter, Captain Lionel Guest, Captain Paul Gore and Lieutenant Roger Jones. Charles Coote and Charles Wilmot had also been first employed as Elizabethan soldiers.[54] There were also ex-army men among the new landlords of Mayo, Roscommon and Leitrim, some of whom served as sheriffs in Sligo. Such army connections were an important source of patronage for provincial and county positions as well as for grants of forfeited land. Unlike in the province of Munster, where the earl of Cork controlled the patronage system, no one man emerged as the dominant patron in Connacht, and so the army network of contacts and connections was a powerful factor in county and provincial appointments.

Conclusion

There is a temptation to compare the Irish local government system with that in England; this, however, can lead to distortions. The Irish system, as it developed in Sligo and probably also elsewhere, was far less complex than in England. There was not the same number of officers in the Irish system, nor indeed was there the same number of landed families looking for patronage and office. Security concerns after 1608 and the problem of recusancy meant that local government was controlled for much of the time by a small group of protestant landlords, not all of whom were resident in the county. Gradually in the 1620s and 1630s catholic landlords acquired more influence in local government, but it is important to note that they were a certain sort of catholic: Old English sympathisers. Few catholic Gaelic landlords held administrative positions in this period.

The establishment of local government in the county was a slow business. In 1632 a complaint was made that there was still 'no certain place appointed in County Mayo for holding of assizes, jail delivery, sessions and other public meetings of ministers of justice'. Reference was also made to the fact that justice 'many times was prevented by the ordinary escape of notorious malefactors' from the jail in Cong.[55] In another county close to Sligo, that of Donegal, the clerk of the peace and the sub-sheriff were assaulted by woodkern in 1636 when travelling to attend the sessions in Donegal town, and the attack prevented the sessions from being held because the clerk of the peace was robbed of the records necessary for conducting the proceedings.[56] Events such as these and the continuing presence of English soldiers in the province in general, and in County Sligo in particular, underline the importance of military and defence matters in seventeenth-century Ireland, despite the growth in civil government. At least three sheriffs were also constables of castles and in charge of small garrisons: Roger Jones, Walter Harrison and John St Barbe.[57] Other Sligo sheriffs, as noted already, had served as soldiers, and their military experience may have been an important qualification for the role of sheriff. The early years of James I may have witnessed the creation of the court circuit, but at the same time provost-marshals were appointed, and Captain Charles Coote began his career in Connacht as provost-marshal in 1606.

The extent to which the indigenous population co-operated and were involved in the new local government is difficult to assess. Clearly there was co-operation at many levels. Local people, albeit mainly landlords, used the courts at provincial and central levels; they served as jurors for inquisitions and other sessions of the courts; they took part in the surrender and regrant commission and paid out money for letters patent. But increased government efficiency and centralisation also meant that more financial demands were made by the government on the local landlords, demands which many found difficult to meet, as the next chapter will indicate.

The meagre evidence also suggests that in the 1620s the leadership role of the indigenous catholic families was being taken over by catholic men from the Pale or men with Old English connections who made use of local government office to gain control of county affairs. This trend reflects the increasingly articulate Old English influence at national level, but it also points to the importance of local office as a vehicle for the spread of Old English ideology. This development assumes a major importance in late 1641 when the Old English on the east coast joined the rising of the north. But it should not be presumed that all remnants of the old Gaelic lordships vanished after 1603. The O'Connor Sligo family, despite their financial problems, remained a focus for strong loyalty and respect, as the experience of the 1640s revealed.

GAELIC ECONOMY AND SOCIETY, *C.* 1585-1641

By 1641 the political structure of the Sligo area had been transformed. The Gaelic lordships of medieval Sligo had given way to the English-style county of Sligo. Political change went hand in hand with changes in the economic and social structure as new landlords appeared in the county and English customs and fashions were gradually adopted. Assessing the nature and extent of these changes is a hazardous task. Evidence is scant and unyielding. In this chapter an attempt is made to piece together the evidence which does exist to provide an analysis of the economic and social structure of the county in the late sixteenth and early seventeenth centuries.

Population figures
One of the greatest weaknesses of early modern Irish history is the inability to calculate any sort of reliable population figures from the surviving documentation. Parish records or poll tax lists are virtually non-existent in Ireland before the second half of the seventeenth century, as are other records used by demographic historians to calculate population figures. Records for County Sligo are no better than for the rest of Ireland. No local parish registers survive for the sixteenth or early seventeenth centuries, and the first poll tax (if that is what it is) dates to 1660.[1] The earliest extant list of the inhabitants of the county can be found in a pardon enrolled on the patent rolls in 1603 which contains the names and addresses of almost 1,000 persons (mostly male) living in County Sligo at that time.[2] It is difficult to ascertain what the list represents. Over half the place-names or addresses provided are those of a tower-house or castle, and the names associated with the castle seem to represent a lord or head of a sept, his immediate family, his household staff and some of his followers or tenants. It is likely that the list excluded many who were not involved in the wars of the 1590s or who did not live in the immediate vicinity of the castle or who were not employed in the service of the lord. The pardon list, therefore, provides some indication of the make-up of tower-house society, but it is of little value for calculating population figures. At the most it represents a minimum figure from which an estimate of the population can be calculated.

Other sources which might yield some information about population statistics are the estimates of land quarters in the county which were not classified as 'waste', i.e. unoccupied, by the composition book of Connacht in 1585; a similar note of the quarters which paid composition rent in 1620; and the land survey of the county which was compiled in the mid-1630s in connection with the proposed plantation.[3] The survey lists the land of the county by quarter (roughly the equivalent of the modern townland), naming the landowner or mortgagee and usually the rent which was due from each quarter. Frequently the rent consisted of a cash payment and what the survey called 'country charges' or 'country duties'. These included labour service and rural produce such as a certain number of muttons, barrels of malt and small portions of butter and oats. The quantities were proportionately calculated and seem to have been normally based on the rent due from a cartron, i.e. one-fourth of a quarter. A typical list of dues was that from the quarter of Carrowvonan: £16 rent, 4 barrels of malt, 4 muttons, 8 medders of butter, 20 medders of meal, and 20 days' labour. The half quarter of Lecarrowcruin paid £8, 2 barrels of malt, 2 muttons, 4 medders of butter, 8 medders of meal, and 20 days' labour. The survey occasionally notes the dues to be paid by one labourer. Thus in Curroghvogan in the barony of Leyny the rent was £9 9s, 1 mutton on every tenant, 1 medder of butter, 3 medders of meal, and 12 'workmen', i.e. 12 days' annual labour were demanded of every tenant. In Dawclonagh in Corran the rent was £10, 3 medders of malt, 1 mutton on every tenant, 4 medders of butter, 8 medders of meal, and 36 'workmen'. The entry for Dawclonagh notes that the landlord had 3 tenants and therefore had to pay 3 muttons.[4]

The rents seem, therefore, to be calculated according to the rent paid by one tenant or family for one cartron of land, and on the assumption that each quarter normally contained four tenants. Katharine Simms has suggested that in medieval Gaelic society rents were often calculated according to the number of people who were to pay them, and the Sligo evidence seems to confirm this suggestion.[5] It might, therefore, be possible to provide some indication of the tenant population by calculating the number of occupied quarters. The figure of one mutton per tenant might suggest that the number of muttons, when given as an amount for the whole quarter rather than for individual tenants, may represent the number of tenants on the land. If, therefore, this figure is added to the number of landlords, it could supply some rough statistics for the landlord and tenant population.

There are, however, a number of problems about this approach. First, not all quarters demanded country charges. This problem might be solved by calculating an average number of muttons per quarter in each barony which could be used to calculate the total number of muttons and possibly, therefore, also the number of tenants per barony. The number of resident landlords can also be estimated from the 1635 survey, and this figure, when added to the mutton/tenant figure, can provide a possible estimate of the number of landlords and tenants in the county in 1635. The second problem with these calculations lies in the proportionate nature of the rents. They are based on the assumption that one quarter contains four tenants. Yet average figures of the number of muttons paid per quarter work out slightly higher or, in the case of the barony of Tireragh, slightly lower. Given the paucity of population statistics, however, the figures which emerge from these calculations, however crude, are worthy of consideration (see table 1).

Table 1: Estimated number of tenants and landlords, *c.* 1635

Barony	*Average muttons per qr*	*No. of quarters*	*Total of muttons*	*No. of landlords c. 1635*	*Estimated total of tenants & landlords*
Carbury	4.6	128	588.8	47	635.8
Leyny	4.3	192	825.6	43	868.6
Corran	4.3	152	653.6	53	706.6
Tireragh	3.5	182	637	37	674
Tirerill	4.5	212	954	105	1,059
Coolavin	4.5	40	180	1	181
Total		906	3839	286	4,125

The result is a total of 4,125 landlords and tenants in the county in the mid-1630s. The 1635 survey is incomplete and omits a number of parishes and therefore quarters. It is impossible to calculate exactly how many quarters were excluded, but a comparison with the quarters noted in the county in the composition book of 1585 and another of 1622 gives some idea of the difference (see table 2).

Table 2: Number of quarters, 1585–*c.*1635

Barony	*1585*	*1622*	*c.1635*
Carbury	150	161	128
Leyny	305	212	192
Corran	158	168	152
Tireragh	133	200	182
Tirerill	305	210	212
Coolavin	20	61	40
Total	1,071	1,012	906

Given the imprecise nature of the calculations, it seems unwise to make too much of the discrepancy in the different figures. All three sets of figures provide an estimate of about 4,000 to 4,500 tenants and landlords. Such a figure compares quite favourably with statistics for the later seventeenth century. For example, in the poll tax of 1660 there were 6,877 persons (probably males only over the age of 15) noted for County Sligo. Given the influx into the county by that time of a large number of new settlers and the more general increase in population in seventeenth-century Ireland which has been noted by demographic historians, the relative increase in Sligo seems not unreasonable.[6] So these figures, however crude and open to question, may bear some relation to reality. A multiplier of 4 or 4.5 gives a total population for the county in the early seventeenth century of between 16,000 and 20,000.

Landed families

The figure of 286 landlords in 1635 is based on the Strafford survey, but it should be acknowledged that, as with all these figures, there are problems involved in calculating with any precision the number of native or locally born landlords in County Sligo in the late sixteenth or early seventeenth century. The documentation is scarce and often difficult to interpret. The earliest list of landowners in the county is the inquisition held in 1616 as part of the surrender and regrant arrangements for Connacht.[7] A comparison of this list with the survey of 1635 is not easy, because a piece of land registered in the name of one man in 1616 might be listed as being shared between several in the later documentation. But a rough calculation (which is all that is possible) suggests that there were about 250 native landowners in the county in 1635. The number of owners may have decreased in the 1620s and early 1630s, but the documentation is not refined enough to calculate this.

Of the 250 locally born landowners, the vast majority were members of the old ruling or lordly families of the area: the O'Connors Sligo, the MacDonaghs, the O'Dowds, O'Haras and O'Garas. Before the arrival of new English and Pale landlords each of these lordly families dominated the landownership of their individual lordships.[8] Thus the O'Connors controlled most of the land in Carbury, the different branches of the MacDonaghs the territory in their lordships of Corran and Tirerrill, while the O'Dowds, O'Haras and O'Garas held most of the land in Tireragh, Leyny and Coolavin respectively. In addition, the O'Connors of Sligo held a castle and some land in each of the other lordships, possibly in recognition of their position as overlord in the region, but also no doubt for strategic reasons: most of the castles lay in the vicinity of Ballysadare Bay.

The composition book of Connacht of 1585 indicates that within each lordship the land was divided into a number of 'cowrin' or *cómhranna*, i.e. sections or segments. Each *cómhroinn* was called after a different branch of the ruling family. Thus in Carbury there were four such *cómhranna*. Genealogical evidence indicates that the Carbury *cómhranna* were called after the four sons of Domhnall O'Connor, lord of Sligo, who died in 1395. The territorial divisions among his sons must have taken place in the early fifteenth century. Similarly, the seven *cómhranna* of Tirerrill are named after men who flourished in the fifteenth century. It is not clear why these territorial divisions took place in the fifteenth century, but as indicated in

18th century engraving of Roslee Castle: tower-house of the O'Dowds.

chapter 2, this was the period when the O'Connors of Sligo were at the height of their power and also the time when Connacht experienced a certain degree of prosperity which manifested itself in the building of tower-houses as residents for individual lords. The tower-houses were associated with specific *cómhranna*, and so the division of the territory and the establishment of permanent dwellings were interconnected. These developments may also reflect a change in society and warfare as Gaelic lords began to live in castles and divide their lordships into territorial units associated with individual castles.

The extent to which the *cómhranna* and the sept divisions which they indicate were an accurate reflection of the landholding pattern of the late sixteenth century varied among the lordships. In Leyny and Tirerrill the divisions do correspond to the division of land among the O'Haras and the MacDonaghs. The MacDonagh lands were still divided between the seven septs noted in the composition book, and the O'Hara territory was also held by the septs which dated back to the fourteenth and fifteenth centuries. This does suggest considerable continuity of landownership within the individual septs. By contrast, in the O'Connor lordship of Carbury and the O'Dowd lordship of Tireragh such continuity is not present. In these lordships, although the composition book indicates that the land was still divided into *cómhranna* which date back to the middle ages, in reality by the late sixteenth century most of the land of the lordship was held by one branch of the family, with the other branches holding only small portions. The lord and his immediate family had been able to oust the other branches from possession, and so continuity of ownership is not in evidence in these lordships. This difference in distribution of land within the ruling families reflects the control which the lords had in their different lordships. In Carbury, Tireragh and Coolavin the lord was sufficiently powerful to acquire and control a large proportion of the land, while in Tirerrill and Leyny the lord's control was weak, so that he was not in a position to control more than the land of his own sept.

Land was also held by families who rendered special services to the lord and his supporters. The mercenary soldier families of MacSweeney and MacDonnell held small portions of land in Tireragh and Leyny, as did the O'Harts, who are described as the cavalry of O'Connor Sligo. The bardic family of Ó hUiginn had land in Leyny, and the legal family of MacBrehon held a small amount of land in the same lordship, while a number of ecclesiastical families were also landholders, although they were later obliged to rent their lands from the bishop in whose diocese the land lay. Apart from these families, the only other notable landowning group were the Creans, the merchant family associated with Sligo town.

In summary, therefore, landholding was confined mainly to lordly families and other families who performed special services of a military, legal, literary, ecclesiastical or commercial kind. Branches of the ruling families (often descended from a different eponymous head from the main branch of the family) might also hold a small portion in each lordship. This land usually lay in peripheral areas, and it is likely that these families had been pushed into marginal lands as the branches of the ruling family expanded. Some families therefore declined in terms of power and influence in the course of the middle ages. But while this type of downward movement can be indirectly documented, it is also clear that other families, such as the MacDonagh or the O'Hara septs, retained ownership of the same land over several centuries. The oft-quoted assertion of the genealogist Mac Firibisigh that in Gaelic society families rose and fell from power very quickly needs to be modfied in relation to Sligo. It was a rule to which there were clearly many exceptions.

Customs of inheritance and land tenure

There has been much confusion among historians about Gaelic land tenure and inheritance practices. Partible inheritance, or gavelkind, as it is sometimes erroneously called, is often regarded as operating in all parts of Gaelic Ireland in a roughly similar fashion. According to this somewhat simplistic perception, land was held by the sept; all male members of the sept were entitled to an equal temporary share in the land; and the land of the sept was redistributed frequently, in many places annually.

The reality was rather different. An examination of Gaelic land law as it operated at local level reveals many variations and deviations from the general description. This is because the essential feature of Gaelic land law was that it was customary law, with no centralising authority enforcing uniformity or regularity. Among Sligo families in the sixteenth and early seventeenth centuries there are examples of one son inheriting the land held by his father, who in turn had received it from his father; of brothers sharing land, and more infrequently of a wider family group dividing the land between them. There is no evidence of annual or even regular redistribution of land, but there are clear indications of considerable continuity of landownership over several generations. Obviously the period under examination is a time of change when English common law and primogeniture inheritance was becoming increasingly popular among landowners. The emphasis on the stem family in land inheritance may be due to this influence, although the evidence does suggest that such practices were already common from a much earlier period.

As already indicated, the land was held by different septs or branches of the main ruling families, and normally inheritance seems to have taken place within each sept without reference to the other branches of the family. For example, in Tirerrill, where inheritance can be traced over several generations down to 1641, seven septs held a certain portion of land which they maintained and transferred from one generation to another without reference to the other septs in the lordship. Obviously this system broke down in the lordships of Tireragh and Carbury, where the ruling lord took over the property of other septs.

The sharing of land among brothers and the passing of land from father to son or sons were the most usual inheritance arrangements. The distribution of land within a wider family or sept group was not common. Some form of major redistribution may have occurred among the O'Dowds, but the evidence to trace this is very poor. There is more positive evidence of a redistribution of lands among a wider family group of a minor branch of the O'Connors Sligo. This sept had lost a considerable amount of property through forfeiture, and the redistribution may have taken place to ensure that all the families in the sept had some land to sustain them. A redistribution of this kind was actually recommended by the authorities to the MacDonagh sept who complained of the loss of Ballymote castle and its lands when it was seized for the crown in 1585.[9]

More usually, however, landholding was confined to a much smaller family group: a father and his sons. There are documented examples of a father leaving land to one son and thereby leaving other sons without land. There were advantages in adopting primogeniture: a father could pass the land on to his heir without subdivision. But there were also disadvantages, as the O'Connor Sligo story illustrates. The O'Connors Sligo clearly followed English common law right through the period, and the problems which they encountered illustrate all the worst aspects of the primogeniture system. Following Sir Donogh O'Connor's death in 1609, there were four heirs to the estate before 1641. Sir Donogh had died without heirs male and was succeeded by his brother Domhnall, who died in 1611. Domhnall's son and heir, Charles, a minor, was made a ward of court for eleven years. He entered into his estate in 1622, but died three years later, also without heirs male. His brother Donogh, who succeeded him inherited an estate burdened with two large widow's jointures (those of the countess of Desmond, wife of Sir Donogh, and of her daughter, who had married Domhnall, Sir Donogh's brother and heir). In addition, a large part of the estate was mortgaged to the Galway merchant family of French. Donogh married Sarah, daughter of Lord Antrim; her dowry was intended to mitigate Donogh's financial problems, but it failed to resolve the difficulties of the estate. Donogh complained that of the 800 quarters in the estate, he enjoyed only 200. His early death without heirs left the estate further encumbered with the jointure of Sarah. Donogh's heir, Tadhg (who was in fact his uncle and a brother of Domhnall who died in 1611), made another attempt to solve the family's financial difficulties by selling to Sir George Radcliffe and Lord Deputy Wentworth a large part of the estate (including the town of Sligo) in return for a completely unencumbered title to the remainder. Tadhg did not live to enjoy his new reduced estate for very long, and four years later his son, another Tadhg, tried to recover the lost family lands following the attainder of the earl of Strafford (as Wentworth had by then become) in 1641. When he and his brothers supported the rebellion in 1641, they forfeited the entire estate.[10]

The failure of the O'Connors to produce direct heirs; the swift succession

of deaths and inheritances, together with the resulting large widow jointures and rapid recurrence of fines for entering into the estate; and finally,
the long minority of Charles (when the profit of the lands went to the
guardian) – all combined to produce a classic case of what could go wrong
with the inheritance system under English common law. The collapse of the
family's wealth was directly related to the inheritance practice which they
adopted.

Another family which practised what seems to have been a form of
primogeniture was the O'Garas of Coolavin. In this case, however, the
custom was probably adopted long before the beginning of the Tudor
administration in Sligo. For much of the fifteenth and sixteenth centuries
the position of O'Gara had passed from father to son. And in the sixteenth
and early seventeenth centuries the land of the family followed a similar
pattern. The result was that the O'Gara had control of all of the lands of his
lordship. It seems unlikely that over several generations successive O'Gara
chiefs produced only one son each. There must therefore have been sons
and other male members of the family excluded from land and power. The
preference of Ulster lords for primogeniture in the late medieval period has
been noted by Dr Katharine Simms, which suggests that the O'Garas'
inheritance practices were not unusual in Gaelic Ireland. As Simms points
out, if a lord and a ruling family had the opportunity of preserving the
inheritance within a small family unit, then they did so.[11]

A minor branch of the O'Connor Sligo family also practised primogeniture.
In a society where definitive titles and ownership of land were not significant
the difference between primogeniture and partible inheritance was perhaps
not important. Other members of the family may have rented land cheaply
or for a nominal rent from the head of the family. This is what happened in
the early seventeenth century among the MacDonaghs of Collooney, where
Brian MacDonagh leased land to his two brothers. His son Brian Óg, who
inherited the estate, continued to rent land to his uncles on the death of his
father. The O'Dowds of Kilglass and O'Haras of Coolaney operated a
similar system where a younger brother was given some land.[12]

It is perhaps wisest to think in terms of a flexible system of land inheritance
which adapted itself to the needs of the family and which might change over
time. An important factor in changing the system was the survival of a large
number of male heirs which might lead to a division of the estate. If the
number of male heirs was small, then a form of primogeniture might be
adopted as the best way of maintaining the unity of the land. High mortality
rates and loss of life through factional fighting meant that the number of
male heirs could be surprisingly low. An analysis of forty seventeenth-
century landed Sligo families, noted in the genealogies of Mac Firbisigh and
another genealogical collection known as the MacDonagh manuscript,
both of which list the number of males in each family, produced an average
of 3.3 males per family.[13] This average may seem low, but it is comparable to
the figure of two or three sons per family which Gearóid Mac Niocaill found

to be the commonest size of male family from his analysis of similar genealogical material. The figures also corroborate what is known about a number
of the main landed families in Sligo in the seventeenth century. Brian Óg
MacDonagh of Collooney, for example, had the good fortune to be the only
surviving son of his father, and the O'Haras of Coolaney also produced an
average of two to three sons over several generations.[14] In such cases it was
easy to accommodate the sons who did not inherit from the father.

If some families confined inheritance to one heir, sharing of land between brothers on a more equal basis was also common among Sligo
families. In the case of the MacDonaghs of Ballindoon, the distribution of
the family land between six brothers is documented, with the eldest brother
taking the largest share and making the division. Subsequently each of the
brothers passed their individual shares to a single son. Thus the family lands
became permanently divided. It is impossible to know in examples such as
these if the transfer from the extended family inheritance to individual
stem families took place under pressure to adopt English common law or
whether it was a Gaelic custom which was practised occasionally in order to
prevent the land being subdivided into uneconomic units. A similar division
seems to have taken place among the O'Haras of Ballyara. Negative evidence
might indicate that care was customarily taken to ensure that land did not
become too subdivided. No Sligo landlord held the tiny fractions of land
into which some parts of neighbouring Mayo were divided. As noted already,
the smallest unit was usually a cartron, i.e. one-fourth of a quarter. Occasional
redistribution of the land held by the sept might prevent land from being
subdivided into very small uneconomic units. Evidence from other Sligo
families also confirms that redistribution was an infrequent occurrence.
Chancery pleadings describe men holding land for their lifetime and passing it on to their son or sons, who in turn held it for their lifetime. In a
society with a low population it was probably not difficult to locate new land
for grazing or farming. This may mean that the need to redistribute did not
arise very often. If family land became too small through subdivision then it
might be expanded through the acquisition of new territory.[15]

In Ballindoon and elsewhere the transfer of land took place on the death
of the father. A chancery pleading concerned with land in Bricklieve also
refers to parcels of land being held by individuals for forty or fifty years and
being inherited by sons after the death of the father.[16] Occasionally, however, the 1635 survey of landowners in Sligo records that a father gave his
son a small portion of land during his lifetime. This seems to have occurred
when the son got married, so the land was presumably to allow the son to
provide separately for his wife and family.[17]

An increasingly common means of transfer, particularly among the larger
landowning families, was the use of a deed transferring the land to one or
very often several men, but retaining the use to the owner and his wife or
son. This was a means of ensuring a safe inheritance to the son and took the
place of a will. It also enabled the heir to avoid fines for entering the estate,

and for this reason this type of land transfer was outlawed by the statute of uses in 1634.[18]

The Sligo evidence therefore suggests that land inheritance among male heirs was a varied business in which no one strategy was preferred to another. Different forms of partible inheritance as well as primogeniture were used. The choice of land inheritance practice depended on the individual circumstances of the family. In their selection of different choices, Sligo families had much in common with families in other countries where partible inheritance flourished. As Margaret Spufford has put it in relation to parts of England, 'the distinction between primogeniture and unigeniture on the one hand, and partible inheritance on the other is a very blurred one'.[19] R. A. Dodgshon has described a similar pattern in Scotland: 'Land law was rarely static over long periods, but constantly shaped itself to the pressures and needs acting upon it.'[20] L. K. Berkner summed up the situation by suggesting that partible inheritance 'always leaves open a wide range of strategies for each individual family, depending on their personal, economic and demographic situation'.[21]

Partible inheritance was under attack in the early seventeenth century. Primogeniture was increasingly adopted in the seventeenth century, but in 1641 it was still only one of a number of inheritance strategies chosen by Sligo landlords.

Women as inheritors and landholders

The 1635 survey indicates that it was common practice by that date for a woman to enjoy a widow's jointure. The land was frequently transferred to the woman by her new father-in-law on marriage. The land was a security for the woman if her husband died before her. It was held during the lifetime of the widow, and after her death it reverted back to her husband's family. The remarriage of the widow did not result in reversion. There are several instances cited in the survey of widows having remarried who continued to enjoy the jointure of their first marriage. Men might also receive land from their fathers-in-law as a dowry or marriage portion, although in these cases the transfer of land was usually permanent.[22]

The widow's jointure could pose problems for the economic viability of the estate. In times of increasing economic pressure in the seventeenth century it is not surprising that landlords were reluctant to lose part of their profits. For example, controversy arose concerning the countess of Desmond's large jointure from her husband, Sir Donogh O'Connor Sligo, and that of his heir's widow (the countess's daughter) which seriously undermined the economic value of an already heavily mortgaged estate.[23] Brian Óg MacDonagh of Collooney inherited only a small estate from his father – the rest was mortgaged to various money-lenders. His mother's jointure thus also deprived him of some of the much-needed income from the estate.[24]

The problem of the jointure and the alienation which it involved, particularly when the widow remarried, could be overcome if the widow handed over the management of the estate to her in-laws, as the survey notes at least one woman did. Another woman, Una O'Hara *née* Gallagher, solved her in-laws' problem by leaving Sligo on the death of her husband and returning to her family home in Donegal. She made an arrangement to lease her widow's jointure to undertenants, on condition that she could return to live on it, if she so desired, on giving sufficient notice of her intention to do so.[25]

If marriage and subsequent widowhood reduced the landed possessions of a family, it could also help to expand the family holding or rescue it from economic penury. Land in the form of a dowry has already been noted as being quite common. Brian Óg MacDonagh of Collooney, who inherited an estate most of which was mortgaged, received a more satisfactory dowry than mere land. His father-in-law, Sir John Taaffe, redeemed one of the largest mortgages on his estate: that of £800 to a Mr Browne of Galway. Thus Brian Óg and his new wife were able to begin married life with a much larger and less encumbered estate than Brian Óg had inherited from his father.[26]

Apart from widows' jointures, a small number of women also inherited land in the early seventeenth century, usually in the absence of male heirs. There is at least one example of this in early seventeenth-century Sligo when Eibhlín O'Hara inherited her brother's estate, a development which probably owed much to the influence of her brother's guardian, Sir Roger Jones. Subsequently Eibhlín married a member of the Jones family, who thereby acquired the O'Hara estate.[27]

Wardship

Another means by which land temporarily left the possession of the family was through the wardship of a minor. If an heir was under age, his custody and that of his family estate was granted to a guardian in exchange for a fine paid to the crown. The guardian was granted an allowance for looking after the ward and was allowed to enjoy the benefit of the land of the estate until the ward came of age. In the early seventeenth century the guardians of Sligo minors were normally New English protestants. Roger Jones's wardship of Seán O'Hara, noted above, is an example of this development. Jones also had the wardship of an O'Connor from a minor branch of the Carbury family, while Sir Charles Coote was the guardian of Tadhg O'Hara of Coolaney, and Sir Theobald Dillon acquired the wardship of Fergal O'Gara of Coolavin. Lionel Guest, an Elizabethan soldier, acted as David O'Dowd's guardian, and Edward Crofton was appointed as guardian to the heir of the main MacSweeney family in Sligo. The guardian not only enjoyed the profits of the land during the minority of the heir, but frequently retained an interest in the estate when the ward came of age. Roger Jones received lands in mortgage from both his wards, as did Sir Charles Coote and Edward Crofton from theirs. The money may have been needed to pay fines for formally entering the estate when the heir came of age and for other expenses involved in taking possession. There were also instances of more intimate connections being established between the ward's family and that of the guardian. As noted already, a relative of Roger Jones married the female heir of the O'Hara estate. Other guardians were also involved in marriages with the families of their charges. Lionel Guest, for example, married David O'Dowd's mother – a marriage which led to a dispute over the inheritance of the family land. Sir Charles Coote put Malby Ormsby in charge of the lands of his O'Hara ward; subsequently a member of the Ormsby family, Thomas, married the young heir's sister, and several other Ormsbys rented lands on the O'Hara estate in the 1630s. The Ormsby influence in Sligo, begun in such an indirect and modest way, was to be substantially expanded in the Cromwellian land settlement of the 1650s.[28]

A wardship could therefore have important consequences for the future development of a family's landholdings. The implications could be detrimental for the estate, but a powerful guardian could also protect the estate from forfeiture or loss. It is probably no coincidence that Fergal O'Gara and Kean O'Hara (heir of Tadhg) were the largest Gaelic landlords in Sligo in 1641. Both had experienced long wardships under the protection of two of the most important men in Connacht: Sir Theobald Dillon and Sir Charles Coote.

Other forms of land transfer

Inheritance and marriage were the most obvious ways of land transfer, but there were others. As indicated above, a chief and his family could simply usurp the land of others, or 'out' them as the 1635 survey termed it. Land could also be taken when it was lying waste and uninhabited, and it is likely that in a region of low population uninhabited land was quite common. The survey refers to an English soldier, Gilbert Green, and some local men moving into waste land in the 1590s.[29] Land might also be given to a lord in return for his protection. In a society where definite land titles and borders were not considered important the transfer of legal ownership by deed to a lord might be viewed as a very sensible precaution. The lord had larger resources to protect the land from seizure or forfeiture. This may explain why, for example, Oilill O'Gara transferred all his property by deed to Sir Donogh O'Connor Sligo in 1603. O'Gara had been threatened with forfeiture after the 1589 rebellion, and he may have feared a similar development after the wars of the 1590s. A number of men made claims to land in Coolavin, and O'Gara may have felt that Sir Donogh O'Connor Sligo, the lord of Lower Connacht, had the support of the crown and might therefore be in a position to defend him against possible land predators. In the event, it was the crown-appointed guardian, Sir Theobald Dillon, who offered the most effective protection to the O'Gara estate.[30] A smaller group of landowners, the MacKeons, attempted a similar agreement with Sir Frederick Hamilton to protect their interests.[31]

Sale of land is a vexed question in studies of Gaelic society. How was it done, and how did it effect the family ownership of the land? The Sligo evidence throws little light on the topic, but sales and mortgaging of land were a fact of life in early seventeenth-century Sligo and were a common method of transferring property. At this time there was a great expansion in the land market in Sligo. An increasing number of small and large land-owners sold or mortgaged parts of their estates. In many cases the form of mortgage agreed meant that the mortgagor took possession of the land until the money was repaid. Frequently redemption never took place, and so the mortgagor became the effective owner of the land. In some cases, indeed, it is likely that a mortgage agreement was used to disguise a sale so as to avoid paying alienation and other fees demanded by the crown. Such transactions could take place within the family (there are examples of an uncle selling land to a nephew), but more usually in the early modern period the transfer of land was to an outsider. Reference has already been made to the mortgaging of large parts of the O'Connor Sligo property to the Frenches, and other sales and mortgaging transactions are described in chapter 6 below.[32]

Although most of the new landowners or receivers of land as a result of mortgaging were Galway merchants, Englishmen or men from the Pale, there were some local landlords who took advantage of the financial troubles of their neighbours. The most important of this group was Andrew Crean, a member of the Sligo merchant family. By the early seventeenth century Crean had a house in Sligo town and an estate in the rural hinterland of the town, and he had expanded his landed possessions by taking land in mortgage in other parts of County Sligo. Andrew Crean's son John and another Crean merchant in the town, Roebuck, were also adding to the Crean estates through purchase and mortgage in the early seventeenth century. By comparison with the Galway merchants, the Creans' outlay on mortgaging was small, but among the local Sligo families, many of whom were sinking into financial debt, their success was impressive. Presumably their commercial transactions gave them the necessary capital for land acquisition.[33]

Use of land

Despite the apparent equality of Gaelic land law, the mortgaging and selling of portions of land on a small and a large scale meant that by the 1630s, at least, there was considerable discrepancy in the size of landholdings. Some were quite extensive, but most were very small, and the use to which the land was put depended on the size of the holding. The larger landholding families rented most of their lands, while smaller landholders with only a small holding were not in a position to do this and kept most of their land for their 'own use' as the 1635 survey put it.

The figures provided by the 1635 survey indicate that by that date over half the landlords either rented no land or else rented a small portion of land which yielded, according to the survey, a rent of less than £9 per annum.

Table 3: Landed Income of Gaelic landlords in County Sligo *c.* 1635*

Rental	%
No rent	25
£1–£10	35
£11–£20	19
£21–£30	6
£31–£50	7
£51–£60	2
£61–£70	0.5
£71–£100	0
£101–£200	2
£201–£300	3
£301–£400	0.5

*Figures exclude country charges (also listed in the 1635 survey)

A quarter of landlords did not rent any land, but 'kept it for their cattle' or their own use, as the survey sometimes indicates. Almost a third of the landlords received an annual rent valued between £10 and £50, and only 7 per cent had a rent roll of over £50 (see table 3). Clearly the Sligo landlords were not, as a group, wealthy. The rent figures given in the survey are deficient owing to the incompleteness of the surviving documentation: a mumber of parishes are omitted. But the omissions could not seriously alter the relative wealth of the Sligo landlords, nor is it likely that any of them received much more than they are credited with in the survey. In any particular year the rent roll was likely to be less than it should have been for various reasons, e.g. as tenants moved around and left land waste, or simply could not afford to pay the rent. It is not at all clear, either, that cash actually changed hands in the form of rent. Cattle may have been the normal means of paying rent noted in money values in the written documentation. A number of surviving agreements made provision for cattle to be given in lieu of cash.[34]

According to the 1635 survey, there were a total of ten landlords with a rental of over £100 (see table 4). The list reflects the survival of local Irish families in the turbulent economic circumstances of the 1620s and 1630s.[35] The situation at the end of the sixteenth century might have been very different, but the figures do at least give some indication of the income of the largest of the local Sligo landlords in the 1630s.

Apart from their cash or beef rent, landlords received country produce in the form of barrels of malt, mutton, medders of butter and meal and sometimes wheat, as well as labour services. As indicated already, the amount of produce was carefully calculated according to the proportions due from one cartron. The amounts of malt (in barrels) and mutton were usually the same : 4 per quarter or 1 per cartron. And the amount of butter was usually half the amount of meal paid. The normal measure for butter and meal was a medder (Ir. *meadar*), a type of drinking vessel. Leases issued by Patrick French refer to the medder being a 'Sligo measure' or an 'Enease crean [Enniscrone?] measure', which suggests that the merchants in Sligo town had a medder of a certain size which was taken as the standard measure for rent collection. Patrick French's leases also instruct tenants to deliver the produce to his house at different times during the year. The muttons, for example, were to be paid on Lammas Day.[36]

Table 4: Rentals of largest Gaelic landlords in County Sligo, *c.* 1635*

Name	Rental	Profitable Acreage+
Fergal O'Gara	£398	*c.* 4,132
Kean O'Hara	£370	*c.* 5,199
David O'Dowd	£246	*c.* 2,476
Andrew Crean	£227	*c.* 3,600
Charles O'Dowd	£155	*c.* 2,708
John Crean	£137	figure not available
Tadhg Og O'Higgin	£132	*c.* 2,185
Tadhg O'Connor Sligo	£111	
Countess of Desmond (widow's jointure)	£289	*c.* 13,755
Lady Cressey (widow's jointure)	£224	

*Figures exclude country charges (also listed in the 1635 survey).
+based on Books of Survey and Distribution

In addition to rent, the chief families were also entitled to collect tribute due to the lord. Although most of these, with the exception of those due to O'Connor Sligo, had been abolished in 1585, there is evidence that some lords continued to collect 'chiefries' in the seventeenth century, and new landlords also retained these traditional exactions.[37]

The cash or beef rent or tribute might be used to purchase food for the landlord's family and retinue, but the 1635 survey notes that some landlords reserved some of their property as demesne land, which may have been worked with the assistance of tenant labour to produce further produce for domestic purposes. O'Connor Sligo kept a quarter of land for his own use, according to the survey; David O'Dowd also kept some land around Lackan, where he had a castle; Fergal O'Gara kept a quarter of land around Copponagh castle; Tadhg Óg O'Higgin kept two quarters of land with a mill for his own use; and Cormac O'Hara, the younger son of Tadhg O'Hara, kept a quarter of land, on which he had a house and a mill. The countess of Desmond kept the four quarters of Ballincar, where she lived in the castle, for her demesne lands. It too had a horizontal or 'low Irish' mill on it.[38]

One of the larger landlords in Sligo in the early seventeenth century was Cormac O'Hara, who died in 1612. Cormac's will has survived among the O'Hara papers and provides an indication of the type of farming and lifestyle which this lord, the O'Hara Boy, carried out on his land.[39] His list of goods included 61 cattle, 52 mares and colts, 60 great hogs, and 30 sheep, as well as 'grayne of corn as well gathered as in the ground'. Among the items which Cormac left to his wife, apart from land, were a hackney, cattle and mares, as well as all his corn in the ground and the free use of the mill of Coolaney for her own 'private' corn for as long as she remained unmarried.

Clearly, then, O'Hara was mainly engaged in pastoral farming, raising cattle, horses, pigs and sheep. But he also grew some corn which, like the corn grown by his widow, was probably for his 'private' or domestic use. The presence of brewing instruments among his household goods also indicates that brewing took place on the estate (malt was commonly included in the country charges). It is likely that most of the other landlords who kept land for their own use worked their demesne lands in a similar fashion to Cormac O'Hara. Thus the Sligo evidence confirms Kenneth Nicholls's conclusion that Irish society was not rigidly divided between cultivators and non-cultivators.[40] Sligo landlords worked their demesne lands and also cultivated crops for domestic purposes.

O'Hara's stock may have been typical of that of other landlords in the region. A late sixteenth-century document suggests that the O'Gara of the time had about eighty cows, which would correspond roughly to the number possessed by Cormac O'Hara. These are small numbers in comparison with the thousands of cattle described in the possession of other Irish lords; but none of the Sligo lords were large or wealthy.[41]

Apart from the dozen or so large landlords in 1635, there were many small ones whose holdings were often under 100 acres. As described already, some held land as individuals, passing their land on to a son; others shared land with brothers. Some small landholders leased out small portions of land and also kept some for themselves, usually for their stock to graze. Some grazed their cattle on land which they had also rented out. For example, Brian MacNogley in Tirerrill rented out land which his own cattle also grazed, and Owen Duff MacBrehon pastured some land 'in common with his undertenants who pay him for their share'.[42] Other small landlords kept all their land for their own use and did not rent it out. While the large landlord families were all associated with a tower-house or castle, some of the smaller landholders were not and may have lived in cabins or cottages similar to those occupied by their tenants.

The extent to which the stock raised by the landlords and received in rent was marketed is impossible to ascertain. In his will Cormac O'Hara left instructions for his son to sell some mares and cows to pay for his debts and the expenses of his funeral as well as for the erection of a monument at Court Abbey, where he was to be buried. This does suggest that the animals were reared for sale, probably in Sligo town, which later gained a reputation for having a good cattle and horse market. Presumably large Sligo landlords participated in and profited from the Irish export market in hides and beef. Small landlords may have disposed of their small surplus either in Sligo town or privately. The complaints of 1589 indicate that private sales were quite common in the sixteenth century; but as the seventeenth century progressed, markets and fairs developed in Ballymote, Templehouse and elsewhere and provided wider facilities for public transactions.[43]

As well as cattle, O'Hara also had 60 hogs and 30 sheep. The prominence of mutton in the rents of the area indicate that sheep were extensively reared. Again, it is likely that many local landlords were able to sell wool in Sligo town, where it was an important export. Indeed, there may be a case for arguing that local Sligo landlords were more directly affected by the problems in the woollen market in the 1620s and 1630s than they were by bad harvests. In a largely pastoral economy where milk products formed a major part of the diet, harvest failure may not have had a large impact on the income of the landlords. On the other hand, a decline in the woollen market for landlords who reared sheep for wool must have had serious economic consequences. The documentation is not, however, detailed enough to trace the impact of the problems in the woollen industry on landlords in Sligo, but it must have been a contributory factor to their growing indebtedness in the 1620s and 1630s.[44]

The quantities of crops received in rent by the Sligo landlords were small; and, as with O'Hara, it is unlikely that many of them were large-scale cultivators. The main crops grown, if the 1635 survey is an accurate guide, were oats and a small amount of wheat and barley. The farming produce in Sligo was therefore very similar to that in other parts of Ireland, with oat-bread, milk and butter forming a large part of the diet. The only contemporary reference to food in the county, which appears in the narrative of Cuellar, the Spanish soldier who travelled through the northern part of the county in 1588 following the wreck of his ship, confirms this impression. He wrote of being given oaten bread and butter to eat and milk to drink.[45]

Apart from rent and the profit of the demesne lands, landholding families could also profit from other natural resources. The 1635 survey notes the presence of a considerable number of mills: over fifty altogether, many of which were associated with a landlord family's tower-house or castle. Most of the mills noted were horizontal or 'low Irish' mills, but six were 'English' or vertical mills, presumably of the type introduced into Ireland by the Normans. Owners of mills charged for the use of them, as is evidenced by Cormac O'Hara's wish that his widow should have free use of the mill in Coolaney for as long as she remained unmarried, and also by the 1635 survey, which noted the additional value a mill gave to land on which it was situated. Occasionally the survey notes that the landowner had leased the mill to a miller. It is not clear, however, if tenants were obliged to use the landlord's mill, as they were in feudal society. It is possible that the quantities of cereal grown by many tenants were so small that domestic grinding was common.

Later in the seventeenth century landlords did begin to insist in writing that tenants bring their corn and cloth to the landlord's mills.[46]

Besides corn mills there were four tucking mills for finishing cloth in the county in 1635. They were all on new landlords' estates, which suggests that tucking mills were not in common use before the arrival of the new landlords in the seventeenth century, and that therefore wool and linen were probably woven domestically.[47]

The 1635 survey notes the presence of fishing weirs on rivers, particularly on the Owenmore and Unshin, where trout and eels were caught. It is impossible to ascertain, however, if the fish was consumed locally or sold to merchants from Sligo, where salmon from the town's weirs and herring from the sea were important exports. Timber was also plentiful, but this was a resource which was exploited by the new rather than the older local landlords. Other natural resources such as quarries and a lead mine which are noted in the 1635 survey may also have yielded a small profit in some form to their owners.

Economic change and the local landlords

The extent to which the large landlords benefited from or adapted to the changes of the early modern period varied and owed much to luck, foresight and sheer cunning. Table 4 lists the largest local landlords in the county by 1635. Clearly survival in the new English world of the seventeenth century was not related to the political status of the family in the old Gaelic world. The head of the O'Connor Sligo family, the old lords of Lower Connacht, was at the bottom of the list, while the O'Gara, the least important of the Gaelic lords of Lower Connacht, was at the top. Both families' fortunes depended on luck. It was bad luck in the case of the O'Connors Sligo, whose story is one of failure to produce direct heirs, long minorities and long-living widows with claims to the estate (for example, Lady Cressey and the countess of Desmond in table 4). In the case of Fergal O'Gara, on the other hand, it was good luck. O'Gara's father had died before Fergal had come of age, and the wardship of the heir and custody of the estate was granted to Sir Theobald Dillon, one of the wealthiest and most powerful men in Connacht. Legal battles were fought over the estate, but Fergal O'Gara emerged as the owner of most of the old lordship of Coolavin in the 1630s, an achievement which can undoubtedly be attributed to the protection and patronage of Dillon. The O'Haras of Coolaney also had the good fortune to produce male heirs and have careful guardians, as did the O'Dowds.[48]

The need for cunning in the effort to survive emerges in the story of the O'Higgin estate. The bardic family of Ó hUiginn lived in Leyny, where they had been given some land by the O'Haras, but their legal title to the land was disputed. In the sixteenth century Tadhg Dall Ó hUiginn co-operated with the new local government while continuing to write bardic poetry, and in the seventeenth century his family forestalled potential property losses by the simple device of falsifying the records. One inquisition refers to

Tomaltach O'Higgin burning documents which disproved the family's right to a certain piece of land, and the 1635 survey describes how another man was kept in prison by Tadhg Óg O'Higgin because he made a claim to their land. Clearly this bardic family was not only in touch with the realities of seventeenth-century Irish life, but was well able to respond to it.[49]

Tadhg Óg O'Higgin displayed a certain degree of foresight in his handling of the family's affairs. So too did Brian MacDonagh in his choice of marriage partner, a daughter of Sir John Taaffe, who brought with her a dowry which redeemed a large mortgage on the estate. The prosperity of the Creans, the Sligo merchant family, was another sign of the times. Commercial success was security against dispossession and enabled the Creans to participate in the land market, by buying up mortgaged territory from their impoverished neighbours.

Survival as a relatively large landlord did not mean abandoning an allegiance to Gaelic culture. An interesting aspect of three of the largest local landlord families in Sligo, the O'Garas, the O'Haras and the O'Higgins is that they were all associated with the promotion of Gaelic literature. The O'Higgin bardic connection is well known; and patronage of the O'Higgin poets by the O'Haras was maintained, despite the latter family's adoption of an English lifestyle in dress and land inheritance. Fergal O'Gara was also a patron of Gaelic literature. He paid the scribes involved in compiling the Annals of the Four Masters and received a fulsome dedication in return.[50]

For many local landlords, neither luck, cunning or foresight prevented their slide into economic decline. Some did try to make use of the new legal processes to have forfeiture decisions reversed or to secure better titles to the land which they possessed. Few, however, were successful, and many small Sligo landlords suffered financially in the 1620s and 1630s.[51] A detailed analysis of the reasons for their financial difficulties is not possible, but it is clear that the fiscal demands of the administration at both provincial and central level posed severe problems for small Gaelic landlords who lacked the cash income necessary to meet government demands.

We have no detailed accounts of the expenditure of a local landlord, but Cormac O'Hara's will gives some idea of the outgoings of a large landlord. His debts included £10 to a Dublin merchant and £1 6s 4d to two Creans from Sligo and £3 to his tailor. Amongst his listed goods were a 'best suit of apparel' which he left to his eldest son, as well as seven guns, a jewel, eating utensils and two table boards. If this was the extent of his worldy goods, he was clearly not living a life of great luxury, though the debts to the Dublin merchant and tailor are examples of expenditure occasioned by the new demands of society. A miniature portrait of Cormac survives in which he is depicted dressed in what may have been his 'best suit of apparel'. Cormac O'Hara's will did not include any cash. Instead, as described already, he left instructions for his son to sell some stock to pay his debts. The absence of money in the will strengthens the view that it was in fact a rare commodity in early seventeenth-century Sligo. Cattle and horses were a more common form of currency.[52]

The fact that O'Hara was one of the larger landlords gives some indication of the poor state of some of the smaller ones. It is easy to appreciate that any sudden demand for cash could give rise to serious problems. Given the small size of most of the landlords' estates, it is not surprising that many of them fell quickly into debt once the government began to collect composition money, subsidies and other payments on a regular basis. Brendan Ó Bric has noted that mortgages increased during the months when the composition money was due (May and October).[53] Paradoxically, therefore, efforts on the part of the small Sligo landlords to conform to the demands of the new English lifestyle by paying composition and other crown revenues or making use of the legal system or adopting English dress and fashions actually threatened their economic survival, as most could not afford the cash expenditure involved.

The proposals for the plantation of Connacht constituted an additional blow to already struggling landlords in Sligo. To their already mounting financial worries was added the threat of partial confiscation. By the late 1630s the prospects for many small landlords looked grim, and, perhaps not surprisingly, it was the small landlords who first supported the rebellion in 1641.

Tenants

Most of the inhabitants of early modern Sligo were not landlords but tenants and their families. We know very little about the lifestyle of the tenants. The 1635 survey was mainly concerned with landowners and provides only incidental information about tenants. It does, however, indicate that just as there were large and small landlords, so also were there large and small tenants. The survey provides the names of some of the more substantial tenants. For example, Murtough O'Cunnegan was noted as leasing thirteen and a half quarters from John Ridge of Boyle. O'Cunnegan sublet most of this land for the rent of £86 11s and kept only one quarter for himself. Thus O'Cunnegan essentially performed the role of a middleman for Ridge.[54] Other tenants did the same. Some of the large tenants were former owners who, after sale or mortgage, remained on as tenants to the new owners and also continued to sublet some of the property. The result could be the existence of several economic layers of interest in the same land. The survey reveals, therefore, that the composition of society below the level of the landowning families was more complex than is usually acknowledged in descriptions of Gaelic Ireland. The phenomenon of the middleman, so often seen as the creation of the eighteenth century, clearly flourished in early seventeenth-century Sligo.

Rent was paid in cash (or cattle) and kind. The leases issued by Patrick French for land which he had received in mortgage from O'Connor Sligo provided for the money part of the rent to be paid in two instalments on May Day and at Michaelmas. Leases usually began on May Day and varied in length from one to twenty-one years (occasionally longer), but the majority were from three to seven years. It was only in 1641 that French issued one-year leases from May Day to May Day, and this was a result of his insecurity of tenure following his dispossession by Wentworth and friends and subsequent repossession in 1641 by Tadhg O'Connor Sligo. It seems therefore that one-year leases were the exception rather than the rule on the French lands.[55] The 1635 survey suggests that longer leases were also common on other lands in the county.

Leases of from three to seven years or longer give the impression of a relatively stable tenant society in which movement from one area to another was not a regular occurrence. This impression is confirmed by a list of tenants on the Ballymote estate in the late 1580s and early 1590s.[56] Continuity of possession relates, however, only to the top level of tenant society. Each of the tenants on the Ballymote estate probably sublet to other tenants, as did many of the head tenants noted in the 1635 survey. Tenants who did not rent directly from the landlord may have been more mobile and inclined to move if conditions looked more attractive in another area.

Increased rents may have been one factor in a decision to move elsewhere. The Ballymote tenants experienced considerable rent increases, and their experience was probably general by the seventeenth century. The French leases reveal that tenants paid the composition money due on land, as well as any additional subsidies and charges. Head tenants were likely to have passed a share of these charges on to their subtenants. As the Binghams frequently complained, tenants tried where possible to settle on lands which were exempt from the composition rent. Wentworth's reduction of such 'free' lands must have meant that more and more tenants were obliged to pay composition money in addition to their contributions to the parliamentary subsidies and other charges introduced in the seventeenth century.[57]

The nature of the rent paid in kind suggests also the type of farming undertaken. As with the landlords, pastoral farming dominated. Most tenants, however small, probably had possession of a few cows and sheep and possibly grew oats and had access to turf for fuel. This would have been sufficient to pay the rent and provide milk, butter, oat-bread, heating and possibly some meat in the form of mutton (beef being reserved for cash payments) for the family. Others may have had some pigs, garrans (small horses) and hens. As noted above, grinding of corn and spinning of cloth could be done domestically or for a fee in the local mill. The 1589 complaints indirectly provide some information about the stock held by tenants. For example, George Bingham seized at various times a total of 8 cows from Dermot O'Beolan, and 2 garrans, 2 mares, 1 cow and 2½ half marks from Shane O'Cahan of Sligo town, while Hugh O'Hart is recorded as having 41 cows in his possession, and Tomaltach O'Hart had 39 cows, a mare and a colt. By contrast, there is a reference to a 'very poor' woman who, along with eight others, was alleged to have been dependent on one cow. She may have been a widow with children.[58] Captain Cuellar described encountering a woman of eighty years of age who drove five or six cows into hiding during the crisis in Connacht in late 1588.[59] The amount of stock held by individual tenants therefore varied, although judging from the available information none possessed large numbers of beasts. Although individual tenants owned small numbers of cattle and sheep, they may have grazed them in common with the lord's stock and with those of other tenants, thus producing the hundreds of cattle which were commonly found in the *caoruigheacht* which were moved to different grazing areas in winter and summer. The amount of land which was cultivated by tenants is unknown, but, as in the case of the landlords, corn and oats were probably grown for domestic purposes. Cuellar's description of the north Sligo region suggests that cultivation of small tracts of land was common. He described coming across a hut full of sheaves of oats where he spent the night. The next day groups of men arrived and spent all day working the land, departing back to their villages in the evening. Similarly, an account of 1642 describes the same area as dotted with small villages where corn was cultivated in the village hinterlands. Near Sligo town, it was claimed, there was an abundance of wheat, rye and barley in the ground.[60]

It is likely that these crops were consumed locally but the extent to which tenants sent goods to market is impossible to estimate from the surviving evidence. If George Bingham's allegation that there were no markets in the county when he arived in Ballymote in the mid-1580s is true, then it is likely that private exchange was the most common means of disposing of surplus goods. Many tenants would have been too far from Sligo town to make use of the commercial services which it offered. Bingham wrote of wheat, barley, oats and malt being sold 'to their own neighbours and from one to another'. Other references in the 1589 documentation described private sales involving horses and suggest that this type of exchange was normal practice.[61] Later, as with the landlords, the development of markets provided another means for exchanging goods.[62]

An additional source of income for a tenant would have been the practice of a craft or skill. The pardon list of 1603 occasionally indicates the presence of craftsmen such as joiners, masons and smiths. Skilled labour was usually associated with a tower-house, and such men may have been employed full-time by the lord or, more likely, would have worked as part-time farmers in addition to following their trade.[63]

Military men

There were also other groups of men in rural society who were accustomed to earning their living not by the land but by the sword. They are sometimes referred to in the documentation as 'kern' or mercenary soldiers. Some of the O'Harts and the MacSweeneys were in this category. These men earned a reputation for continuous cattle-raiding. Cuellar wrote of the cattle-raiding of such groups in north Sligo who when chased by the English soldiers had 'no other remedy but to withdraw themselves to the mountains with their women and cattle, for they possess no other property nor more moveables nor clothing'.[64] The impression of a countryside where encounters with such bands was likely is conveyed by Cuellar; significantly, the territory through which he was travelling was that of the O'Harts, the traditional cavalrymen of the O'Connor Sligo family. The presence of bands of kern in the lowland parts of south County Sligo was probably less common. It is also likely that the numbers of such groups declined in the seventeenth century as society became less military-minded. Nonetheless, the eagerness with which men enlisted in Strafford's newly established army in 1640 suggests that there were still a large number of men in society who were attracted to a military lifestyle and were not prepared to settle down as tenant farmers.[65]

Conclusion

Society in Sligo in the sixteenth and early seventeenth centuries was a complex one with many different groups and economic levels. Gaelic law may give the impression of a society divided between the landed and the labourers, but the reality was very different. The landed class was divided between large and small landed families, some of whom rented out large parts of their estates while others retained their small portions of land for their own use. Below the level of landlord there were several economic groups, ranging from large, wealthy tenants to small subtenants who leased a small portion of land from a head tenant. There were also groups of men who lived by the sword rather than by the land, but their existence is more shadowy and difficult to document. The pardon list of 1603 reflects in English social terminology the complexity of Irish rural society. It distinguishes between gentlemen, yeomen, husbandmen, labourers and kern, and these distinctions might be interpreted as indicating the different economic levels of rural society in Sligo at the time. 'Gentlemen' refers to the landholding families; 'yeomen' to the large tenants; 'husbandmen' to the smaller tenants; and 'labourers' and 'kern' to the subtenant and military groups in society. A small number of clergy and skilled craftsmen are also listed.

Land inheritance was usually confined to small family groups and rarely included the extended family noted in the theory of Gaelic land law. The distinction between the lord of the land and the lord of the people is a blurred one, as traditional tributes were by the late sixteenth century virtually indistinguishable from land rents. Nonetheless, the traditional prestige of the old lordly families survived, and new landlords continued to collect chiefry charges when they could.

Society was overwhelmingly rural, and the economy was centred on agricultural production, largely for home consumption. Private sales were probably the most common form of exchange. None of the landed families was significantly wealthy, and most were relatively poor. They received enough in rent to retain their position in Gaelic society, but encountered difficulties in paying for all the demands of the new administration.

The financial demands of the government were the most direct way by which the new socio-economic system made an impact on society in Sligo. The result for many of the smaller landlords was disastrous, and many were forced to mortgage or sell lands to acquire the necessary cash. Survival depended to a large degree on external assistance in the form of a guardian during a minority or a marriage alliance with a wealthy landlord's family. But the success story of the Creans and the O'Higgins, who prospered through their own ability, proved that economic decline was not the inevitable fate of Gaelic Ireland.

CORMAC O'HARA † 1612

Cormac O'Hara in his 'best suit of apparel'.

NEW LANDLORDS IN
COUNTY SLIGO *C.* 1585–1641

In 1560 there were no New English landlords in Sligo, nor did any Palesmen own land in the region. Just over thirty-five years later Sir Richard Bingham compiled a list of new landlords in Connacht and included in it twelve Englishmen and Palesmen who had purchased or received grants of land in Sligo and another twelve who held leases of land in the county. In 1616 there were twenty-four new landlords recorded in the county, a figure which amounted to about 10 per cent of the total number of landlords; by 1635 the figure had risen to almost forty and by 1641 to about fifty. By that time the new landlords owned about 50 per cent of the land in the county. For an area which was not subject to an official plantation the change was substantial.[1]

An examination of the names of the new owners reveals, not surprisingly, that many of them were officials and soldiers of English and Pale origin who were in crown service in Connacht. Others were merchants from Dublin, Galway and Sligo, and a few were Dublin-based administrators. The Church of Ireland was also a substantial landowner as a result of taking over the property of the secular clergy. County Sligo was divided between four dioceses, so there was a bewildering number of church officials with claims to land in the county.

There were several ways in which land was acquired from local owners. The most common were: the receipt of a grant of crown land; a mortgage of land in return for a cash loan; direct purchase; or, in the case of the church, the identification of diocesan property.

Crown land

The accumulation of crown land in Sligo began during the presidencies of Fitton and Malby, when several surveys were made of monastic property in Connacht. County Sligo's monastic land included the small properties attached to Sligo abbey and Ballysadare abbey, as well as the more extensive estates belonging to large monasteries based outside the county, such as Boyle abbey, Inishvickerin and Holy Trinity abbey, all situated in north

Roscommon.[2] As indicated already, Sir Richard Bingham established his presidency at Boyle and administered the Boyle abbey estates on behalf of the crown, but despite his frequent pleading, he was never given a grant of it. It remained part of the crown's store of lands until the early seventeenth century, when it was granted to a rising official, Sir John King, a former servant of Bingham's.[3] Although Bingham never received a grant of land from Queen Elizabeth, he did contribute to the store of crown land by seizing Ballymote castle in 1584. The castle was claimed, rather belatedly, as part of the Tudor inheritance from William de Burgo, earl of Ulster. George Bingham, Richard's brother, resided in Ballymote for a number of years, but like his brother he was not rewarded with a grant of it. Like Boyle abbey, Ballymote remained in crown hands until the beginning of the reign of James I, when it was granted to James's former spy and courtier, Sir James Fullerton, who subsequently sold it to William Taaffe.[4] Another former Connacht administrator, John Crofton, received grants of Inishvickerin and Holy Trinity Abbey, which laid claim to Templehouse, the residence of the O'Hara Boy, as part of its inheritance. Having served for a short time as a member of the Connacht administration, Crofton had been appointed escheator general, a position which no doubt facilitated his acquisition of a substantial amount of former monastic land in Counties Sligo and Roscommon.[5]

Apart from the lands of dissolved monasteries and land which might, usually for contemporary strategic reasons, be claimed as part of the Tudor inheritance, crown land also included any land forfeited to the crown through the attainder of its owner or because of the failure of heirs. Gradually in the late sixteenth and early seventeenth centuries the amount of such forfeited land in County Sligo increased as its owners were found to have died in rebellion in the wars of the 1590s or in earlier rebellions such as that of 1589. Occasionally land was forfeited through failure of heirs – although under Irish land law this was virtually impossible. The store of this type of crown land was built up over the years and consisted of small portions of land scattered around the county. No territory of the larger lords was confiscated, although several of them, such as O'Gara and O'Dowd, were threatened with confiscation after the 1589 rising. The Binghams also tried unsuccessfully to seize most of the property of the O'Connors Sligo. The main victims of the seizure of crown land were, therefore, the smaller landlords.[6]

The government was assisted in locating potential crown property by local resident officials and soldiers. For example, John Baxter was an Elizabethan soldier who had served with Bingham and later with Sir Henry Docwra at Ballyshannon, and in the early seventeenth century he was able to present to the government a list of small Sligo landowners who had participated in the rebellion of the 1590s. In return Baxter received a grant of the land he had 'discovered'.[7] The 'discovery' of concealed crown lands – either in this form of rebel lands which had not been legally forfeited or lands

which had been excluded from a crown grant through error or ignorance –
was encouraged by the central government because poor surveys and bad
communication made it difficult for centrally based officials to keep an
accurate record of all crown property. In return the local officials often
received a grant or a lease at low rents of the land they had discovered, as
Baxter had done. However, as Terence Ranger has demonstrated, this
system was ingeniously exploited and abused by Richard Boyle to acquire
large quantities of crown property at low rents for himself and a small group
of friends. Some Sligo land was included in the Boyle transactions, and the
local official William Taaffe was used by Boyle in his acquisition of crown
lands in Sligo.[8]

By the beginning of the seventeenth century most of the potential crown
land had been discovered in County Sligo, and James I made use of any
ungranted property to reward supporters and creditors such as Sir James
Fullerton. As Ranger has explained, there simply was not enough crown
land left in Ireland to satisfy all the soldiers and officials to whom James
promised grants of Irish land. It was this predicament which led Boyle and
his cronies to transform their discovery of crown land into a sophisticated
and complex business of dealing in 'books' of Irish crown land. James
issued a 'book' to his creditor or supporter granting him a certain amount
of unspecified Irish crown land at a certain rent. The 'book' was in effect a
blank form allowing for the receipt of a grant of unspecified Irish land at a
stated rent and tenure. It was up to the grantee to find the land to fill up the
form or 'book'. Frequently the terms by which the land was to be held were
generous: in fee farm and in free and common socage, i.e. there were no
liabilities such as military service attached to the land. And it was the
generous tenure which proved so attractive to the Dublin officials. They
were able to use these 'books' which they bought from the grantees to get
more liberal forms of tenure for land which they already held either by lease
or by military tenure. In other words, they transferred land which they
already held by lease or by more onerous tenures to the new 'books' and
in this way transformed their tenures to the fee farm specified in the
'books'. Thus the official named on the grant of crown lands enrolled on
the patent rolls became irrelevant as James's courtiers jumped at the opportunities to sell their 'books' to Irish administrators. For example, Sligo
lands were included in grants to Sir Francis Gofton, Sir Edward Southworth
and Sir Henry Brouncker. None of these men ever owned the land officially
granted to them. Their grants of crown land from James I were sold to
landowners in Ireland who made use of them to secure better titles to Sligo
estates. These included the landlords who had acquired lands in the sixteenth
century, such as Richard Boyle, John Crofton and John King. By 1616 the
crown lands of County Sligo were in the possession of a small number of
men whose family ownership of the land in most cases dated back to the
sixteenth century, despite the impression to the contrary given in the
enrolled grants.[9]

Mortgaging and purchase

Apart from dealing in crown property, land might also be acquired through mortgaging and purchase. It is, however, at times difficult to distinguish between the two processes, because, as noted already, mortgaging frequently led to the mortgagor acquiring permanent possession of the property involved. It may, indeed, have often been used as a legal fiction to avoid alienation and livery fines due when land was sold. (In the survey of 1635 the terms 'mortgage' and 'sale' are used interchangeably.) There was a considerable amount of land mortgaged in County Sligo in the early seventeenth century. Most of it was mortgaged by native-born Sligo landlords, although there are also some surprising names among the mortgagees. Richard Boyle, earl of Cork, mortgaged several parcels of land in County Sligo; and such an action by one of the wealthiest men in Ireland adds to suspicions that mortgaging was used as a legal device to conceal a sale of the land. Mortgaging might not, therefore, always be a sign of impoverishment.[10]

The most common type of mortgage was the delivery of possession of the land to the mortgagor, who often rented it back to the mortgagee or owner of the land. Redemption was possible but seems to have occurred only rarely, so that receiving land in mortage effectively amounted to a purchase of the land. For example, Patrick French included a clause in leases of land (which he had received in mortgage from Donogh O'Connor Sligo and subsequently leased to O'Connor) that the lease would be void if O'Connor redeemed the land – although this never in fact happened. The French papers also reveal evidence of another type of mortgaging in which the money was lent and the rent from the land was then paid to the mortgagor until the rents paid amounted to the sum lent plus interest (which was normally set at 10 per cent).[11]

There are over a hundred mortgage transactions noted in the survey of 1635 for land whose total value amounted to over £1,300. The amount of money mortgaged is only occasionally given, but the average of the examples noted amounts to about seven times the value of the land. (Of course, the amount of cash provided varied considerably depending on the location and quality of the land in question; but, as Brendan Ó Bric noted, seven times the value of the land serves as a rough guide.)[12] Using this figure, the total amount of money given in mortgages in County Sligo by 1635 amounted to about £10,000. About 40 per cent of that figure was lent by merchants from Galway – about £3,600 in total – and of that sum over £2,600 was provided by two members of the French family, Patrick and John.

The Frenches were the largest mortgagors of Sligo land, and most of their transactions involved the land of the O'Connor Sligo family. In the 1620s and 1630s a large proportion of the O'Connor Sligo estate came into the possession of Stephen French and his son Patrick. By the late 1630s they claimed to have spent over £3,000 on it, although in 1636 there were strong allegations that they had only in fact paid £900 of the money promised in the mortgage deeds. The Frenches also claimed to have disbursed over £1,700 on other land in Sligo: mainly to Cormac O'Hara, uncle of Kean, (£800) in 1638, and £600 to John Taaffe in 1639.[13]

The French connection with Sligo was significant in the sense that it established a strong link between a prominent Galway 'tribe' family and Sligo. Patrick French lived on the family's Sligo lands, where he built a house in O'Hara's country at the foot of the Ox mountains. He leased out the lands for a mixture of cash and country produce and the leases specified, as indicated in chapter 5, that the produce was to be delivered to his Sligo residence. When his father died, Patrick seems to have returned to the family house in Galway. The French connection with Sligo was retained, however, and was maintained even when the French Sligo lands were confiscated in the 1650s.[14]

Another large mortgagor was Roger Jones (£1,600), the merchant entre-preneur living in Sligo town. Perhaps, surprisingly, an anglican minister (Mr Dodwell) also figures among those lending money in Sligo: a total of about £1,500. Jones's mortgaging was systematic and concentrated on two areas: Sligo town and Banada, where he had acquired the abbey lands. Dodwell, on the other hand, was more opportunistic and clearly provided money in return for small portions of land scattered around the county. In addition, he sometimes acquired very small shares in land as one part owner offered his share in the family land for mortgage. Dodwell's mortgaging pattern had much in common with that of the many Galway merchants (apart from the Frenches), who also acquired small portions of scattered land, mainly in the northern part of the county, from a variety of minor landowners. Other mortgagors included the Sligo merchant family, the Creans (£600). Clearly, however, it was the Galway merchants who had access to the largest sums of ready cash for mortgage purposes; the Sligo merchants operated on a much smaller scale. The new landlords as a whole, apart from the merchants, did not involve themselves in mortgaging trans-actions to any large degree, probably because they did not have the finance to do so.[15]

Purchasing of land is difficult to document because no deeds or instru-ments of sale survive, but several examples are noted in the 1635 survey. One of the most notable was that of the soldier Patrick Crawford, who was given a grant of lands in and around Markree castle. Crawford sold his Sligo lands to Patrick Plunkett, second son of Christopher Plunkett of County Louth. Plunkett took up residence on his new estate and subsequently played an important part in the rebellion of the 1640s in Sligo.[16] William Taaffe also sold much of his sixteenth-century landed estate in Sligo to O'Connor Sligo in the early seventeenth century. He may have been under political pressure to do this, but it was also for him an attractive proposition. His titles to the land were vague, and there were allegations that he had acquired much of it by force.[17] The land sale by Tadhg O'Connor Sligo to Lord Deputy Wentworth and Sir George Radcliffe has already been noted.

There are other changes in landownership, such as the Taaffe acquisitions of the sixteenth century, for which no documentation exists to explain how they came about. There were allegations in the 1589 complaints, and later in the list of new landowners compiled by Bingham, that Elizabethan officials acquired land by illegal methods or that the land was simply taken by force from local owners.[18] However, it may well be also that the Gaelic ownership to the land was not clear (in one case two Englishmen claimed to have made agreements with different local owners for the same land),[19] or that the land lay unoccupied and 'waste'. As already noted, the 1635 survey reveals that the Elizabethan soldier Gilbert Green took possession of land in the south-west of the county when it was lying waste, and William Taaffe and other Elizabethan servitors may have done the same.[20] Acquisition of Sligo estates by new landlords before 1641 rarely involved eviction.

The occupation of such land by soldiers also, of course, suited the government and made military sense. Colonisation through the establishment of garrisons was an important part of the history of County Sligo throughout the seventeenth century. In the early part of the century the tradition was continued through Captain John St Barbe, in charge of the garrison at Ballinafad, who also established himself as a landowner in the county.[21] Later in the century soldiers were to make a more dramatic impact on the colonisation of Sligo.

Permanent transfer of land through marriage (as opposed to a widow's jointure, which was only temporary) was also a means by which the landed wealth of a family could be enhanced. The Jones family, in particular, appear to have been building up a network of connections through marriage. The marriage of Brian MacDonagh to Sir John Taaffe's daughter also assisted the stabilisation of the MacDonagh property. Wardship, as has been already noted, provided opportunities to influence the marriage of the ward and was used by guardians to increase their own family's landed wealth.[22]

Estate management

Although we can document the acquisition of land in early modern Sligo with reasonable accuracy, it is more difficult to discover what the new owners did with their lands. The survey of 1635 does, however, provide details about leasing of land by landowners and notes if the owner kept some land for his own use. If the land was leased, the survey lists the rent received, and sometimes gives the tenant's name, and occasionally his occupation.

From this survey we can at least compile a list of the new landowners and the rents which they claimed in the county (see table 5). Clearly, in trying to analyse the way in which estates were managed, it is necessary to distinguish the resident landlords from the non-resident. The majority of the new landlords were in fact absentees, either living in other parts of Connacht or further afield in Dublin or, in the earl of Cork's case, in Munster. In 1616 only six of the twenty-four new landlords were resident. In 1635 the number of new resident landlords had risen to about thirteen, and although the number of new landlords increased between 1635 and 1641, the number of resident landlords remained the same.

Table 5: Rentals of the main new landlords, *c.* 1633-5*

Name	Rent	Profitable Acreage†
Viscount Taaffe	£527	c.3,361
Patrick French	£324	c.4,485
Sir Roger Jones	£307	c.4,164
Sir William Crofton	£293	c.1,988
Sir Thomas Wenman	£169	c.2,428
Sir Robert King	£148	c.5,579
Earl of Westmeath	£146	c.3,017
Mr Dodwell	£135	figure not available
George Crofton	£100	c.1,560
John Fagan	£93	c.1,317
John Nolan	£93	c.3,920
John Crofton	£84	c.402
John French	£70	c.792
Thomas Crofton	£57	c.1,057
Patrick Plunkett	£57	c.969
Andrew Kirovan	£32	figure not available
Mr Lynch	£32	" " "
Mr Broonagh	£13	" " "

* Figures exclude country charges (also listed in the 1635 survey)
† based on Books of Survey and Distribution

Of the resident landlords, the Taaffe family (William, succeeded by his son John) were the largest, and the history of their landed possessions, in so far as it can be discerned, reveals a conscious attempt to develop a consolidated and profitable estate. By 1603 William Taaffe already had land in Sligo, mainly situated around the castle of Bunannaden in the south-west, but also in small scattered parcels elsewhere in the county. Instead of trying to develop these rather poor and scattered lands in the early seventeenth century, William Taaffe embarked on a series of sales and purchases which completely transformed the Taaffe estates in Sligo. There were several stages and transactions involved. First, as already noted, Taaffe sold to O'Connor Sligo most of the Sligo lands he had acquired in the sixteenth century. Taaffe received £1,000 for the land. He then bought Ballymote castle and its demesne lands from the crown grantee, Sir James Fullerton, for £1,500. In addition, he purchased other lands in the vicinity of Ballymote from Richard Boyle, as well as some abbey lands in Ballymote which had been granted to other patentees. He also accquired the valuable property of the abbey of Sligo, on which some of the town was built. The result was that by 1616 Taaffe had a much more attractive Sligo estate than he had had in 1603.[23] There was undoubtedly more status and social standing attached to the castle and lands at Ballymote than to his former property. Ballymote had been the headquarters of George Bingham, and the references to the castle in the state paper documentation suggest that Bingham restored the impressive medieval castle, cultivated its demesne lands, and encouraged the growth of a town and market in Ballymote.[24] Bingham's increase in the rents on the demesne has already been noted in chapter 3, and it may not be unconnected that Taaffe's rent from the Ballymote lands were also higher than those collected in other parts of Sligo. In particular the country charges demanded were more varied and more demanding than elsewhere. Horses for carriage, beeves and wheat were included with the other more typical duties of malt, mutton, butter, meal and labour services. The butter was measured in the larger unit of a quart rather than the more normal and smaller unit of a medder. These higher demands were probably inherited by Taaffe from Bingham.[25]

Apart from his Ballymote estate, Taaffe also acquired through mortgage some land in the vicinity of Sligo town and redeemed his son-in-law's large mortgage with a Galway merchant. But on the whole the Taaffes were not involved in the mortgage business on a large scale. Taaffe's only other major landed property was in the east of the county, around Ballintogher. This was probably acquired in the sixteenth century but not sold with the rest of his property in the seventeenth century. The reason for retaining this land is clear from the 1635 survey's reference to its valuable woodlands which, according to the survey, were by that time almost all decayed through sale to Sligo. The profits from the timber may in fact have assisted Taaffe's purchase of Ballymote.[26]

Another possible source of income was the growth of the town at Ballymote. Much of the land around the castle was leased to men describing themselves as merchants. Most had Scottish names. They include, for example, James Smith, who is described as a merchant, Andrew Ferguson, also referred to as a merchant, and William Wilson, a tailor.[27]

The 1635 survey also reveals that William Taaffe's son John rented nearly all his land to tenants by leases which varied in length from seven to thirty-five years. He reserved a small demesne around Ballymote castle for his own 'ploughing', which indicates that he was actively involved in farming some land of his own. The rents for his property, according to the survey, amounted to over £520, in addition to considerable quantities of rural produce and labour. A combination of direct farming and the food rents probably provided for most of the needs of his household. The Taaffe rent roll would have placed the family in the middling ranks of the gentry in England. Regrettably, no comparable figures for landlords' income are available for other parts of Ireland.[28]

One of the more interesting aspects of John Taaffe's tenants when they are named in the survey, is the number of Palesmen living on his estate. Apart from members of his own family, his tenants included members of the Brett, Dowdall and Nugent families – all from Taaffe's own native county of Louth. Some of these tenants became landowners as John Taaffe sold them small portions of land, mainly in the south and some distance from the main estate around Ballymote.[29] It is intriguing to speculate whether there was a conscious policy to bring tenants from the Pale to occupy the Taaffe land in County Sligo. The Pale and particularly County Louth connections of the Taaffes were clearly of great importance to the family. Both William Taaffe's wives (a Brett and a Bellew) were from County Louth, and about 1620 he returned to live there, leaving his Sligo estate to his son John. William subsequently served as sheriff of County Louth and died and was buried in Ardee in 1631. The connection with Louth also emerges in the marriages of his children: two daughters were married to other Taaffes from Louth, and even in the next generation the link was continued with one of John's children marrying Randal Plunkett, brother of Baron Dunsany.[30] These connections ensured that the Taaffes maintained their social and, equally importantly, their political connections with the Old English on the east coast. The arrival of new residents from the Pale such as Plunkett would have reinforced these contacts. Indeed, it is likely that membership of the Old English community was of more importance to the Taaffes than any notional involvement in the community of County Sligo. The importance of the Old English connection emerges in 1641, as the next chapter will indicate.

The Taaffes also established links with members of large landowning Gaelic families in the area. As explained in chapter 4, one of John Taaffe's daughters was married to Brian MacDonagh, an M.P. in 1613–15, and another to Fergal O'Gara, a process which is likely to have brought the Gaelic men into the Old English sphere of influence rather than gaelicising the Old English family.[31] There is no evidence of intermarriage between this group and the new English landlord families.

Despite the large sums expended by William Taaffe in purchasing his estate and his son's seemingly large rent roll, there are indications that the family was in some financial trouble by 1641. Land was sold to some of the Pale tenants noted above and also to a number of Galway merchants. The reasons for this are not clear. In the 1610s William Taaffe borrowed money from Richard Boyle to finance his land purchases, which, as Boyle noted in his diary, remained unpaid for a number of years. Taaffe pleaded the problem of having to finance the marriage dowries of two daughters, and his son John made a similar complaint to Wentworth in the 1630s – with some justification, considering the amount he paid to redeem Brian MacDonagh's property. Apart from family duties, another large financial expense must have been the long court cases which William Taaffe pursued for possession of the Ballintogher lands and other property. The Ballintogher case lasted for over ten years and involved suits in a number of local and central courts. Maintaining two households in Sligo and Louth must also have been a burden on the estate.[32]

The financial problems of the Taaffes may have been a contributory factor to the participation of some members of the family in the rising in the 1640s. In the 1620s and 1630s, however, the social standing of the Taaffes in County Sligo was unquestioned. William's knighthood in 1604 was followed in 1628 by the bestowal of a baronetcy on John. They were the largest landowners in County Sligo, and William was prominent in the early establishment of the county administration. The family network also helped to establish control of parliamentary representation in the county. The family's political prominence was, however, overshadowed by their catholicism, and it is noticeable that William's son John was not as involved in local government in the seventeenth century as his father had been in the sixteenth century. John's name was crossed off a list of potential J.P.s for the county, probably because of his catholic and Old English connections.[33] It was for this reason also that the Taaffes did not achieve a higher status in central affairs in Dublin, a fact which may have contributed to their financial problems, being excluded from holding potentially lucrative offices. On the other hand, the Taaffe family by the opening of the seventeenth century clearly identified with the Old English group who, as chapter 4 described, were beginning to play an important role in local government despite their catholicism.

John Crofton's estate in County Sligo was almost as large as that of the Taaffe family, but it was scattered throughout the county and consisted of a mixture of different monastic and church lands. Crofton, who died in 1610, divided his Connacht estate between his sons, so that in 1616 three members of the family, William, Edward and John, held land in County Sligo. Subsequently Edward's lands were further subdivided between his two sons, George and Thomas. Of all the Crofton landlords in the county, William held the most land and was the only one of the three brothers to live in the county, although Thomas, his nephew, also lived in Sligo.[34] In 1635 William had a rent roll of about £300 for his lands, which were situated in and around Templehouse in the barony of Leyny. Like the Taaffes, he rented most of his lands, but he kept some lands in the vicinity of Templehouse 'for his sheep' and presumably also as demesne land.[35] Unlike the Taaffes, he received most of his rents in cash rather than kind and would therefore have needed farm land to provide household produce. The reference to keeping land for sheep indicates one of the sources of Crofton's income. There was a tucking mill on the estate, and it would appear that the Croftons, like many other landlords, were involved in the sheep and wool market. William's nephew Thomas was also noted in the survey of 1635 as building a tucking mill on his Sligo lands.[36] Other sources of income derived from the development of Templehouse as a market town, as well as the profits of three grinding mills and the fees from the ferry which crossed over Templehouse Lake. Like the Taaffes, Crofton was not very active in the land market, but he did avail of the opportunity to purchase small portions of land in the vicinity of Templehouse.[37]

Although William Crofton's rent roll was not as high as that of the Taaffes, he did have access to other means of income which were not available to the Taaffes, whose religious affiliation was regarded as suspect by the government. William Crofton was granted the wardship of a number of Sligo heirs, which meant that he enjoyed their estates until they came of age. In one case he was granted the wardship of an heir whose estate later became the possession of his nephew Thomas. William Crofton was also appointed to a number of positions in the Dublin administration: clerk of the first-fruits and later auditor of accounts for Connacht and Ulster, an office which he may have acquired through the influence of his father-in-law, Sir William Ussher. Crofton also developed wider Dublin connections through his wife, who brought him as a marriage dowry some property in Dublin. In 1616 he was made a freeman of Dublin, as subsequently was his son, who also married a daughter of a Dublin official.[38]

As an indication of his growing status, Crofton, like many other socially ambitious gentlemen, built himself in the mid-1620s a house at Templehouse, or at least remodelled and extended the existing castle on the site. One of the most significant aspects of the new building was that the Crofton coat of arms was placed over the front door. This is the earliest instance of the use of the Crofton arms, and it is a striking indication that Crofton was in the process of establishing himself and his family as landed gentry. The motto over the door was appropriate: 'The generation of the righteous shall be blessed.'[39]

Socially, therefore, and possibly also economically, William Crofton and his family were typical of many rising gentry families in early modern Ireland and England. His landed estate was not large, but he made the most of his opportunities to consolidate it and to develop connections in the wider world of Dublin politics. It is likely that for a man such as Crofton membership of the New English community based in Dublin was more important than membership of the community of County Sligo.

Another new landlord who was also clearly trying to improve his social status but who went about it in a different way to Taaffe or Crofton was Roger Jones. Jones's Sligo connections, unlike those of Taaffe and Crofton, cannot be traced back to the sixteenth century. A Derbyshire man, Jones served in the army in Ireland in the 1590s as a lieutenant, and his first known connection with Sligo was in 1607 when he was appointed constable of the new jail there. In 1611 he was given a reward of £20 for discovering sixty quarters of concealed land in Connacht. His discoveries came just too late. A few years earlier the discovery of such property might have been rewarded with a grant of it, but by 1611 complaints had resulted in the banning of such practices. So Jones did not begin the century with a landed estate. Nevertheless, by 1616 he had property in and around Sligo town and in the vicinity of the former monastery of Banada. By 1635 he had further extended his property in these two areas. The survey of that year also reveals how, for the most part, Jones acquired the land: he received it in mortgage. By 1635 he had about thirty quarters of land, and just over half of it had been received through mortgage transactions which are described above. By 1635 his rent roll of over £300 with country charges placed him among the top landlords in the county.[40] His landed acquisitions, particularly in Carbury, were carefully selected: property in and around Sligo town was clearly valuable as the town developed and prospered. Jones also leased land at Rosses Point from the bishop of Elphin; this property included a 'good lead mine' which he sublet to John Watkins, who was probably Scottish.[41] Jones, like Taaffe, may have been selective about his tenants: if the Taaffes encouraged Palesmen to live on their estate, Jones seems to have attracted British families to his lands. As the appendix to this book indicates, by 1641 a substantial number of British settlers were living in Sligo town, and some of these were probably tenants of Jones. Jones was associated with the Ulster plantation as well as the plantation in Leitrim and perhaps made a conscious attempt to plant his Sligo property with British settlers.[42]

Jones also had many connections with settlers elsewhere. His sister was married to Robert Parke, a settler in the new plantation in County Leitrim; his son to the daughter of Henry Hart of Doe castle, County Donegal; and his daughter to John Ridge, who lived in Boyle. Other members of the Jones family married into the O'Hara family, and, perhaps more importantly, one of them married Roebuck Crean.[43] The Crean and Ridge connections were of great importance for Jones. Ridge was one of the wealthiest and probably the most enterprising of the new generation of settlers in Connacht. At Boyle Ridge had an extensive farm settlement with a French 'kill house', 'wool house', cow-house and five dwelling-houses, as well as a twenty-five-bedroomed house in which he lived. He also had extensive property elsewhere in Connacht and in Dublin and Wicklow. He had about 10,000 sheep on his Connacht lands which were managed by resident agents. Clearly for Ridge sheep-grazing was a large business affair. The 'kill-house' and 'wool-house' suggest that he was involved in the woollen industry on an extensive scale and that he possibly also exported mutton, sheep-skins, beef and cowhides.[44]

Ridge may indeed have exported wool through the port of Sligo, where his father-in-law played a leading role in the town corporation. Jones lived in the town and had a 'shop' there in addition to his house. The marriage between Roebuck Crean and Elicia Jones (probably Jones's niece) was as profitable and as shrewd a match as that between his daughter and John Ridge. Roebuck Crean was one of the most prominent merchants in the town and in the 1620s joined with Jones in exporting and importing goods in Sligo. The Creans, as the established and known merchants in Sligo, had experience and knowledge of the trade pattern of the town, and it was a wise move to ally with them rather then try to establish a rival business.[45]

As with William Crofton, Jones's official status made him suitable to act as a warden for minors, and, again like Crofton, he benefited from his charges. Jones's rising social status was acknowledged in 1624 when he was knighted. Another symbol of Jones's elevated status was the townhouse which he built in Sligo. He was also wealthy enough to finance the building of a chapel in St John's church, where he was later buried with an impressive gravestone.[46]

In summary, Jones is in many ways an early example of a gombeen man: a tradesmen and farmer and money-lender who built up sufficient capital to develop a leading position in the commercial and political milieu of his locality. Unlike Crofton, he never achieved a position in the Dublin administration, but in the 1620s and 1630s he was expanding his landed interests outside Sligo into Leitrim and further afield. For Jones, perhaps, the county community had more significance than it had for Crofton or Taaffe, but his main connections were with the new generation of settlers coming into the north-west in the early seventeenth century – settlers who were intent on exploiting the resources of the country in a commercial and profitable way. Such businesslike attitudes had no ideological objection to financially profitable marriage alliances with Irish families. It was indicative of this attitude that Jones's brother-in-law and business partner, Robert Parke, expressed his reluctance to get involved in attacking supporters of the rebellion in the autumn of 1641. His business depended on good relations with Irish as well as English neighbours.[47]

The Taaffes, Crofton and Jones were all in the process of establishing themselves and their families as landlords and members of the county gentry in Connacht. They all contributed to the introduction into Sligo of new fashions, as in the new houses built by Jones and Crofton and the development of the commercial potential of the villages and towns of the region. In a broad sense, they contributed to the anglicisation and modernisation of the area, using English breeds of cattle and other stock on their lands.

Another group often overlooked who contributed to this process were the Church of Ireland ministers who held benefices in County Sligo. Four sees owned land in the county, and during the early seventeenth century the church began to recover some property formerly granted out to lay grantees. The bishop of Elphin had the largest holding, with a rent roll of over £300, according to the 1635 survey. Most of it was rented to local tenants. Significantly, perhaps, one quarter of land was set to the bishop's son, who sublet it to a Michael English on condition that he build an English grist mill and also a tucking mill on the land.[48] This suggestion that church ministers were actively involved in encouraging English agricultural methods and techniques is further reinforced by the 1644 deposition of William Brown, the registrar of the dioceses of Killala and Achonry. He described how he had built on his Sligo lands in the four years before 1641 a dwelling-house, barn, dairy-house, stable and cow-house and had spent £200 enclosing fields. Among his goods lost in the rebellion were thirty-six English cows and over 130 other beasts, as well as books worth £20 and stacks of wheat, barley and oats.[49] Brown also had a mill on his land. Most of his property was that which was attached to the registrarship, but other Church of Ireland ministers were involved in the land market. The 1635 survey notes a number of ministers receiving land in mortgage as well as purchasing property. Among the most prominent was Mr Dodwell, whose transactions have already been noted. Dodwell had an extensive property in Connacht by 1641 and claimed to have lost large stocks of animals and crops as a result of the rebellion. The 1635 survey noted that he kept some of his Sligo lands for his mares, which he must have been breeding for sale.[50]

Non-resident landlords

The majority of the non-resident landlords rented out their lands in Sligo – very often to the former owners. The most important politically were Sir John King and his son Robert, although in the seventeenth century they were clearly in the process of consolidating their Roscommon estate and selling off some of the more distant Sligo lands. Another significant element among the non-resident landlords was a group of Galway merchants (about seventeen in number), of whom the most important – in terms of landed interest in the county – were the Frenches. The number of merchants with an interest in land in Sligo increased after 1635, but none were on the same scale as the Frenches. As noted already, the French estate consisted mainly of the lands of the O'Connors Sligo, but they had also received in mortgage lands from other less important families. The Frenches were also unusual among the merchants in that, as noted already, they maintained a family house on their Sligo estate.

The Sligo land of most of the other Galway merchants lay in the northern coastal regions of Tireragh and was mainly rented out, although the 1635 survey noted a number of merchants who kept land for sheep and probably, like John Ridge, had an agent looking after their herds for them.[51]

Those absentee landlords who simply rented land received in mortgage were in effect receiving an annual interest for their investment. This clearly explains the interest which two Dubliners, William Crow and John Fagan, had in Sligo lands. Another absentee landlord who made an annual profit from his Sligo lands without too much effort on his part was the earl of Westmeath; he leased all his Sligo lands to one man, Walter Terrill, who sublet it and made a small profit in return. Westmeath leased the land to Terrill for £145, and Terrill sublet it for £171 and country charges – evidence of another more rapacious type of middleman in seventeenth-century Sligo.[52]

New tenants

Of perhaps more importance for the development of County Sligo than the absentee landlords were the new tenants who came to live on the land of the resident and absentee landlords. These included the Palesmen on the Taaffe estate; the tenant agents on the sheep-farming lands, such as Thomas

Coote on Ridge's lands, or Robert Brown, who managed a small estate at Dunierin in Tireragh for two brothers who lived in Boyle; and a group of other tenant settlers, many of whom had Scottish surnames.[53] According to the depositions taken after the outbreak of the 1641 rising, there were men and women of British origin living right across the northern part of Counties Sligo and Mayo in 1641. It is difficult to estimate the number of people involved in this settler movement, but two deponents estimated that there were about 140 families of British origin living in County Sligo in 1641. Another suggested that there were about sixty British families living in the town of Sligo.[54] The appearance of these settlers in Sligo formed part of a wider movement of Scottish settlers into north Connacht in the 1620s and 1630s which was in turn connected with the revivial of emigration from Scotland at that time.[55] The depositions also reveal a surprisingly large number of settlers in County Leitrim despite the assumed failure of the plantation there. There was also a large settler community in County Roscommon. Most were tenants rather than landlords, and many were also part-time craftsmen. For example, in Leitrim the depositions indicate the presence of a tanner (with a tanyard), a claypotter, glover, joiner, clothiers (with a shop) and a feltmaker, while elsewhere millers, smiths, carpenters and clothiers were among those who made depositions.[56] The depositions give the impression of the existence of a small but very active settler community engaged in building houses, leasing land and developing the commercial possibilities of the land, particularly in relation to the woollen and leather industries. Many also seem to have accumulated cash reserves and introduced into the north-west new material goods. The possessions of the settlers listed in the depositions stand in stark contrast to the rather meagre and simple goods listed in Cormac O'Hara's will thirty years earlier. William Walsh of Sligo town, for example, included gold jewellery, silver cutlery and bowls among the items which he lost in the rebellion. Jane Stewart, who with her husband had a general store in Sligo town, recorded that beds, curtains, pillows and cupboards had been taken from her and her husband.[57]

The gap between the rising prosperity of the new settlers and the declining fortunes of their Irish neighbours must have been increasingly obvious in the late 1630s. While conflict between the two groups was not the inevitable outcome of such a discrepancy, it did provide the basis for local jealousy and envy which might all too easily spill over into sectarian conflict, as the 1640s were too prove.

Conclusion

There are a number of points which can be made about the new landlords at this time. First, their number was increasing throughout the period. The number of new resident landlords remained small, although the larger ones such as the Taaffes, Croftons and Roger Jones were all in the process of developing the commercial value of their land and establishing their families as members of the landed gentry. But there is no indication that the new resident landlords were beginning to come together as a coherent group. If their marriage connections are any guide, then the three main landowning families went three different ways. The Taaffes looked largely to the Pale, and particularly to County Louth, for marriage partners, while the second generation in Sligo began to develop contacts with locally born catholic landed families. William Crofton married the daughter of a prominent Dublin administrator and tried to involve himself in Dublin affairs, and his son did likewise; other members of his family retained connections with the established settler families of north Roscommon. Roger Jones, on the other hand, himself a new arrival in seventeenth-century Sligo, developed contacts with other new arrivals in Ulster, Leitrim and the new generation of administrators such as John Ridge, Henry Hart and Robert Parke. And, as a shrewd businessman, he matched his family also with local merchant families, a practice which seems to have been avoided by the older generation of settlers. The new landlords were not therefore a united group with shared economic experiences and political views. Religion was one obvious source of division, but there were others which are not so easily classified. Personal ambition and and career opportunities could lead men to look for marriage partners in different circles. The divisions within the new landlord community emerged more strongly in the 1640s, but the potential for division had clearly older roots.

The non-resident landlords, among whom the most prominent group was the Galway merchants, were clearly acquiring land for the financial return which they received from it, although some of them did keep land for sheep. Sheep-grazing, as John Ridge's deposition of 1641 indicates, was big business in early seventeenth-century Connacht and was ideally suited for absentee landlords. It did not involve a great deal of expense: poor, scattered parcels of land could be bought cheaply and made to yield a profit very quickly. There was little labour involved, and the sheep could yield a 'variety of marketable commodities' such as wool, mutton, tallow and skins. It has been calculated that from wool alone 1,000 sheep could yield an annual profit of £140 in the 1630s in England.[58] John Ridge's 10,000 sheep could have been very profitable indeed.

The relations of the new landlords with local Irish landlords and tenants are difficult to assess. There is evidence of intermarriage between the catholic Taaffes and local families, but Roger Jones's family was unusual among the new protestant landlords for marrying into local Irish families. Co-operation at local government level enabled the administrative system to function, but there is no evidence of a sense of common purpose emerging among the landlords of County Sligo in the 1630s. This is perhaps not surprising given the contrast between the prosperity of the new landlords and the financial problems of the older resident landlords. The catholicism and political identity of the Old English group in the county, as described in chapter 4, appears to be the only socially cohesive development in society, and that by its very nature was exclusive and divisive.

REBELLION AND WAR, 1641–52

Shortly before Christmas in 1641 the town of Sligo was besieged by an army of men from Counties Sligo and Leitrim. The army included some of the principal gentlemen of the county: Tadhg O'Connor Sligo and his two brothers, two sons of Sir John Taaffe, Brian MacDonagh, Patrick Plunkett and other members of the O'Connor and MacSweeney families. Andrew Crean, the high sheriff of the county, and his son John, a justice of the peace, and James French, another justice of the peace, and his son Jeffery were also involved in the siege. The small crown garrison quickly yielded up the town, and articles of agreement were signed, arranging for the safe convoy to Boyle of the protestant residents of the town who wished to leave. Led out by the Church of Ireland minister, William Roycroft, most chose to go, but a small group of about forty opted to stay. About three weeks later, on or about 13 January 1642, the British settlers who had remained in the town were, at O'Connor Sligo's command, put into Sligo jail. That night followers of O'Connor, including two of his brothers, entered the jail and attacked the prisoners with 'swords, knives and skeans'. By morning most of the settlers were dead or seriously wounded.[1]

These two events, the military and ordered seizure of a valuable strategic site and the bloody and disorderly attack on British settlers, were characteristic of the outbreak of the 1641 rising, not just in Sligo but also in many other parts of Ireland. It is tempting to dismiss events in Sligo in 1641–2 as simply a product of the rebellion elsewhere. It could be argued that rebellion had spread to Sligo from neighbouring Ulster counties and therefore took a similar form there as in other parts of the country. However, looked at from the perspective of the history of County Sligo, it is possible to identify a number of long- and short-term factors which help to explain why the rebellion received support in Sligo. In other words, although Sligo was no doubt caught up in the general spread of the rebellion throughout the country, there were also specific local events which determined the way in which resistance manifested itself and developed in County Sligo.

The politicisation of the Old English

In County Sligo, as elsewhere, the last years of the viceregency of Wentworth gave rise to considerable dissatisfaction and hostility towards the central government. In particular, the project for the plantation of Connacht created an atmosphere of fear and uncertainty among landlords in the west of Ireland.[2] Although the scheme initiated in 1635 was never implemented, it was not until the spring of 1641 that the king finally agreed to abandon it. For six years, therefore, the landlords of Connacht lived under the threat of partial dispossession. For large and small landlords the prospect was not enticing, but for those landlords already in financial trouble (as many of the smaller Sligo landlords were) the threat of the plantation helped to exacerbate an already deteriorating situation.

Wentworth's inquiries into the validity of the Connacht surrender and regrant scheme of 1616 and his subsequent introduction of the plantation scheme was a grievance taken up by the Old English in their negotiations with the crown.[3] The Old English discussions and attempts to win concessions from the king were concentrated in Dublin and London, but the impact of their activities could be surprisingly direct at local level. As a result of the land acquisitions of the previous century, there were established landed families related to the main Old English families scattered around the country, but particularly in Connacht. In County Sligo there were many connections between local landlords and the political leadership of the Old English group. Patrick Darcy, for example, was a landlord in Sligo, as also was the earl of Westmeath. Both Darcy and Westmeath were key figures in the Old English negotiations.[4] Another Old English connection was through the French family, prominent among Old English supporters in Galway.[5] As was shown in the preceding chapter, resident landlords in Sligo also had direct contact with Pale families: the Taaffes maintained close links with their ancestral home in County Louth, and several of Sir John Taaffe's children married into prominent Pale families. Other Sligo landlords, such as Patrick Plunkett, second son of Sir Christopher Plunkett of County Meath, the Dillons, Nugents, Bretts and Dowdalls, had relatives in the Pale. Gaelic landlords were also linked to the Old English network: Brian MacDonagh was married to a Taaffe, as was Fergal O'Gara, while Donogh O'Connor Sligo married the daughter of the earl of Antrim, who supported the Old English position. The existence of these connections helped to spread support for Old English political views, and they also meant that the Old English were not simply a pressure group based in the Pale with outposts in some of the major towns. They had supporters throughout the country.

There were therefore a significant number of landlords in Sligo who were likely to have sympathised with the views of the Old English. In addition, the increased politicisation of the Old English in the 1620s and 1630s seems to have been reflected at local level, as chapter 4 has already described. As will become clear later, Old English sympathisers played an important part in the beginning of the rebellion in the winter of 1641.

Apart from the impact of the increased politicisation of the Old English, there were other developments in Sligo in the 1620s and 1630s which contributed to an atmosphere of unrest and hostility to the establishment. Most important of these was the ecclesiastical reorganisation which occurred in the Church of Ireland and the Roman Catholic church.

Ecclesiastical organisation in County Sligo, 1603–41

In the sixteenth century the Church of Ireland – with the exception of Galway town – was not well organised in Connacht. The ministers of the church – including the hierarchy – were mainly locally born Irishmen, many of whom were recognised by Rome as well as by the established church. Thus Eoghan O'Hart, appointed bishop of Achonry in 1562 while attending the council of Trent, was also recognised as bishop by the established church. Eoghan O'Connor Sligo, brother of Sir Domhnall, who was appointed bishop of Killala in 1591, may have been a more committed protestant than O'Hart. He had attended Oxford University for a number of years and was recommended for the see by Sir Richard Bingham and other prominent government figures. But O'Connor did litle to improve the state of the established church in his diocese.[6] Following his death in 1607, the two bishoprics of Achonry and Killala were granted to the infamous Miler Magrath, who was at the same time archbishop of Cashel. Magrath, a convert from catholicism, had a reputation for greed and self-aggrandisement rather than spiritual sanctity. Magrath's appointment to the two western dioceses underlines the chaotic state of church affairs in Connacht, as well as pointing to the indifference of the authorities to do anything about it.[7]

The poor state of the church in Killala and Achonry was revealed in the 1615 visitation. In the two dioceses there was a total of six clergy, of whom five were only reading ministers and not fully qualified preachers. Only two resident clergy were recorded for Achonry. The non-resident clergy claimed to serve in the parish on occasional Sundays. The quality of the ministers in the dioceses was also questionable. According to Alan Ford, Achonry 'seems to have been used by Magrath to support those clergy . . . thrown out of his other dioceses'.[8]

In Elphin the condition of the church was relatively better. In 1615 nineteen clergy were recorded for the diocese, and eighteen of these were resident. The larger number of resident clergy in Elphin was partly due to the presence of a substantial English settlement in the southern part of the diocese, and also to the efforts of Edward King, appointed bishop in 1611. King, who had been educated at Cambridge, was a fellow of Trinity College, Dublin, and he attracted to Elphin a mixture of English and Irish graduates. Among his appointments were William Roycroft, the vicar of Drumcliff and other parishes in north Sligo, and William Newport, vicar of St John's in Sligo town, both graduates of Trinity College, Dublin.[9]

In the years between 1615 and 1634, the year of the next visitation, there was a notable increase in the number of Church of Ireland ministers in the

Sligo dioceses. In Elphin Bishop King continued to appoint qualified ministers. Most, however, were of English birth. In Killala and Achonry the
growth in numbers of clergy was less dramatic, but there was a similar trend
towards the appointment of non-Irish clergy. The new men were mainly of
Scottish birth. This was because Magrath was succeeded in the united see by
two Scotsmen: Archibald Hamilton (1623–30) and Archibald Adair (1630–
40). Under them 'the diocesan clergy were transformed from a wholly
native body in 1615 to a largely Scottish ministry in 1634'.[10] And the trend
towards increased numbers of English and Scottish clergy continued after
1634.

There were three important implications for the Sligo region of this
growth in the established church. First and most simply, it brought into the
area more British settlers. The ministers came with their immediate families
and also often with more distant relatives and friends who frequently set up
separate households in the area. They were thus an important factor in the
growth of the settler community in County Sligo. Many of the Scottish
ministers also had considerable sympathy with Scottish presbyterianism,
and although Wentworth tried to rid the church of such ministers, there is
little evidence that he had achieved much in this direction in Connacht
before 1641. In 1640, indeed, Bishop Adair of Killala and Achonry was
deprived on suspicion of sympathising with the Scottish covenanters.[11] The
strong Calvinist views of the Scottish ministers were unlikely to have made
them tolerant of their catholic neighbours.

The second implication of the strengthening of the church involved its
impact on church property and the general wealth of the established
church. One of the major concerns of successive bishops was to identify the
property which belonged to their sees. With considerable government
support they fought in the courts against recalcitrant landlords who, they
claimed, held property which belonged to their episcopal sees. Edward
King was particularly successful at reclaiming church property for Elphin.
King, and probably the other bishops, also raised the rents collected from
diocesan property. In the 1630s the rise in rent on ecclesiastical land was
quite striking: by 1638 King could claim that the value of his land had risen
from £300 to £700 through increased rents. He, along with other Church of
Ireland bishops, was given government permission to change the form of
their tenures from fee farm (i.e. at a fixed rent in perpetuity) to sixty-year
leases, thereby making a rise in rent on episcopal land possible. King
calculated that this concession raised the value of the see's lands by another
£640. The result was that by 1638 the bishopric of Elphin was worth an
impressive £1,340. The other bishops in the area were involved in a similar
process, although their success is less well documented.[12]

The third implication of the increase in the number of protestant clergy
in Connacht was the corresponding increase in the amount of tithes which
were collected. In the western diocese the established church inherited a
very 'archaic' system of tithe collection. The tithes were divided into four

18th century engraving of Sligo Abbey.

parts: one part going to the bishop, two parts to the sinecure rector or, in many cases, the impropriator, and one part to the resident vicar.[13] In medieval times monasteries took over the functions of parochial clergy and collected tithes and appointed parish priests. This meant that in the seventeenth century a receiver of dissolved monastic land from the crown also received the right to collect the impropriator's share of the tithes and the right to appoint a rector to the living. This was a serious problem for a growing church with more and more ministers dependent on the tithes for their income. And in the 1630s efforts were made to reform the tithe-collecting system. The commissioners of the court of high commission received numerous petitions from newly appointed ministers complaining that lay landlords were depriving them of the profits of their benefices. In Sligo the Crofton and King families, with their grants of Boyle, Inishvickerin and other monasteries, were the main culprits in this regard. The commissioners were usually sympathetic to the minister, and the impropriators were frequently ordered to provide for the clergy on their lands, or, alternatively, the ministers were permitted the right to collect the tithes of the parish, as well as the right to the 'book money', i.e. money charged for services performed, or some sort of compromise arrangement was agreed. In a typical dispute between William Oliphant, the newly appointed vicar of Ballysadare and Enagh, and the Crofton family, it was resolved by the commissioners that the Croftons should pay to Oliphant an annual sum of £30 and permit him to collect the 'book money'. In order to provide further income for the ministers, the bishops also agreed to forfeit their right to a fourth of the tithes and remit it to the parish clergy.[14]

Thus in the course of the 1630s an increasing number of English and Scottish ministers held the right to collect all the tithes in their parish. It created a unique situation in the Sligo region and in many other parts of Connacht also. For the first time tithes were collected on a regular basis by Church of Ireland ministers and not by lay impropriators. The tithes were also probably collected more efficiently because the ministers were often dependent on the tithes for their subsistence. There is evidence to suggest that tithes were frequently farmed out to lay proctors in return for a fixed sum of money. The methods of collection used by the proctors led to many complaints. For the first time too tithes were collected on a regular basis for a church to which the majority of the people did not belong. In the eighteenth century changes in the tithe system were to cause considerable agrarian unrest, so it is not surprising that the introduction of the effective operation of the system in the seventeenth century gave rise to great resentment.[15] Hostility towards the clergy was made manifest at the outbreak of rebellion in late 1641 and early 1642, when ministers were often singled out for particularly abusive and violent treatment.[16] For example, the earl of Clanricard reported in January 1642 that many clergy wanted to go to England because they feared the people 'not so much for religion as their great extortions under them' and particularly the 'greediness of some'.[17] The efficient collection of the tithes and increased rents imposed by the bishops contributed to the development of a general sense of animosity which was to provide much popular support for the rebellion in 1641. Resentment at the activities of the Church of Ireland was no doubt also considerably encouraged by developments within the catholic church.

Coinciding with the strengthening and reform of the Church of Ireland was a remarkably similar growth in the ministry and organisation of the Roman Catholic church. In the sixteenth century, apart from the small number of secular clergy who straddled the two churches, the main centre for catholicism in the Sligo region was the Dominican priory of Sligo abbey. The abbey escaped dissolution in 1568 when Sir Domhnall O'Connor Sligo's grant from the queen included a clause permitting the priory to continue to function on condition that the priests became secularised. It seems unlikely, however, that this happened, and in the early seventeenth century the abbey continued to house a small community of Dominican priests. In 1622 there were eight priests and three or four novices in the abbey. The prior was Daniel O'Crean, who, like many other priests in the seventeenth century, had returned to Ireland after a continental catholic education. Small communities of Franciscans also began to re-emerge in north Connacht in the early seventeenth century.[18]

But the main development in the catholic church in the early seventeenth century was the strengthening of the diocesan structure and the appointment of secular clergy, sometimes recruited from the ranks of the regulars. This development was slower in Connacht than in other parts of the country, but by 1630 a resident bishop had been assigned to Elphin and, more siginficantly, a resident archbishop of Tuam, Malachy O'Queely, had been appointed.[19] One of O'Queely's first acts as archbishop was to summon a provincial synod in 1631 which issued decrees concerning the organisation of the dioceses in Connacht and the correct behaviour for the parish clergy. By 1635 O'Queely was claiming considerable success in appointing parish clergy in the eighty-nine parishes in his province as well as carrying out the duties of a bishop in administering sacraments such as confirmation, performing yearly visitations, preaching and, he claimed, reconciling many protestants to the church. In 1640 O'Queely held a second synod at Galway, where the 1631 decrees were republished and additional decrees about procedures in the church were agreed.[20]

O'Queely's success in Connacht was confirmed by the remonstrance which the Church of Ireland hierarchy of Tuam presented to parliament in June 1641. They complained of the very public carriage of O'Queely as he travelled 'up and down with great companies'. The remonstrance also pointed out that every church in the diocese of Tuam had a priest and that 'the friars swarm everywhere and are often met in the highways in their habits'. The main grievance of the remonstrance was, however, that the people being subject to payments to the protestant and catholic ministers were not paying to 'our clergy as willingly as to their own, and think their tithes and so forth very burdensome, though they willingly give far more to the Papists'.[21]

The catholic clergy were not in possession of temporalities, but they were supported by local gentry and received payments for performing religious services. The remonstrance suggests that they were well looked after by local people. Given the strongly based counter-reformation training of many of the catholic clergy, it seems unlikely that they would have encouraged local people to pay tithes to their protestant counterparts. The strengthening of the catholic church thus exacerbated the hostility created by the collection of tithes.

Clearly by 1641 both church institutions had become better organised in terms of administration and personnel than they had been in 1603. The late 1620s and 1630s, in particular, had witnessed a notable increase in the number of clergy in both churches. It is hardly surprising that these developments created problems. For the first time there existed in the west of Ireland two rival sets of clergy making claims both on the spiritual loyalty and on the financial support of the people. Given the strength of the counter-reformation movement (in numbers of clergy, apart from any other factor), the protestant clergy lost the first battle, but they retained the government-backed authority to force people to support the established church financially. For the first time, therefore, people were obliged to pay tithes to a church to which they did not belong and to which the majority of the clergy in the province did not belong. It was also, it should be stressed, the first time that tithes were collected on a regular basis in every parish, and it is likely that the strong commitment of clergy in both churches made the tithe issue a crucial area of conflict between them. The remonstrance presented to parliament in 1641 revealed both the hostility between the clergy of the two churches and the repugnance felt by lay people towards the payment of tithes. There is no evidence of the seizure of tithes by catholic clergy before 1641, but after 1641 there are a number of instances in Sligo and elsewhere in north Connacht where catholic clergy were given the temporality of local parishes.[22]

The growth and development within both churches therefore created a considerable amount of popular resentment which manifested itself in attacks on protestant ministers and general support for the rebellion in the 1640s.

The new Irish army and County Sligo

Apart from developments in the church and the local impact of the politicisation of the Old English, there were also more short-term developments which contributed to the tension existing in Sligo by the late summer of 1641. The most important of these was the formation of a new Irish army by Strafford. The idea for a new Irish army had arisen from Charles I's conflict with the Scots which began in 1638. As the struggle became more serious, Charles was urgently in need of military reinforcement. Strafford planned to provide this through recruitment of an army of 10,000 men from Ireland.[23]

Preparations for the army began in the spring of 1640. Officers were appointed, recruitment undertaken and arrangements made for bringing the soldiers together for military training in the north. In Connacht two regiments were raised by Sir Charles Coote and Sir Henry Bruce. In both regiments officers included members of landowning families of English and Irish backgrounds. From Sligo, Theobald Taaffe, son and heir of Viscount Taaffe, was appointed lieutenant-colonel to Colonel Coote, and two of his brothers were issued with captain's commissions. Their brother-in-law Brian MacDonagh was a captain in Sir Henry Bruce's regiment.[24] Recruitment to the army was the responsibility of individual officers, each being commissioned to raise 100 men. Recruitment was voluntary, but it is likely that most captains formed their companies from tenants and other men living in the vicinity of their family estates. On 18 June 1640 the two Connacht regiments were assembled at Boyle, and from there they marched northwards towards Belfast and Carrickfergus.[25] There, however, they remained. Developments in Scotland and England made it unwise for Charles to make use of the Irish army, and so at the beginning of the winter in 1640 it was decided to reduce each company to fifty men, a move which would have reduced the Connacht regiments from 2,000 to 1,000 men.[26] As far as the military activity of the army was concerned, the reduction was of no consequence because on 8 May 1641 Ormond, the commander-in-chief, was ordered by the king, under pressure from the English parliament, to disband the new army completely.[27]

The king and his advisers were, however, very aware of the 'disorder which the soldiers . . . might hereafter commit, to the disturbance of the peace and quietness of our subjects', and so permitted eight selected officers to transport 8,000 of the soldiers abroad to serve with 'any prince or state in amity with us'.[28] Among the eight chosen officers was Theobald Taaffe. The plans to transport the soldiers abroad (to Spain) met with opposition – for different reasons – from the Irish and English parliaments. Eventually, in August 1641, Charles was forced to reduce the number of men to 4,000 and the officers to four. Theobald Taaffe was still included, and he was given permission to take 1,000 men to Spain.[29]

But even with the halving of the number of men and officers, the English parliament was not satisfied, and on 28 August 1641 it declared its opposition to the levying of any men in Ireland for the service of a catholic power. In Ireland the prohibition of the parliament seems to have been ignored, for soon afterwards Taaffe, with the assistance of Sir James Dillon, another officer from the abortive army for Scotland, formed two regiments in Connacht, part of which, at least, Taaffe was trying to ship to Spain through the port of Galway as late as November 1641. It is not clear if they were actually permitted to go, for despite a special licence from the lords justices and the earl of Clanricard, the customs officer of Galway was reluctant to allow the soldiers to depart.[30] He may have succeeded in preventing them from leaving; at any rate, the depositions for Sligo reveal that a number of men recruited by Taaffe were involved in attacks on British settlers in the winter of 1641 and obviously did not travel to Spain.[31]

The raising of the new army, its subsequent disbandment and re-enlistment have been seen as 'an essential part of the context within which a rebellious conspiracy secretly matured' in the summer of 1641. Some of the eight officers who were originally given permission to take soldiers to Spain conspired for a short time in a plot to overthrow the government in Ireland. There is no evidence that Theobald Taaffe was involved in these plans, although his undoubted loyalty to Charles I would suggest that if Charles was involved in the plot (and there is some evidence to suggest that he was), then Taaffe would have been a willing supporter of it.[32]

As far as County Sligo was concerned, however, the main importance of the raising of the new army and its subsequent development lay not in its implications for the colonels' plot but in the less sensational and more prosaic effect of the recruitment of the soldiers on life in the county. For almost a year and a half before October 1641 there was a considerable amount of enlisting and arming of men in the region. The initial uncertainty about when the soldiers would be used, followed by the staggered disbandment of the army in the winter and spring of 1640 and 1641, took place against a background of political instability and created a potentially explosive atmosphere in the area. The authorities were well aware of the problems presented by disbanded soldiers, particularly when, as in this case, they had been badly paid, fed and clothed. The decision to allow men to be transported abroad arose out of this awareness, and the officers involved in the transportation were given special warnings on the dangers of the assembling of large groups of men in one place. They were advised to keep the men dispersed until the time of their departure. In fact the confusion over whether or not the men were to be allowed to go meant that in one instance (and possibly others) the men were mustered for the purpose of embarking on arranged shipping which never arrived because it was stopped by the English parliament. The resulting frustration for the assembled, waiting troops must have created exactly the sort of dangerous situation which the authorities had tried desparately to avoid.[33]

In Sligo the process by which the army was disbanded and men recruited for Taaffe's transportation is unclear, but it was not simply a question of the transfer of soldiers from one command to another, for Taaffe was issuing local officers with commissions for new recruitment in the late summer of 1641.[34] It is highly likely, however, that many of the men who had been recruited for the new army were also recruited by Taaffe's officers. The recruitment and assembling of the different companies of men under individual captains undoubtedly created problems for the local population. It is clear from the depositions that in the late summer of 1641 bands of soldiers were demanding food and lodging from local residents.[35] The outbreak of the rising in the north in October added to an already tense situation. Although it was not until December that Sligo became involved in the rebellion, the evidence of the depositions suggests that the enlistment of soldiers in the summer of 1641 helped to increased tension and fear in the area. When the rising did begin in Ulster in October and spread quickly to the neighbouring county of Leitrim, many settlers in Sligo feared for their lives and quickly took refuge in the Crofton house at Templehouse or moved to safer areas.[36]

Apart from the disruption caused by hungry and impatient soldiers, the outbreak of rebellion in the north provided a legitimate justification for soldiers to vent some of their frustration through violent attacks on English and Scottish settlers. Patrick Dowd, for example, had a commission from Taaffe to recruit soldiers and tried to lodge some men with Sir Robert Hannay at Moyne castle. When Hannay refused to entertain so many soldiers, Dowd joined up with his father and brothers and attacked and evicted the family of John Nolan in Enniscrone castle, which had formerly been a possession of the O'Dowd family. Another officer commissioned by Taaffe, Brian MacSweeney, was named by many deponents as being responsible for attacks on settlers in north Sligo in October and November 1641, before the rebellion officially began in Sligo.[37] There is thus a direct link between the recruitment of the soldiers and the indiscriminate attacks on settlers. Such attacks are often seen as the spontaneous eruption of violence by catholics against their protestant neighbours. In the case of Sligo, at least, the initial violence against settlers is more accurately seen against a background of one and a half years of military recruitment but no military action.

The connection between the attacks and the disbandment of the soldiers was recognised by some contemporaries. In 1643, the author of *Mercurius Hibernicus* included the prohibition on the transportation of the army among the reasons why the rebellion occurred. He wrote of the fact that when the army for Scotland was disbanded the country 'was annoyed by some of these straggling soldiers, and not one in twenty of the Irish, will from the sword to the spade or from pike to the plow again'.[38] It was this type of man, perhaps typified in Sligo by Brian MacSweeney (from the former galloglass family) and his followers, who was on the rampage in Sligo and elsewhere in the autumn of 1641. The signal for rebellion for them was the long-awaited signal for military action.

Strafford, Sir George Radcliffe and the O'Connor Sligo estate

The recruitment of the army was, therefore, a crucial factor in the way in which the rebellion began to make an impact on County Sligo in the autumn of 1641. There was one other local event which contributed to the general atmosphere of unrest.

Donogh O'Connor Sligo had died in 1634 without heirs. His death resulted in yet another sucession crisis in the O'Connor Sligo family, but it also had far more wide-ranging implications. Donogh had had an unfortunate time as head of the family. His attempts to revive the family fortunes had failed, and one account reported that he died in disgrace and shame at the size and number of his debts and creditors in Ireland and England. As described in chapter 5, his successor Tadhg endeavoured to rid himself of his inherited debt by selling a large part of the estate to Lord Deputy Wentworth and Sir George Radcliffe. The land was sold on condition that the purchasers should pay off all the encumbrances on the land and that Tadhg should receive back 3,000 acres free and unencumbered. To what extent these conditions were fulfilled is unclear, but there is evidence that some of the estate's creditors were paid money owed.[39]

Patrick French, who had received a large part of the estate in mortgage, strongly objected to these transactions which in effect deprived him of any interest in the O'Connor estate. Having failed to resolve the problem through the local administration, French brought his protest to the council table in Dublin in June 1638, where it was agreed that Sir Philip Perceval (who had acted on Wentworth's and Radcliffe's behalf) should pay French £2,000 compensation. French complained bitterly about his off-hand treatment by the council and accused Wentworth of intervening in the legal proceedings concerning his claims. He also alleged that Perceval, on being asked by French what he should do with all the documentation which he had brought with him to prove his ownership to the land, responded: 'Goe out of our sight and stop bottles with them.'[40]

French was outraged at what he saw as his dispossession by Wentworth, and two years later he and his father seized the opportunity of the growing hostility to the earl of Strafford (as Wentworth had now become) and his supporters to travel to England and present a petition to the house of commons in November 1640 which claimed that he had been dispossessed by Strafford. The commons concluded that French should be restored to the land in dispute, but that Perceval should be reimbursed with any money which he had paid to Tadhg O'Connor for the lands. O'Connor followed French to London to protest that Perceval, Strafford and Radcliffe had not in fact performed the conditions of their agreement, and that therefore the land was rightfully his. O'Connor was drowned in the course of his journey to England, but his son, another Tadhg, followed up his father's argument in a more practical way by seizing possession of the lands in April 1641.

By that time hostility to Strafford was so strong that there seems to have been considerable local support for O'Connor's action. Two court inquiries were held into O'Connor's seizure, but neither found possession of the estate for Strafford and Radcliffe. O'Connor also had the backing of Patrick French, to whom he returned possession of the lands which he had formerly held. In the summer of 1641, following Strafford's attainder, the king issued instructions to the Irish privy council to grant the lands in trust to Joshua Carpenter, George Carr and Guildford Slingsby, an action which can have done little to relieve the tension in Sligo, since Carpenter and Carr were close asssociates of Strafford and Radcliffe and were obviously acting for their respective families. A more acceptable compromise was agreed in August 1642 by means of a clause inserted in the bill to annul the plans for the plantation of Connacht; it stipulated that Sir Philip Perceval was to be repaid the money which he had given to O'Connor for the Sligo lands. The bill, however, was never enacted.[41]

The main importance at this time of the involvement of Strafford and his associates in the Sligo land dispute was that it must have added considerably to the atmosphere of unrest and growing hostility to the government in Sligo. O'Connor's seizure of the lands in April 1641, followed by Strafford's execution in May 1641 and the refusal of the two local court sessions to prosecute O'Connor, suggests that events in Dublin and London were beginning to have a direct impact on the Sligo area.

There may also have been a local political aspect to the support which O'Connor Sligo received in the quarter sessions which refused to find the title for Strafford. The purchase of the Sligo estate enabled George Radcliffe to sit for the county in the parliament summoned in 1640, and a relative, Thomas Radcliffe, represented the borough of Sligo in the same parliament. The purchase of the O'Connor estate gave Radcliffe, and therefore Strafford, a direct form of political influence and control in the county.[42] Thus O'Connor's seizure of the Sligo lands in 1641 could have been interpreted as symbolising the end of the Strafford regime and may have been applauded as such by Old English sympathisers in the town and county at large.

Outbreak of rebellion

By October 1641 there was, therefore, the potential for serious and violent disturbances in County Sligo. Many of the necessary preconditions for rebellion existed: popular discontent at the Church of Ireland collection of tithes, encouraged by the expanding and well-organised catholic church; a number of landed gentry with financial and other grievances and an increased political awareness; and a large body of men ready and anxious for military action. Yet Sligo in October 1641 lacked one essential element for rebellion: a leader or leaders willing to participate in the rising begun in the north. The immediate reaction of the landed gentlemen of the county to the rising in the north was to try to prevent it spreading into Sligo. Andrew Crean, the high sheriff, called a meeting of the chief gentlemen of the county at Ballysadare. Two resolutions were agreed: to repress the incursions of foreigners into the county, and to suppress the violent course of idle persons within it. Clearly, then, the concern was to stop men from other areas fomenting rebellion in the county and to deal with the problem of marauding soldiers within the county.[43] The main direction from which the rebellion was likely to spread into Sligo was from the north-east, as men in County Leitrim had joined the rebellion of the northerners in

October. The main targets of the rebels were the successfully planted parts of Leitrim: around Sir Charles Coote's ironworks in the north of the county, and Manorhamilton, the home of Sir Frederick Hamilton. Shortly after the rebellion began, Tadhg O'Connor Sligo, who had attended the meeting at Ballysadare, sent a letter to Hamilton assuring him of his loyalty.[44] However, the expression of loyalty and agreement at Ballysadare to suppress idle persons had little effect on the soldiers who continued to attack British settlers.[45] The outbreak of disturbances is hardly surprising because, even while the gentlemen of the county were resolving to control the idle men, Theobald Taaffe, through his brother Luke, was still continuing to arrange to transport his alloted 1,000 men to Spain, and the resulting assemblage of large groups of soldiers inevitably created problems and added to the confusion in the county.[46]

The pillaging of the soldiers continued throughout November: the earl of Clanricard heard rumours that 500 of them had burnt the quarters occupied by the crown garrison at Ballinafad, and by 17 November he reported that in Sligo 'loose people' had plundered the English and were now falling on well-affected natives.[47] Yet the county was still considered loyal and not involved in the rebellion. The situation changed in early December. Andrew Crean summoned a second general meeting at Ballysadare, and from this meeting, according to one deposition, 'most of the gentlemen of the country went towards Sligo and there remained until the said Sligo was taken'.[48] The siege and taking of Sligo was followed by the siege and capitulation of Templehouse, the house of William Crofton and probably, apart from the Taaffe residence of Ballymote, the largest house in the county. It was in Templehouse that many of the protestant settlers took refuge when the rebellion began in October.[49]

The sieges of Sligo and Templehouse were carefully plannned military operations. They were led by members of some of the main landowning families in the county. As indicated already, at the siege of Sligo were members of the Taaffe, O'Connor Sligo and MacDonagh families, as well as men from some of the O'Rourke families and others already in rebellion in Leitrim. John Crean, son of Andrew, and members of the MacDonagh and O'Hara families as well as the Taaffes were involved in the siege of Templehouse. The timing of the siege of Sligo is important: about 10 December, after the Old English in the Pale had joined the rebels and begun to organise support for the 'catholic army'.[50] Clearly the Old English action on the east coast was decisive and gave the signal to the Irish catholic gentlemen in County Sligo to join the rebellion. The fact that the siege of Sligo was begun as a result of a meeting arranged by Andrew Crean, together with the fact that men with Old English connections (Brian MacDonagh, Patrick Plunkett and the Taaffes) played an important leading role in the beginning of the rebellion in the county, suggests strongly that the Old English action was the main factor leading to the rebellion in Sligo. Prominent men were now prepared to provide leadership and organisation

– the vital element which transformed the disturbances of October and November into rebellion in December.

Theobald Taaffe's issuing of captains' commissions and the recruitment of soldiers in the late summer of 1641 also proved advantageous when the decision was finally taken to besiege Sligo. Among those who took part in the siege were Brian MacSweeney and David Dowd, who had been issued with commissions from Taaffe.[51] There were probably also many other officers at the siege. The rebels appointed Brian MacDonagh as their commander, no doubt in recognition of his military expertise. (According to one deponent, Tadhg O'Connor Sligo was initially asked to act as leader, but he refused to accept the position.) MacDonagh had been one of the officers in Coote's regiment of the new army and would have received some military training as a result. Luke Taaffe, another of Coote's former officers and in charge of his brother's soldiers, also quickly became one of the most important commanders among the rebels.[52]

In other words, the formation of the new army in 1640 and the subsequent plans to transport many of the soldiers involved to Spain considerably aided the military plans of the rebels in Sligo. They had at their disposal an already assembled army of men, some of whom were armed and had been trained as soldiers. Clanricard summed up the situation in December 1641 when he wrote of the royalists being 'daily robbed of many proper young men for want of means and employment who, I believe, would have served faithfully and are now forced to take the worst course, being stopped from foreign service, and no use made of them here'.[53]

The military organisation of the leaders, however, did not prevent the continued attacks on settlers. The random violence of the soldiers was also joined by what seems to have been a more ritualistic maltreatment of protestants, particularly ministers. At both sieges protestants were violently attacked and their possessions looted. At Templehouse two ministers and a woman were attacked. One of the ministers, William Oliphant, the vicar of Ballysadare and Enagh, was stripped, hanged, and his body dragged naked through the district and buried in a ditch.[54] Another minister, George Wray, was stabbed and later died of his wounds. Jane Brown, wife of the registrar of Killala and Achonry, was also physically abused, but was rescued by Fergal O'Gara.[55] In Sligo, as in other Connacht counties (apart from Leitrim), no distinction was made between English and Scottish settlers. The most violent attack on British protestants in the area, however, was that which took place in Sligo town in January 1642.

Massacre

As already explained, after the siege of Sligo many British people left the town, but about forty British settlers chose to stay on in Sligo after the siege. For three or four weeks they were allowed to travel freely about the town, but on or about 13 January they were put into Sligo jail, allegedly for their safety. Later that night they were savagely attacked and most of them were

119

killed; only a small number survived to tell the tale. The attackers were named by deponents (who included some survivors) as two brothers of O'Connor Sligo, members of the O'Hart family, and some other men (including three or four butchers) who lived in the town.[56]

The deponents who survived the massacre or who had escaped being put into jail, alleged that the atmosphere in the town had changed when two men from Donegal came to Sligo and killed some Scots in the street. The killings coincided with a meeting held in Sligo abbey which was attended by Tadhg O'Connor Sligo and his brothers and other followers, as well as by members of the O'Rourke family from County Leitrim. After the meeting a number of men remained together drinking and then later in the evening perpetrated the attack on the jail. The killings might therefore be seen as the actions of a drunken mob excited by the murder of the Scots. But they must also be viewed in the context of the activities of Sir Frederick Hamilton in County Leitrim.

Hamilton, almost singlehandedly, by his own account, was trying to suppress the rebellion of the O'Rourkes and others in County Leitrim. In October he formed a troop of horsemen from his own tenants and proceeded to launch a series of assaults on the O'Rourkes and their supporters. His military strategy seemed to be one of burning houses, destroying crops and stealing cattle, presumably in order to starve or frighten the rebels into submission. Prisoners were usually hanged as an example to others. In the first couple of weeks of January Hamilton began to concentrate his military tactics in areas near the border of County Sligo. These attacks began just before the assembly in Sligo abbey and the subsequent massacre in the jail. The O'Rourkes had already worked closely with the Sligo rebels, and the presence of Owen O'Rourke – their commander-in-chief – at the Sligo abbey meeting suggests that they were looking for military assistance from the Sligo men. This seems to have been agreed, because about 20 January – less than a week after the meeting – Luke Taaffe and Brian MacDonagh led a large force of men towards Manorhamilton, where they retaliated against Hamilton's military tactics by burning his corn and driving away his cattle.[57]

The killing of the settlers in Sligo jail took place, therefore, against the background of Hamilton's military campaign in Leitrim. There must have been real fear in north Sligo that Hamilton was in a position to take over Sligo town and control the surrounding area. The settlers may have been put into jail in a genuine attempt to protect them following the murder of the two Scots in the town; but if so, the plan gruesomely backfired. In the atmosphere of the time, the temptation of so many British protestants together in one place was too much to resist. The decision of the leaders to launch a military attack on Hamilton was precipitated by some of their followers through the attack on the settlers in the jail. As will be made clear later, the ramifications of the massacre in the jail – and particularly the involvement of the O'Connor Sligo family in it – were to rebound on the rebel leaders in Sligo.

Rebellion and war

By January 1642 County Sligo was clearly in rebellion. In the early months of the rebellion the earl of Clanricard was still optimistic that the situation in Connacht could be contained. There were, he asserted, still enough loyal gentlemen in the province willing to give support to the government forces. In December 1641 he was of the opinion that if he were sent arms for 1,000 men, he could deal with the rebellion. The problem was that the Dublin government was not in a position to send arms for 500 men, let alone 1,000. It needed all the help it could get to defend the Leinster region. To Clanricard's alarm, instead of sending him aid, the government actually summoned some Connacht troops to Dublin. The lords justices, for their part, hoped that local landlords armed with commissions for martial law and authority to raise troops from their own tenants would be able to cope with the situation in the west.[58] The reaction of many of the protestant landlords to the rebellion, however, was not to recruit troops from tenants, as Sir Frederick Hamilton had done, but to barricade themselves and their families into their castles and not to become involved on either side in the rebellion. Robert Parke, the business partner of Roger Jones who lived at Newtown on the border between Leitrim and Sligo, tried to ignore the outbreak of the rebellion and to avoid taking sides in the conflict between Hamilton and the O'Rourkes, much to the anger of Hamilton. Parke was alleged to have said when asked for help by some of Hamilton's men that 'it was well for him if he could defend himself and his till aid come, without provoking or doing anything to draw the country upon himself'.[59] Similarly, Sir Henry Bingham in Castlebar refused to give protection to John Goldsmith, the parson of Burrishoole, because he was afraid that it would provoke an attack on the castle.[60] In Sligo Edward Crofton, son and heir of George Crofton, raised a small troop of twenty horse and fifty foot, having received authorisation to do so in April 1642. It seems, however, to have been primarily for the 'better defence of his house and the neighbouring garrisons'.[61] William Crofton allowed Templehouse to be used as a refugee centre for protestants, but again no offensive against the rebels was organised. The divisions within the New English community evident before 1641 emerged very clearly during the war years and were to become even sharper as the war progressed. Many of the landless settlers resident in Sligo before the rebellion left the county to serve as soldiers elsewhere in Connacht. County Roscommon and south Leitrim became the main bases in the province for British forces, but it was not until the summer of 1643 that Sir Charles Coote received a commission to form a troop in Connacht.[62]

The failure of the pro-government landlords to come together in a united force undoubtedly meant, as Clanricard repeatedly alleged, that Irish landlords who wanted to remain loyal were forced to take the side of the rebels in order to protect themselves. He perceptively pointed to the lack of 'confidence or community' between the 'English of quality shutting themselves up in forts' and the Irish 'gentlemen of quality of the country'.[63]

A good example of the lack of confidence and community was the experience of the Irish gentlemen of County Roscommon who asserted in January 1642 that they had been forced to take up arms 'being left subject to the spoil and destruction of the forces in action in the counties of Leitrim and Sligo, oppressed and mistrusted by the English garrisons in their own county.'[64] Similarly, the then protestant Lord Mayo complained about the lack of support which the state had given him. He considered the possibility of receiving into his protection the rebels who were rumoured to be beleaguering his castle, and making use of them for the crown's service. Mayo, apparently despairing of government help, eventually joined the rebels, although his commitment to their cause was always open to doubt.[65]

Fear was therefore an important factor in influencing some men, particularly landlords, to support the rebels. But as already indicated, there was also considerable ground for discontent in Sligo by late 1641. If the background of the individuals who participated is analysed in more detail, some of their reasons for participation become clearer. Three main social groups can be identified.

The original leaders of the rebellion in Sligo identified with the position of the Old English and, as noted already, only took up arms after the Old English in the Pale had declared their support for the rebels. Men like Andrew Crean and his son John, the Taaffe brothers, Patrick Plunkett or even the Frenches did not have major financial problems or other strong material motives for participating in the rebellion. They undoubtedly shared in the general dissatisfaction created by Strafford's lord deputyship and were unhappy with the prospect of the plantation. At a local level, they may have been incensed at the manner in which the Radcliffes tried to dominate the parliamentary representation of the town and the county of Sligo. The Frenches were also upset at the way in which they had been dispossessed by Strafford.[66] However, it is unlikely that any of these factors would have been strong enough to persuade them to take up arms if it had not been for the leadership and initiative of the Old English on the east coast. Patrick Plunkett explained his involvement in the rebellion in December 1641 as being due to 'the justness of our cause, which is for the maintenance of His Majesty's Prerogatives, our liberties and religion, which is so much trodden under foot, that most of this kingdom are resolved to sacrifice their lives in defence thereof.'[67] The leaders of the Old English in the Pale could not have phrased it better. Awareness of and involvement in the wider world of Old English politics was the main reason why this group of Sligo residents took up arms. They brought with them into the rebellion families who had previously been linked with the Old English group, such as that of Brian MacDonagh. Other Irish families like the O'Garas and the O'Dowds were more cautious in their support of the rebels.

Another identifiable group on the rebels' side came from local landlord families who supported the sieges of Sligo and Templehouse and who had encountered financial problems in the previous twenty or thirty years. This group would have felt particularly threatened by the plantation plans. Tadhg O'Connor Sligo undoubtedly resented the gradual erosion and loss of his family's estates, which had culminated in the sale to Radcliffe and Wentworth. Cormac O'Hara, uncle of Kean, and his sons Oilill and Brian had also lost much land in the 1620s and 1630s. The men from minor branches of the O'Connors who were present at the siege of Sligo were also not successful in retaining their estates intact in the seventeenth century. Other small landlord families who participated in the rebellion could also be said to have had problems with their landed possessions.

Yet to draw a simple equation between financial difficulties and participation in the rebellion would be too crude. To begin with, it must be asked what these landlords hoped to gain by participation in the rebellion. Were they hoping that the rebellion would bring about an improvement in their financial position? If so, it must be asked how this was to be achieved. Repossession of land lost through sale, mortgage or forfeiture might be the simplest method of recovering lost fortunes. But if this was a motive, then it would have involved the dispossession of some of the local rebel leaders. Andrew Crean had received land in mortgage from the O'Haras, the O'Connors and the MacDonaghs. Patrick Plunkett lived on the confiscated estate of the MacDonagh family, as did, of course, the Taaffe family.[68] It seems unlikely that these two groups would have co-operated together while one group had a long-term aim to dispossess the other. Undoubtedly for some there may have been hopes of regaining lost estates, and some attempted to put these hopes into action. The O'Dowd action of ejecting the Nolans in Enniscrone is the clearest example in Sligo of this type of motive being important. But, on the other hand, the estates of other new landlords were not seized. The rebels needed to at least distinguish between Old English and New English landlords; and to recognise that a simple restoration of lost land was not possible.

In the case of some of the small landholding families who joined the rebellion, there is evidence, as noted already, that they had been issued with captain's commissions to take troops abroad by Theobald Taaffe, and they may also have served in the new army formed in the summer of 1640. A military career might have been attractive to small landholders who saw little prospect for a change in their family fortunes. Their participation in the rebellion may have owed as much to the group spirit and sense of common purpose encouraged through association in the army as it did to their financial problems. Group loyalty may also have been inspired by Tadhg O'Connor Sligo's seizure of the Sligo estate and his subsequent involvement in the siege of Sligo. Loyalty to the old Gaelic lords was still a powerful force in the area. The fact that the rebel army was organised around the old family units of the area was a recognition of the continued strength of the traditional system. Financial problems, therefore, can have been only one of several reasons for involvement in the rebellion.

More cautious in their attitude to the rebellion were a small number of landlords from Gaelic families who are noticeable both for their absence from the list of initial rebels in Sligo and their later involvment in the assembly at Kilkenny. These men, such as Fergal O'Gara, Tadhg Óg O'Higgin and Tadhg Riabhach O'Dowd and their families, had much to lose through rebellion. Their survival as relatively wealthy landlords owed much to a cautious and conservative outlook which endeavoured where possible to co-operate with the government. They had connections with the Old English group in the county and had served with them in local government, but do not appear to have shared with them the initial enthusiasm for identifying with the cause of the Old English on the east coast. They were from families who had successfully survived one rebellion in the 1590s and were reluctant to risk all by becoming involved in another. Their attitude to the rebellion was probably similar to those described by Clanricard when he wrote of Irish men of quality who wanted to remain loyal but were forced to take sides with the rebels because of lack of military support from the government. Repre-sentatives from these large landowning families in Sligo only began actively to support the rebellion when the confederation of Kilkenny was established in 1642, and it was from this group that the representatives for Sligo for the provincial council set up by the Kilkenny assembly were chosen: Tadhg Óg O'Higgin and Tadhg Riabhach O'Dowd. It is therefore likely that for this small group of larger landlords the establishment of the confederate system and the emergence of a united catholic front was the determining factor in their support. They tried to remain neutral for as long as possible and only joined when it was safe to do so. Fear of what might happen if they did not must also have contributed to their decision. They did not play an important part in the military aspects of the war, and their ultimate aim may have been nothing more that the preservation of their existing landed wealth and the maintenance of law and order. [69]

Notable absentees among the large local landlords who supported the confederates were Kean O'Hara and Theobald Taaffe, who succeeded his father, John, as Viscount Taaffe in 1642. Kean O'Hara is not referred to in any records relating to the period and either locked himself and his family quietly away or else removed them elsewhere. His allegiance to protestantism remained sound, and there was never any suggestion that he had participated in the rebellion. Theobald Taaffe, on the other hand, remained catholic but loyal and was very similar to the earl of Clanricard in his loyalty to Charles. He attended the Irish house of commons in November 1641, but thereafter he went to England, where he developed a role as adviser to the king on Irish affairs, returning to Ireland several times as the king's repre-sentative in his negotiations with the confederate assembly. Like Clanricard, he had many relatives on the rebel side.[70]

More generally, religion and support for catholicism undoubtedly were important issues for those who supported the rebellion. There is clear evidence of clergy travelling through the countryside urging support for the war in late 1641. The unity of all catholics was one of their main messages.

For example, Brian MacKeoghan, guardian of the Franciscans in Creevelea, County Leitrim, was preaching in Killoran, County Sligo, in October 1641. He told William Brown, the Church of Ireland registrar of Killala and Achonry, on whose land he was preaching, that the blood shed by the Binghams was to be revenged, as were the fines levied against recusants. When Brown pointed out the failure of the Irish in previous rebellions, MacKeoghan replied that on those occasions the Irish of the kingdom were divided, whereas now there was scarcely an Irish catholic who would support the protestants.[71] Similarly, Tadhg O'Connor Sligo in a letter to Sir Frederick Hamilton wrote of the union among all Roman Catholics who had vowed to help each other.[72]

Clerical pressure on individuals was very real. The catholic but loyal Clanricard wrote in 1642 of the clergy forcing men to take the oath of association and threatening excommunication if they did not. They also threatened to 'set all others upon them' if they did not support the rebellion.[73] Clerical support for the rebellion undoubtedly influenced all sections of society, but their hostility to the collection of tithes and their seizure of protestant ministers' church livings probably received considerable popular support from the lowest levels of society. It is difficult to get any clear idea of the nature of the support which the rebellion received at the lower end of the social scale, but the impression given from the evidence is that support was widespread. Priests no doubt played an important part in encouraging popular support. And as the rebellion progressed the catholic church strengthened its local organisation and took advantage of the chaos in the established church to improve its economic position and fill vacant ecclesiastical positions.[74]

At popular level, garbled versions of the more sophisticated Old English ideology and rumours of anti-Irish legislation in England combined with catholic sermons to produce a strong anti-English and anti-protestant ethos which helps to explain the viciousness of the attacks on the protestant ministers and their families. One Mayo deponent reported a rumour that there was an act of parliament in England that all the Irish should be forced to go to church, and others that the English had plans to destroy all Irish catholics. Brian MacDonagh was alleged to have said in response to this that 'I hope before it be long that this hand of mine ... should squeeze the blood out of the hearts of many hundreds of the Englishmen.' The same deponent reported a resolution of the rebels that the Irish wanted to 'root out all the English and Scots out of Ireland and then have all their own chief governors, judges, justices, and great officers to be of the mere Irish and to be governed by their own laws: further saying why should not they have it so in Ireland as well as the Scots had it in Scotland'.[75] In Mayo mock courts were held in derision at the English legal system.[76]

There were therefore many different reasons for participating in the rebellion. Some wanted the fulfilment of the limited aims of the Old English: fair administration and religious toleration. Some wanted to restore law and order. Others had vague hopes that the war would improve their economic standing and restore lost family lands. Others responded to the loyalties of Gaelic Ireland, and many undoubtedly joined for the excitement of the long-awaited military conflict or because of resentment at the collection of tithes, or they were persuaded by the catholic clergy to participate.[77]

Confederate control

The confederate control of Connacht began in the summer of 1642 when, following a meeting of many of the main landlords in Ballinrobe, a provincial council was formed, with two representatives from each county. The representatives from County Sligo were, as noted already, Tadhg Óg O'Higgin and Tadhg Riabhach O'Dowd, two substantial landlords. The provincial meeting also nominated county and borough representatives to attend the assembly at Kilkenny. Luke Taaffe and Patrick Plunkett were chosen for County Sligo.[78] There is no evidence that the borough of Sligo was represented at the assembly in Kilkenny. Taaffe and Plunkett were involved in the rebellion from the initial stages and had led military campaigns against Manorhamilton and Boyle earlier in the year. Their selection as representatives at the Kilkenny assembly is not therefore surprising, but it did help to emphasise the Old English leadership of the rebellion in Sligo. Although in many counties there may have been a strong continuity between parliamentary representation and membership of the general assembly, in County Sligo this was not the case. The assembly seems to have preferred to select Old English representatives rather than choose from the Gaelic families who had previously served as M.P.s for the county.

The choice of O'Dowd and O'Higgin as members of the provincial council was paralleled in other Connacht counties by the selection of large landlords. The main tasks of the provincial council were the restoration of law and order and the regularisation of the confederate army. The confederate assembly in Kilkenny was particularly concerned to be seen to be imposing control at local level, and it was for this reason that early in 1643 instructions were issued to Brian MacDonagh and Luke Taaffe to arrest sixteen men in County Sligo because there had been complaints that they had committed 'massacres, outrages and robberies'.[79] The sixteen included Tadhg O'Connor Sligo and his two brothers and other O'Connors and O'Harts, as well as Andrew Crean and, most surprisingly of all, Fergal O'Gara. It is not clear if the order to arrest all these men was carried out, but Tadhg O'Connor Sligo and his brothers were certainly apprehended. There were reports that O'Connor Sligo was to be executed, but he was later released.[80] The main effect of confederate control and its dislike of the way in which the rebellion had developed in Sligo was the exclusion of some of the initial leaders from any further decision-making role during the subsequent war. The O'Connors were in disgrace, and Andrew Crean, who had played an important part in co-ordinating affairs in late 1641 and in early

1642, was ignored by the confederates. In their place no clear county leader emerged. It is noticeable that the provincial council appointed Viscount Mayo as governor of County Mayo, while Clanricard's control in County Galway was recognised, and a commander of County Leitrim was also appointed; but no one was put in charge of County Sligo. The obvious choice, from the assembly's point of view, if not from that of the local inhabitants, was Viscount Taaffe, but his departure for England ruled him out. In his absence, the assembly may have been unwilling to appoint a rival, but Taaffe's brother Luke was given a prominent role both as representative at Kilkenny and as commander of the forces in Sligo following the death of Brian MacDonagh in 1643. Thus the massacre in the jail at Sligo and the random attacks on settlers had a lasting effect on the progress of the conflict in the county, excluding many from leadership roles and eventually causing division and faction-fighting among the Irish forces.

The provincial council also made arrangements for the raising of soldiers and their maintenance through levies on local people. In addition, John Burke – a Mayo man who had served as a soldier on the continent – was appointed colonel-in-chief of the army in Connacht by the assembly in Kilkenny, an appointment which was strongly resented by Viscount Mayo, who was reluctant to yield his county control (authorised by the provincial council) to Burke. The fact that Burke was a Mayo man considerably increased Viscount Mayo's hostility to him and led eventually to a feud in County Mayo, with the county divided in support for the two men. Sligo hostility to the new confederate control was not as clearly expressed as in Mayo, but it did eventually emerge.[81]

Initially the formation of the provincial council and the establishment of the assembly at Kilkenny seems to have made little difference to the situation in County Sligo. The war continued on two fronts: Brian MacDonagh and Luke Taaffe concentrated on Hamilton's forces at Manorhamilton, while Patrick Plunkett launched assaults on Ballinafad and the garrison at Boyle.[82]

The cessation of arms agreed in September 1643 between the confederates and Ormond did not bring the military conflict to a halt, but instead seems to have contributed much to the emergence of a chaotic and, according to Clanricard, an almost anarchic situation in Sligo and in north Connacht in general. By the time the truce was agreed it was clear that many of the English soldiers based in north Roscommon supported the parliament in England in its conflict with the king. One week after the truce was announced the English parliament published the 'solemn league and convenant' which it had entered into with the Scots. Both groups disliked the truce with the Irish catholics. The parliament instructed the commanders of the forces in Ulster (a mixture of English and Scots) to ignore the cessation and accept the covenant. Most of the Scottish commanders were prepared to do this, and their actions were supported by officers and troops in north Connacht, particularly by Sir Frederick Hamilton in Leitrim. The garrisons under the command of Sir Charles Coote and Robert Ormsby in

County Roscommon also began to hint strongly at their sympathy for the Scottish covenanters and the English parliament.[83] Robert King, a commander at Boyle, told Clanricard in 1643 that 'he could not command one man of his troop, his brother Captain Francis King and Captain Ormsby having seduced them all, by assuring them all of the immediate advance of the Scots [i.e. of the army in the north], who were (as they affirm) the only preservers of honesty and religion'.[84]

The refusal to observe the truce and the plundering carried out by soldiers from the northern and western garrisons in north Connacht during the cessation led to much confusion and no doubt great frustration among the Irish troops in the region. Under the terms of the truce, the Irish forces were prohibited from retaliation, and Ormond refused to authorise action against the soldiers in the west who were still in theory considered supporters of the king. The situation in Sligo was further exacerbated by the cessing in the county of the Ulster forces of Owen Roe O'Neill in 1644. The failure to reach a permanent settlement also contributed to the general instability and sense of frustration.[85]

The situation in Sligo had deteriorated to such an extent by 1645 that confederate control of the region appeared to be very shaky. Clanricard wrote of 'another sort of people risen into a new rebellion in the counties of Sligo, Leitrim and Mayo'. The new group, which he claimed was growing daily, 'neither regard the royal power, the parliament covenant nor the confederate association, but adore liberty, spoil and rapine'.[86] It seems likely that the inhabitants of Sligo were taking the law and the defence of their property into their own hands. Clanricard's report also suggests that the area was suffering from the activities of soldiers who had been prevented from venting their frustration in military action, as had happened before at the beginning of the rebellion.

The loss of control in north Connacht was initiated and encouraged by the behaviour of Viscount Mayo. Mayo's resentment at the appointment of John Burke as commander-in-chief eventually developed into a refusal to accept Burke's authority and culminated in Viscount Mayo's breaking away from the confederation and taking control of a number of castles in Mayo. The situation was considered sufficiently serious by the confederates for the earl of Castlehaven to be sent to Mayo to seize the occupied castles in April 1644. Viscount Mayo was arrested and brought to Kilkenny, but he escaped early in 1645 and returned to the west, where by that time discontent had spread from Mayo into Leitrim and Sligo.[87]

Shortly after Mayo's return Sir Charles Coote declared his support for the parliament, and in the summer of 1645 he received a parliamentary commission to be president of Connacht. He returned to Ireland determined to take control of the province. The first step in this plan was to take Sligo castle which he accomplished with a large army composed of northern and local Connacht men in June 1645. Tadhg O'Connor Sligo was in the town at the time and was criticised by the confederate commanders for yielding up the town without a fight. In reality, the lack of confederate control in the area made Coote's task easy.[88]

The taking of Sligo was followed by the seizure of other castles in north Sligo. These events finally persuaded Ormond that it was legitimate to proceed against Coote and his allies because their public support for the parliament was a clear act of treachery. He therefore commissioned Theobald Taaffe to raise an army to resist Coote and his supporters. Taaffe succeeded in taking many of the garrisons in Roscommon, but failed to take Sligo, which remained in parliamentary control until 1649.[89] The seizure of Sligo by Coote and the formation of the army by Taaffe seems to have distracted attention from the chaos in north Connacht and no doubt also helped to channel the frustration of the soldiers into positive action against the English garrisons. Resentment at confederate authority in the region remained, however, and no doubt helps to explain why most of the local Irish supported Archbishop Rinuccini in 1646 when he rejected the peace finally agreed to and proclaimed by Ormond. Neither Ormond nor the confederates had done much to win supporters in Sligo.[90]

The incidents in north Connacht are also a reminder of the localised nature of loyalties. Even loyalty to a provincial authority seemed to be problematic. Viscount Taaffe encountered a similar resistance among the Burkes in Galway as John Burke experienced in Mayo.[91] Old family pride and loyalties remained strong, a fact which the confederate assembly at Kilkenny does not appear to have appreciated. Viscount Mayo was treated with a lack of sensitivity to his social status and family background. In Sligo the authority which O'Connor Sligo could command was also disregarded. The unrest in 1643–5 also reveals a certain confusion of authority between the provincial council of local landlords, who gave Viscount Mayo the command of County Mayo, and the supreme council at Kilkenny, who wanted the army organised at provincial level by John Burke.

When Sligo was taken by the parliamentary forces in 1645, the history of the region reverts to a familiar wartime pattern, with both sides recognising the strategic merit of the area and trying to seize Sligo castle. The confederate forces made several attempts to take the castle. The Leinster military leader, Thomas Preston, was told by the supreme council in Kilkenny on 11 August 1646 that the taking of Sligo would 'give the lord nuncio [Archbishop Rinuccini] more satisfaction and draw more help from his holiness than all the inland forts of Connacht'.[92] But the problem of the formidable border presented by the Curlew mountains once again assumed a major importance. Preston failed to take Sligo, and although Owen Roe O'Neill had plans to seize the castle and his 'pioneers were at work five or six weeks through Rockey mountains to make way for his guns', he never succeeded in doing so.[93] It was not until 1649 that the confederates regained control of Sligo when the English garrison surrendered to the earl of Clanricard, who by then had taken command of the royalist and confederate forces in Connacht. The parliamentary forces tried to retake the castle but failed because

129

Clanricard by then had wisely taken control of the passes in the Curlews and so could block any advance of enemy troops into the county.[94] But Clanricard's resistance in the west was of little value in the wider context of the war in Ireland. Oliver Cromwell's military campaign in 1649 recovered much of the country for the commonwealth regime, and in the spring of 1652 the castle of Sligo and the surrounding garrisons finally surrendered.[95]

Conclusion

A study of the causes and progress of the war in County Sligo in the 1640s reveals the importance of viewing events from a local stance. Concentration on the Old English in the Pale and their involvement in the confederate assembly at Kilkenny overlooks the impact of their actions in the localities. The Sligo evidence reveals how direct that impact could be. In particular, the politicisation of the Old English was manifest in local government and was a crucial factor in the outbreak of rebellion in County Sligo. Reasons for supporting the rebellion, initiated by the Old English, were complex and varied according to the social group involved. Consequently recognition of the confederate system of local government was not without qualification. The confederates never established total control over the north-west where, despite forty years of local government, loyalty to old Gaelic families such as the O'Connors Sligo was still very strong. The Kilkenny assembly was insensitive to such loyalties and preferred to rely for county and provincial representatives on men associated with the Old English group in the county. It did not, as is sometimes assumed, nominate men who had represented Sligo in the Irish parliament. The weak local government structure of the confederates undermined the solidarity of their support and in Sligo facilitated the progress of the parliamentary troops under the command of Sir Charles Coote. And it is Coote and his soldiers who eventually emerged victorious in the county in the 1650s.

LAND AND SOCIETY, 1652–88

When the war ended, Sligo, like the rest of Ireland, became the focus for commonwealth reform plans. These were actuated by a mixture of religious zeal, greed, and concern for the security problem presented by the country. In the case of Sligo, it was the latter consideration which dominated government policy in the 1650s. The strategic importance of the county was a continuous theme throughout the commonwealth period. Fear, rather than religious faith or acquisitiveness, was thus the main motivating force behind Cromwellian involvement in the county.

Military plans

The initial military proposals of the commonwealth for the county formed part of the general scheme to secure the province of Connacht from a military point of view. The aim was to create around the entire province a four-mile border where soldiers were to be settled. The border zone was therefore to be excluded from the other major plan for the province – the transplantation scheme. In addition, a system of new forts was to be constructed within the four-mile border and also in other strategically important areas.[1] In County Sligo a new fort was planned for Bellahy on the 'pass from Galway to Sligo' in the southern part of the county, while Castleconnor in the north-west was to be repaired, and two other forts were to be built on the coast of Carbury. These new garrisons were in addition to the existing garrisons stationed at Sligo, Ballinafad and Ballymote. Other Connacht counties were also to have a number of new forts.[2] Not all of the projected forts were built, but by 1655 the engineer, William Webb, was in the process of building at Bellahy, where the new fort was called Fort Cromwell, and by 1659 there was a report of a new fort in Sligo town. A garrison was retained at Ballinafad and probably also at Ballymote and Castleconnor.[3]

The land settlement

The land settlement of County Sligo implemented during the commonwealth era also reflected the security concerns of the government. As with the rest of the country, all catholic-owned land was forfeited to the government. The initial plan for the redistribution of the forfeited territory involved dividing the county of Sligo into two parts. The northern part (i.e. the coastal area), consisting of the baronies of Carbury and Tireragh, was to be allotted to soldiers in payments of their arrears. This would help to fulfil the plan for securing the borders of the province by means of military occupation of the border zone. The southern baronies of Leyny, Corran, Tirerrill and Coolavin were to be included in the general transplantation scheme for Connacht as a whole. The lands alleged to belong to the estates of the earl of Strafford and Sir George Radcliffe were to be excluded from both schemes and reserved for their heirs.[4]

The procedure by which the northern baronies were divided among the soldiers is not clear, but by January 1654 a number of officers were authorised to divide the land and set it out by lot. Most of the soldiers awarded land in Sligo had served in Connacht during the war, mainly in the regiment of Sir Charles Coote or in that of his brother Richard. They were a mixture of local English landlords (largely from County Roscommon), men from families who had lived in the province before 1641 as tenants rather than as landlords, and English and Scottish men recruited in the north of Ireland, Scotland and England to serve in the army.[5]

Many of the soldiers were owed arrears for serving in Sir Charles Coote's regiment since the summer of 1645. The land allotted in north Sligo to these men did not by any means meet all the arrears due, and in 1654 and 1655 the soldiers pressed for more land to be awarded to them.[6] For many of the officers who had served in Connacht during the 1640s the demand for land was complicated by the fact that most of them wanted land in Connacht. This was understandable, as many of them were already landlords in the province or came from families who were. They requested that their new estates be as close as possible to the existing landed possessions of their families. Their expectations of having their requests granted were high because in the late 1640s the parliament had already leased out, on a temporary basis, lands of known rebels in Connacht. For example, the lands of Brian MacDonagh and Patrick Plunkett were leased to serving soldiers in 1647.[7] The hopes of the soldiers for land in Connacht were further encouraged by the statement of the general council of the army in Ireland in the summer of 1653 that the soldiers should be 'settled in those quarters where they have served and are best acquainted'.[8]

For the officers and men who served in the war in Connacht the government's scheme for massive transplantation and resettlement in the province must therefore have been a bitter blow. It not only cut across any plans which they may have had for receiving their arrears in the form of land in Connacht, but it also threatened their existing family lands in the province. There was in theory provision for protestant landlords in Connacht to exchange their Connacht estates for land elsewhere, but, given the acute shortage of available land in the country as a whole, this was of little practical value.[9] In 1652 Robert King, one of Coote's officers, was quoted as expressing his opposition to government interference on his lands in Connacht by claiming that 'I hope the states of England have not more right to my lands than myself; who besides by birthright have purchased my freedom and interest by my sword as well as given them a power to govern.'[10]

The Connacht landlords were eventually allowed to retain their lands in the province, and in the middle years of the commonwealth the soldiers began a campaign to pressurise the government into giving them more land in Connacht. Agents for the army included Francis Gore and Robert Ormsby, both of whom had served with the Scots and had received estates in County Sligo. The agents met with some success. By the late summer of 1655 much of the remaining part of County Sligo was awarded to the soldiers. The final triumph of the soldiers came in 1659 when they secured the estate of the earl of Strafford and proceeded to divide it out among themselves. This included, of course, the town of Sligo and valuable land in the vicinity of the town.[11]

The withdrawal of County Sligo from the transplantation scheme can therefore be attributed to the influence of the officers of Coote's regiment who demanded and eventually got a large part of their arrears paid with land in Connacht. Their success must also be related to the undoubted importance of Sir Charles Coote in the post-war period.

Charles Coote (whose father had been an important official in Connacht earlier in the century) rose to prominence in Ireland largely as a result of his command of the Connacht army and its joining up with the so-called Laggan army from the north (which consisted of about 4,500 English and Scottish men recruited in the mid-1640s). The combined forces under Coote operated in Ulster and Connacht on behalf of the English parliament. After the war Coote was rewarded for his military achievements by being given virtual control over the province of Connacht. He was president of the province; he was also one of the commissioners involved in supervising the transplantation scheme, and he was a commissioner in charge of taking depositions which found that many of the native Irish landlords of Connacht had taken a prominent part in the rebellion. He was therefore very influential in determining which land in the province would be forfeited.[12]

Not surprisingly, Coote was careful to look after the interests of the officers and men who had served him loyally during the war. The interests of Coote's army are, in fact, crucial to the ultimate failure of the transplantation scheme in Connacht, and crucial also for the land settlement in Sligo. The drawing-board plans of the act of settlement were upset by the very human fact that the soldiers could not be moved as easily around the country as the planners had imagined. Indeed, in the initial plans for the transplantation, the presence of resident protestant landowning families who were also entitled to army arrears had not been seriously considered. In the end the victory went to the officers who acquired lands in County Sligo and the neighbouring barony of Tirawly in County Mayo, which was also withdrawn from the transplanted area.

The officers and men of Sir Charles Coote's regiment therefore dominated the division of lands in Sligo. However, it could also be added that the soldier-dominated settlement suited the overall plans of the government. The initial attempt to secure a four-mile border around Connacht free of catholic landowners may have failed, but the strong military presence in County Sligo at least secured some of the key strategic parts of the province.

There were thus four main stages to the commonwealth settlement of Sligo: the occupation of military garrisons and the building or repairing of forts; the distribution of Carbury and Tireragh to the soldiers *c.* 1653-4 (excluding the Strafford estate); the distribution of much of the rest of the county to the soldiers by 1655; and finally the distribution of the Strafford estate in 1659.

Catholic landowners

All catholic landlords officially forfeited their landed possessions as a result of the commonwealth settlement. In theory they were to be compensated with lands in other parts of Connacht which were reserved for the transplantation scheme. Proof of ownership before 1641 was certified by the commissioners sitting in Athlone, and land was then allotted proportionate to the amount forfeited. A total of fifteen Sligo landlords were given some land in Galway, Mayo and Roscommon; just over half of these were of Old English or New English background. The Creans and John Nolan received the largest portions. There was a similar concentration of Old English families among those who received transplantation lands in County Clare.[13] Few Gaelic landed families, therefore, received compensation from the Athlone commissioners. This may have been because the Creans and the Old English families in general had better legal assistance and documentation to prove their ownership to the commissioners. Accusations of corruption and misconduct were levied at some of the commissioners in Athlone, and the Sligo evidence could support these allegations in the sense that families with Old English connections were treated more favourably than families of Gaelic origin.[14]

The complicated legal processes involved in the settlement meant that Old English families (particularly those with professional lawyers in the family) had a legal knowledge which could be exploited to their advantage, albeit sometimes in rather unusual ways. From the point of view of the commonwealth authorities, the more catholic-owned land which could be legally identified, the more land was available for them to distribute among the adventurers and soldiers who were owed money by the government. In the case of Sligo, legal assistance of local lawyers was essential to unravel the complex ownership of the O'Connor Sligo estate, which had become heavily encumbered with mortgages and debts. In order to seize the estate, the commonwealth authorities had to prove it was in catholic possession in 1641. The purchase of much of the estate by the earl of Strafford and partners in the late 1630s meant, however, that catholic ownership was not

Barony of Carbury by William Petty, surveyor for the commonwealth land settlement.
Sligo town, lying between St John's Church and the Dominican Abbey, is clearly
depicted. The dotted line represents the roadway through the area. The bridges at
Drumcliffe, Sligo, Ballysadare and Collooney are also marked.

easily proved, and initially the estate was reserved from forfeiture. As was outlined in the previous chapter, Patrick French had always disputed Strafford's right to the land, and in 1642 he had received a possession order from the English house of commons. French's lawyer and agent in London during the dispute was Geoffrey Browne from Galway. In the 1650s and 1660s, Browne's acquisition and knowledge of the documentation relating to the estate was eagerly sought by soldiers anxious to acquire a share of the property. Geoffrey Browne provided legal assistance for soldiers who claimed possession of the O'Connor Sligo estate on the grounds that in 1641 it had belonged to Browne's client, the catholic Patrick French, and not to the protestant earl of Strafford and his partners. Browne produced the legal documents to support the case of the soldiers – a rather ironic role for a prominent member of the confederate assembly at Kilkenny.[15]

It is not clear what reward or compensation was given to Browne or the French family or other Old English landlords who assisted the forfeiture process in this way. Favourable treatment by the Athlone commissioners of the Frenches' claims to other lands in Connacht proportionate to those which they had lost in Sligo is one likely reward. Leases of land forfeited and permission to remain on forfeited property are others. As is shown in the appendix to this volume, members of the French and Crean families continued to live and trade in Sligo town in the 1670s and 1680s. Secret or clandestine deals during the commonwealth period may have been responsible for this continuity of possession, but this cannot be proved by the evidence.

Geoffrey Browne was promised a reward for his services by Francis Gore, and it is perhaps worth noting that the only catholic M.P. elected to the Irish parliament in 1661 was Geoffrey Browne representing Tuam.[16] This unusual collaboration between the catholic dispossessed and the new landlords reflects the complexity of the land settlement of the 1650s. It also perhaps reveals the ingenuity and pragmatism of men like Browne and his fellow Galway lawyers and merchants. Browne had been at the centre of the negotiations between the confederates and Ormond and the king in the 1640s and would have had plenty of time to contemplate the consequences of the failure of the negotiations and to identify means of survival for himself and other catholic families in the west.

Those catholic landlords who did not receive lands under the transplantation scheme virtually disappear from the historical record. Some were executed for their part in the war, and some chose to go overseas.[17] But it is likely that a number remained living as tenants on their former lands and tried unsuccessfully to regain their lands through the court of claims, although many Sligo landlords were excluded from this process because they had been named as rebels in the act of settlement. The fact that so many Old Gaelic families re-emerge very quickly in the 1680s suggests strongly that many stayed in the county living quietly on their former possessions as tenants to the new landlords. A list of barony deputies in the

1670s suggests that they also retained some power in their localities, and the events of the 1680s would seem to corroborate this suggestion. James II's army was commanded by men from many of the same families who had fought on the confederate side in the 1640s.[18]

The restoration settlement

The land settlement which followed the restoration of Charles II seriously undermined the distribution of the land of County Sligo among Coote's soldiers. Three royal grants considerably reduced the quantity of land held by the soldiers. First, Charles II questioned the French title to the O'Connor Sligo estate and wanted to restore it to the heirs of the earl of Strafford and Sir George Radcliffe. This gave rise to a lengthy legal dispute which eventually ended in defeat for the soldiers, despite the legal assistance of Geoffrey Browne. As a result, the second earl of Strafford and Thomas Radcliffe, son of George, received a grant of over 18,000 acres of land in Sligo, including the town of Sligo.[19] The second major royal grant by Charles was to his loyal supporter Theobald Taaffe, the earl of Carlingford, to whom he restored about 11,000 acres of land, mainly in the vicinity of Ballymote castle. Finally, smaller grants were made to supporters of the Stuarts and a number of men who had lost land elsewhere in Ireland as a result of the restoration settlement. Thus Sir Theophilus Jones received a grant of about 4,000 acres in compensation for giving up his County Dublin estate which had been restored to the Sarsfield family. The Crofton family, dispossessed in the 1650s, were also restored to their Sligo lands in the 1660s.[20]

The result, therefore, of the restoration settlement was to considerably dilute the soldiers' control of the county. The grant to Strafford and Radcliffe was the biggest setback, but the estates of some officers were also reduced by the grants to Taaffe and others.

The final land settlement, as revealed in the enrolled grants and the Books of Survey and Distribution, meant that there were about eighty-five landlords in the county.[21] Of these, three peers, the earls of Strafford, Collooney (i.e. Richard Coote, brother of Charles) and Carlingford, were by far the largest, with estates of over 10,000 acres each. Lord Kingston, Kean O'Hara, Sir Francis Gore and Jeremy Jones each held over 4,000 acres, while four more landlords had estates of over 3,000 acres, and thirteen had grants of over 1,000 acres. The majority of landlords had, however, much smaller estates of less than 1,000 acres, some considerably less.

Of the eighty-five or so landlords in the county by 1680, about half were from families who owned land in the province before 1641, and the majority of these were from the Roscommon families who had garrisoned the forts of Roscommon, Boyle and Castlecoote and later took commands under Coote. None of the old landlords of County Sligo benefited from the changes of the 1650s and 1660s. The Croftons and the Taaffes succeeded in holding on to their property, but did not expand it. The lands of Roger Jones were inherited by the Parke family, but were not increased during this period.

The O'Haras of Annaghmore were the only family of Gaelic stock to survive as landowners, and the Taaffes were the only pre-1641 catholic landlords to survive into the second half of the seventeenth century.

An interesting phenomenon among the new landlords is the number of brothers or members of the same family who received grants of land in County Sligo. There were three Gore brothers, six members of the Ormsby family, three Nicholsons and two King brothers, as well as Richard Lord Collooney, brother of Sir Charles Coote. Clearly the commonwealth settlement enabled existing landlord families not just to expand their family estates but also to provide for younger brothers and establish cadet branches of their families. Through the settlement the Gores, Ormsbys and Cootes developed a network of marital links and consequently of social and political influence throughout the northern part of Connacht.[22]

About half the landlords in the county were from families who had not held land in the county or province before 1641. Most of these, presumably, had come to Ireland during the war years as recruits to the army in the 1640s or with Cromwell in 1649. If owning a house in the county was an indication of residence, then about half of the landlords were resident in 1662, and of these the majority (23 out of 39) came from the newly arrived landlords.[23] Most of the new resident landlords only owned land in County Sligo, while many of the absentee landlords held land elsewhere in Connacht, and a small number, such as the Kings and the Cootes, owned property in other parts of Ireland. Thus, in terms of landed possessions, many of the new resident landlords in the county were relatively poor.

There were, therefore, three main divisions among the resident landlords: first, a small group of families who were resident in the county from the late sixteenth or early seventeenth century; secondly, a group of landlords with family connections with landlords in other parts of the province, mainly Roscommon; and thirdly, a group of new English and Scottish men who had earned their land through service in the wars of the 1640s. It is the third group who formed the majority of the resident landlords in the county.

Many of the new landlord families intermarried with one another. This was particularly the case with those whose landed possessions were confined to the county or province. The larger landed families had wider contacts. Such intermarriage gradually led to more consolidated and some very large estates, but this was a process which had only begun in the late seventeenth century and its main results were not seen until the eighteenth century. Thus the Gore family built up their estate around Lissadell through the marriage of Sir Francis Gore to Anne, the daughter of Robert Parke, and subsequently added to their Sligo lands and wealth through marriage to a member of the Booth family, one of the new merchant families in Sligo town.[24]

T. C. Barnard has suggested that the process by which the older generation of English settlers and the new Cromwellian landlords assimilated together in the late seventeenth century was important for the development of landlord society thereafter.[25] To the extent that the Roscommon families who got land in Sligo belonged to the former group, this analysis is valid for Sligo. But the intermarriage and connections between the new and established landlords seem to have excluded those families who were royalist during the war: the Croftons, Taaffes and O'Haras. Dr Tom Bartlett has described the way in which Kean O'Hara was never quite accepted as a social equal by his fellow-landlords in Sligo, despite his protestantism.[26] The Croftons retained their loyalty to Charles I throughout the war, as did the head of the Taaffe family, and both families were dispossessed by the commonwealth regime and restored to their property by Charles II. Henry Crofton of Longford converted to catholicism in the late seventeenth century, which undoubtedly made him socially unacceptable, while the Taaffes retained their strong catholic links.[27] On the other hand, the Parke family fitted easily into the new social scene in Sligo. The Parkes, however, after much initial hesitation, had supported the parliamentary forces.[28] In other words, the divisions of the war had a long-term effect on landlord society in Sligo. Landlords who had served in the parliamentary and commonwealth armies formed a dominant and exclusive social grouping. The military nature and influence on society was reinforced by the ex-soldiers who continued to reside in Sligo on land leased from their former officers, and also by the continued military presence in the county. Throughout the 1660s the county was still garrisoned with soldiers based in Sligo town, Bellahy and elsewhere.[29]

Many of the landlords also maintained positions in the army long after the war ended. Dr Frederick Riegler has indicated the manner in which Sir Charles Coote after 1659 packed the army with his own relations and supporters. He took two regiments for himself and gave others to each of his three brothers (including Richard Coote, who maintained his troop partly in Collooney), to a cousin, a member of the St George family, as well as to Arthur Gore, a landlord in Sligo and Mayo. Other Sligo landlords, Sir Francis Gore and John King, Baron Kingston, also maintained positions in the army after the cessation of the war, as did several members of the Ormsby family. The army gave status to these small Sligo landlords, and it also provided an outlet for younger sons. The lower ranks of these regiments would have been filled with tenants of the commanding officers, many of whom, as noted already, were men who had served in the wars of the 1640s. Dr Riegler also stresses the marriage connections between army officers, which again would have reinforced the solidarity of the Sligo veterans and serving officers and men.[30]

The Coote influence in the army in Connacht was complemented by a similar control of civil affairs in the province. Even after Charles Coote's death in 1662 the family retained its influence in the province, largely because the president of Connacht, Lord Berkeley, was an absentee. In 1666 Lord Kingston was made joint president with Lord Berkeley. So the new landlords in Sligo were supported by the provincial authorities; and clearly they dominated local county affairs, monopolising the office of sheriff and the parliamentary representation of the county and borough. Only for a brief period in the 1660s and again in 1687–9 did the Crofton family secure the position of sheriff. Similarly, the O'Haras rarely held the position. The society of former officers and their families linked to the Coote provincial network controlled county affairs in Sligo.[31]

The shared military and war experience of the resident landlords also gave them a sense of community and solidarity. It is worth noting in this context that the first clear expression of the community of County Sligo was the formation of the Sligo Association in 1688 to resist the expected attack from the new army of Richard Talbot, Earl of Tyrconnell.[32] As Dr Riegler has pointed out, the officers in the Irish army were among the first to experience the changes in Irish society authorised by Tyrconnell as he attempted to replace the protestant ascendancy of late seventeenth-century Ireland with a catholic equivalent. Among the protestant officers dismissed by Tyrconnell were members of the Coote and King families, who were also active in the Sligo Association.[33] By the 1680s the protestant landlords had developed a community consciousness which enabled them to join together to defend their society against the triumphalism of catholic Ireland in the 1680s. Their reaction to the conflict of the late 1680s stands in sharp contrast to the response of the new landlords in the county at the outbreak of rebellion in the 1640s, when there was no unity or identification of a common interest.

Economic development

As in earlier times, it is difficult to calculate population figures for the county in the late seventeenth century, but it is possible to get some idea of the relative strength of the new British population in the area. In the 1660 poll tax returns 538 English and Scottish people out of a total of 6,877 were enumerated, i.e. almost 8 per cent were English or Scottish. In a hearth money roll of 1662 about 312 of the 1,682 hearths which were taxed can be identified as belonging to British people, i.e. about 18 per cent of the total.[34] The discrepancy between the two figures can be partly explained by the different nature of the two documents. The 1660 figure is deficient because a number of parishes are missing from the poll tax document. It is therefore likely to represent a minimum figure. The 1662 figure, on the other hand, is too high and probably reflects the higher number of newcomers with taxable houses. It omitted poorer and non-taxable houses belonging to many Irish inhabitants. The correct figure is therefore likely to be somewhere between the two estimates, i.e. between 10 and 15 per cent of the total population in the county was of English or Scottish origin. It is a relatively high percentage for a county outside the province of Ulster, and it was higher than for any other Connacht county. As J. G. Simms noted, in late seventeenth-century Sligo the 'proportion of protestants was higher than in any county outside Ulster'.[35]

The settlers were not evenly distributed around the county. The majority of them were in Sligo town. Elsewhere, there was a concentration of settlers around the garrisons of Ballymote, Ballinafad and Bellahy. There was also intensive settlement along the northern coastline. It was in this area that many of the army officers received grants of land and took up residence.

Along the coast there was a line of residences, usually with two or sometimes three hearths (according to the hearth money roll of 1662), occupied by former or serving army officers such as Robert Morgan in Cottlestown, Thomas Wood in Lackan, John Bourke in Dunneill, Captain Watts in Scardan, Henry Griffith in Ballincar, Francis Gore in Court, and Thomas Sodden in Grange. Some had taken over older tower-houses, but others had begun to build new houses. Most were modest affairs: the large house which Richard Coote had built at Collooney with ten hearths was unusual.[36]

It is more difficult to assess what landlords did with their land in Sligo after 1641 than before than date. The available evidence suggests that economic development was slow and that most landlords did not derive large incomes from their lands. As already indicated, the majority of landlords in Sligo had relatively small estates of less than 1,000 acres, and the majority also were dependent on their Sligo estates for their entire income. Charles O'Hara, in the middle of the eighteenth century, wrote a very gloomy description of the economy in Sligo at the end of the seventeenth century. He wrote of tenants who only paid rents in kind because they had no cash, and of landlords consequently being too poor to travel abroad. They had enough to keep them at home but not for travel. The only money which came into the county was through the army or the occasional Leinster grazier buying some lean cattle in the county.[37]

Other evidence confirms O'Hara's description. In 1667, for example, there were complaints that rents were slow to come in to landlords. Furthermore, at this time rent was still paid in a mixture of cash and kind, so that even when rents were paid, they may not have considerably increased the landlords' cash supply.[38] As late as the mid-eighteenth century Charles O'Hara described village tenants as being 'bound by contract to a sort of slavery to which old custom gives some sanction, that of duty work'. Another, perhaps surprising, legacy of the pre-1641 situation was the collection by the agent on the Strafford estate of 'chiefries' from lands which had paid these small charges to O'Connor Sligo under the terms of the composition book of Connacht.[39]

Tenants on the Strafford and O'Hara estates were a mixture of British and Irish families, (although there were considerably more British tenants on the Strafford lands). They were as much in short supply in the second half of the seventeenth century as they were in the first half. Kean O'Hara complained of the shortage of tenants among landlords in Sligo in the 1690s, commenting that "'Tis the same case with all the gentlemen in the country that have lands here and will be so till some tenants come from the north or other places to inhabit this country for there is not half enough people in it to take half the land that is [here].'[40]

The overall economic and social picture which emerges is of a protestant landlord class with small incomes banded together by a common war experience and military connections. Their solidarity was further strengthened during the Williamite war when Sligo played an important, if familiar, strategic role. The subsequent land settlement after the war did little to alter the already solidly protestant landownership pattern in the county. Thus the commonwealth land settlement established the framework for the political and economic development of Sligo in the eighteenth and nineteenth centuries.

9

CONCLUSION

I

This study has attempted to describe the experience of the Sligo area as it was transformed from a Gaelic political and social entity into an English-style county in the sixteenth and seventeenth centuries. Politically, the change from Gaelic lordship to English local government was not a simple process, largely because the two systems were not mutually exclusive. English administrators adopted some of the methods of the Gaelic lords in collecting revenues, and remnants of the old lordships continued to exist alongside the new county government in the seventeenth century.

The political transformation was also complicated by the fact that concepts of lordship were not uniform in the Gaelic world. They varied from one lord to another, and they also changed over time. The lordship exercised by the great lords at the end of the fifteenth century was far more exacting than those of lordships in the early medieval period. Several layers of lordship could also overlap and exist in the one area. Thus in the later middle ages three different types of lordship can be detected in the Sligo region. The overlordship developed by the O'Connors Sligo in the fourteenth century was not a demanding form of lordship, and their sublords retained a considerable degree of autonomy within their own territories. These small local rulers were the real lords of the land: controlling its distribution and inheritance, administering justice and dominating the local ecclesiastical structure. The more ruthless and exacting nature of the O'Donnell overlordship of the late fifteenth and early sixteenth centuries upset the equilibrium established by the O'Connors Sligo and introduced a new style of lordship.

Oppressed by the O'Donnells, the O'Connors recognised the advantage of attaching themselves to the powerful lordship of the Tudors and eagerly accepted Queen Elizabeth as their sovereign lord. Yet their expectation that the Tudors would provide a lordly defence on their behalf was to be disappointed. The Tudors never resolved the dilemma of the hegemony of the O'Neills in Ulster, and throughout the sixteenth century they

143

continually relied on the O'Donnells to divide the power of the O'Neills in the north. The hopes of the O'Connors for defence against O'Donnell could not be fulfilled until the O'Neill problem was resolved.

Although the Tudors shired County Sligo, they did not introduce a system of civil county government. In many ways Tudor rule in Sligo can be interpreted as the imposition of a new form of military lordship. The newest element was the collection of an annual land tax in the form of the composition, but the manner in which it was collected was very similar to the tribute-collecting system of O'Donnell. The composition money was usually collected in kind rather than cash, and there were frequent complaints about local officials riding up and down the county with bands of armed men seizing stock. Their behaviour was not much different from that of Gaelic lords on a cattle-raid. The crude and violent actions of the officials, combined with the military rule of the Binghams (which became more ruthless after the Armada emergency gave the president freedom to govern as he pleased), alienated the inhabitants from the Tudor regime and explains the support which Hugh O'Donnell received in the area in the summer of 1595.

The war abolished government by lordship, and the Stuarts succeeded in establishing a system of county government; but it was a slow process, and loyalty to older forms of personal lordship remained an underlying threat to the new county government, as evidenced in the 1640s and again in the 1690s.

Changing concepts of economic and social relations ran parallel with new ideas of government and political control. A study of Gaelic economy and society in Sligo before 1641 reveals a complexity which is not often stressed in commentaries on Gaelic society. The apparent egalitarianism of Gaelic land law is belied by the reality of large and small landholders and different levels of tenantry. The complex structure of society makes it difficult to gauge effectively the impact of the appearance of new Irish and English landlords in the area. Some seemingly modern customs such as primogeniture had existed in the medieval period, while on the other hand new English landlords continued to collect the 'chiefries' due to their lordly predecessors. The new landlords also retained the pastoral economy of the area, using their new estates largely for stock grazing. An analysis of the financial income of the locally born landlords in the county in the 1630s suggests that many of them had little or no cash income. The financial demands of the government in the form of composition money, crown rents, parliamentary subsidies and fines for alienating lands or receiving letters patent inevitably undermined their financial position. By 1641 many had sold or mortgaged substantial parts of their small landed estates.

Yet it was not this group which initiated or led the rising in the county in 1641. The rising was begun by a group of Old English landowners who had in the course of the late 1620s and 1630s become increasingly influential in local government in County Sligo. They were the local manifestation of the politicisation of the Old English at central level; and they were encouraged

144

in their dislike of political events in Dublin and London by local developments such as the proposed plantation of Connacht and Lord Deputy Wentworth's and Sir George Radcliffe's purchase of much of the O'Connor Sligo estate, including the town of Sligo. The purchase gave Wentworth and Radcliffe political influence in the town and county, as the Radcliffes represented both in the Irish parliament of 1641, a development which exacerbated the existing lack of trust between the government and the Old English.

Apart from the Old English group, support for the rising in the county varied in terms of motivation and in intensity from one economic group to another. Landlord indebtedness fused with the frustration of disbanded soldiers and increased religious tension to provide initial widespread popular support. But after 1642, when the confederate assembly at Kilkenny began to control and supervise the progress of the war, divisions among its catholic supporters in the north-west emerged. The Old English at Kilkenny preferred to select men from Old English backgrounds or with Old English connections as county and provincial representatives, and thereby excluded many local families from involvement in their affairs. The dislike of the Kilkenny assembly which was evidenced in County Mayo can also be detected in County Sligo. In the mid-1640s the confederates lost control of the whole of the north-west as it was overrun with a variety of disorderly factions: local men protesting against the assembly; Scottish soldiers enticed into the province by British landlords who supported the English parliament; and the Ulster forces of Owen Roe O'Neill looking for food and plunder. The assembly's lack of control in the area considerably facilitated the parliamentary seizure of Sligo castle in 1646.

When the war was over, two recurring themes in the history of the region become more marked. There had long been a tradition of Scottish settlement in the area. In the early seventeenth century Scottish immigrants had come to Sligo, often as a result of disenchantment with the more structured settlement in Ulster. In the 1650s the Scottish influence in the county increased substantially as its lands were distributed among the soldiers of Sir Charles Coote's and his brother Richard's regiments. Many of the new landlords were resident, and retained as tenants soldiers who had served during the wars. The presence of such a relatively large number of British settlers changed the religious demography of the county, and by the end of the seventeenth century Sligo was the most protestant part of Connacht.

The settlement of the soldiers and the presence of several garrisons in the county, notably in Sligo town, underlined the strategic importance of the area, another recurring theme in its history. The army also provided social cohesion and a sense of common purpose and experience among the new settlers, as manifest in the formation of the Sligo Association in 1688. It was an exclusive community, and families who had remained royalist during the 1640s were not included. The divisions within the protestant community between parliamentarians and royalists were not as easily healed as historians have suggested.

145

Despite the racial, cultural and religious divisions in society, catholic and protestant, Irish, English and Scottish merchants and tradesmen continued to live and to work alongside one another in Sligo town. There is a strong continuity within the merchant community in the town throughout the seventeenth century. The names of the mercantile community in the 1680s is testimony to the resilience of local business families who, by whatever means, retained their commercial involvement in the town throughout the wars and land forfeitures of the 1640s and 1650s.

II

The land settlement at the end of the seventeenth century did not fix the contours of Sligo society into an unchanging mould for the next two hundred years or even for the next century. Rather the commonwealth, restoration and Williamite settlements initiated a process of change which continued into the eighteenth century. The overall pattern of landownership changed as marriage, death and sales consolidated, divided and transformed ownership of estates. The high level of resident landlords continued, but their sense of cohesion and community was strengthened by intermarriage and by continuing association with protestant families elsewhere. Links with Scotland and Ulster were reinforced by the arrival of new settlers and by marriage and commercial alliances with families from the north. The wealth of the landlords improved as the county merged into the expanding Ulster economic region created by the boom in the linen industry.

Sligo town retained its role as a market centre for the north-west, and it further expanded and prospered in the eighteenth century through the provisions trade and the linen industry. Trade with England, Scotland and the northern ports of France and Spain continued to form (as it had done since medieval times) the bulk of the town's trade, but steam power increased the volume of its commercial activity.

The strategic importance of the area continued to exercise an underlying influence on the life of the region. The army and local militia groups were an important aspect of life in the county. Military connections gave social rank and status to small landlord families and access to a wider social world. More importantly, association with military institutions continued to give a sense of coherence and community identity to the protestant community of Sligo. There were four barracks in Sligo town in 1766 and others elsewhere in the county. Joining the Volunteers and later the yeomanry was a popular pastime. In the 1790s there was, as the local historian W. G. Wood-Martin wrote, a 'mania for military service' which 'seized upon all ranks and classes amongst the protestant population', and in the late 1820s the Sligo Yeomanry was still attracting a large number of recruits. Wood-Martin also documents the fact that the yeomanry in the county was funded by the local Church of Ireland, underlining the importance of the military institution for the

Assault on the 'Green Fort' by the forces of James II in 1689. The town of Sligo can be seen in the background.

protestant community in the county. Other institutions which strengthened the identity of Irish protestants, such as the Orange Order and masonic lodges, were also popular in the county in the late nineteenth century. Similarly, commitment to an active protestant faith was strong, and John Wesley's mission in the county was particularly successful.[1]

The career and writings of William Gregory Wood-Martin, who wrote the first history of the town and county of Sligo, demonstrate the awareness of and pride in its military tradition which existed in nineteenth-century Sligo. Wood-Martin, a landlord descendant of men who had fought in the wars of the 1640s and 1688–91, commanded the Sligo Rifles and from 1883 to 1903 was lieutenant-colonel in the Sligo Artillery. In 1880 he published a book entitled *Sligo and the Enniskilleners from 1688–91*, which was designed to 'chronicle the deeds of the Sligomen in the Revolution of 1688 more distinctly than has been done by other writers, and to remind the Enniskilleners of the services rendered them by their faithful allies at a momentous crisis in the history of our country'. An active Orangeman, Wood-Martin was a member of the County Grand Lodge of Sligo and at the time of his death was its Grand Master. The fact that Wood-Martin was the first historian of the county of Sligo is perhaps indicative of the self-confidence of the protestant community in the county by the nineteenth century.[2]

The corollary of this strong sense of protestant group identity was the existence of a high level of sectarian tension in the county, which was noted by visitors and commentators on life in Sligo in the eighteenth and nineteenth centuries. In 1798, after the arrival of the French at Killala Bay (finally fulfilling Tudor fears that a continential army would land in the north-west), many protestant houses were attacked in north County Sligo and protestant churches were plundered. Just over thirty years later, in 1829, the year of catholic emancipation, a mob broke the windows of almost every protestant householder in Sligo town. Political elections throughout the nineteenth century frequently provoked sectarian conflict, although often the main political division was between liberal and conservative rather than catholic and protestant candidates, a remnant perhaps of the division perceptible among landlords in the seventeenth century.[3]

W. B. Yeats depicted in his *Autobiographies* the social world of the merchant and small resident landlord families of Sligo in the late nineteenth century. His family moved within the small and rather inward-looking protestant community of the county where everyone 'despised nationalists and catholics', and the young poet 'thought he would like to die fighting the Fenians'. His grandfather, William Pollexfen, carried a pistol in his pocket when he went to church in case of an attack by Fenians.[4]

Yeats's family background, in fact, encapsulates many of the principal developments in Sligo's history from the seventeenth to the nineteenth centuries. His self-conscious pride in his Anglo-Irish ancestry was formed by his Sligo origins and by the history of the area since the sixteenth century.

Appendix

URBAN GROWTH AND DEVELOPMENT:
SLIGO TOWN

Medieval Sligo

Sligo town was given borough status by King John, and by the end of the thirteenth century there was a castle, abbey, hospital and parish church in the new town.[1] It was a sufficient basis for the development of an urban settlement, but there are few indications of the functioning of Sligo as a town before the end of the fourteenth century. The wars of the thirteenth and fourteenth centuries, during which the O'Connors of Sligo took possession of the castle, did little to create an environment in which trade could flourish. But in the fifteenth century, coinciding with the strengthening of the lordship of O'Connor Sligo, the town of Sligo developed as a trading centre. From the early fifteenth century Sligo begins to appear on the portolan maps of continental traders, and other evidence also indicates that there was an increasing amount of direct trade between the town and merchants from France and Spain. English merchants are also recorded trading with Sligo in the fifteenth century.[2] The reason for the growth in Sligo's commercial activity at this time was the attraction of the fishing resources of the north-west region. In the early fifteenth century the salmon resources of Sligo began to be exploited by English and continental adventurers; by the middle decades of the century shoals of herring from the Baltic appeared in increasing numbers off the coast of Ireland, particularly in the Atlantic. With the boom in herring fishing came a new way of storing and preserving the fish: salting them in barrels, a process which transformed the herring fishery into a very profitable industry. The result was an expansion in the number of ships fishing and trading off the west coast of Ireland. They came mainly for fish, but traded in agricultural produce such as hides, meat and wool as well.[3] In exchange for these goods the Irish merchants imported wine and salt and small quantities of other goods. The salt was used to preserve fish and meat and to tan hides. In 1400, for example, a Bristol ship was licensed to bring twenty tuns of 'old wine', six lasts of salt and five packs of cloth to Sligo. In Sligo the master was to buy salmon, salt it, and bring it back for sale in England.[4]

Direct trade between the west coast of Ireland and the continent was more important than trade with English port towns in the late medieval period, although the pattern of trading could involve a three-cornered trade between Ireland, England and the continent. For example, in 1453 a Bristol ship, laden with English produce in Bristol, sailed to Lisbon, where the English goods were sold in exchange for wine, honey and salt. The ship then sailed to the west coast of Ireland, calling at Galway and 'Legge de Breon', which was probably somewhere in the vicinity of Sligo, where the wine, honey and salt were exchanged for hides. The vessel subsequently travelled to Flanders, where the hides were to be sold, putting into Plymouth, Winchelsea and Sandwich on the way.[5]

The prosperity which the increased trade brought to Sligo is reflected in the growth in the building of tower-houses and monasteries. As Timothy O'Neill has indicated, much of the west of Ireland experienced a building boom during the second half of the fifteenth century. The town of Sligo profited from this building expansion. A Franciscan friary was established in the town, and the abbey was also rebuilt. Both the friary and abbey had fishing weirs which must have brought in a profitable income. The merchant houses and a house of the bishop of Elphin, which Sir Henry Sidney later found in ruins in the town, probably also dated to the fifteenth century. The merchant houses were of the tower-house variety, similar to those built in Galway at the same time. Another indication of the increased wealth of the region is reflected in the rise in the valuation of Boyle abbey in the mid-fifteenth century. The abbey of Sligo experienced a similar growth in prosperity as the building was added to and improved during this time.[6]

The fifteenth century also witnessed the appearance in the records for the first time of the local merchant family of Crean. The genealogical origins of the family are unclear, but they seem to have originated in Donegal and moved to Sligo as clients of O'Donnell, who claimed the customs duties of the town. The Creans were also prominent in the church, and members of the family frequently held the bishopric of Elphin, an ecclesiastical office which the O'Donnells tried to control. The Creans are the only recorded merchant family in medieval Sligo, although it is likely that the friars in the abbey and other groups and individuals traded directly with the foreign merchants who came to the town.[7]

As noted in chapter 3, O'Donnell's claims to the customs and cocket of Sligo was challenged by the Clanricard Burkes. The subsequent competition between the two lords for the profit of the customs mirrors the political and military conflict between them for control of the north-west. At the same time it is a reflection of the prosperity of the town that both sides considered the customs worth fighting for.[8]

The conflict between Clanricard and O'Donnell also raised a continuing dilemma for the growth of Sligo town. It had to compete with Galway and the ports in Tyrconnell. Few of the continental or English merchants who came to Sligo traded exclusively with the town. It was included among a number of ports to be visited on the west coast of Ireland from Dingle to 'La Foyle'. In the surviving documentation, Sligo is frequently associated either with Galway or with the north-western territories of Tyrconnell such as Killybegs or Lough Foyle.[9]

Sixteenth-century Sligo

The wars of the early sixteenth century hindered the growth of Sligo town, but the arrival of the English administration in the area in the second half of the sixteenth century raised hopes for renewing the prosperity of the fifteenth century. Sir Nicholas Malby reported meeting merchants from Sligo who traded with France and Spain and who asked him for assistance to wall the town. Malby favoured the idea, as did his successor, Sir Richard Bingham, but nothing came of the proposal.[10] Sligo remained unwalled at the end of the seventeenth century. The military atmosphere of the 1580s and 1590s left little time for civil affairs, and Sligo seems to have declined rather than developed in the sixteenth century. In 1576 Sidney described the town as:

> upon a good haven and hath been a greate towne full of marchauntes howses, all which are now disinhabited and in ruyn, therein is a large monasterie of White Friers, and a busshops house. The Busshops See is in O'Connor Roes countrie called Elphin.[11]

Further destruction occurred in the 1590s when Sligo castle was razed by O'Donnell. Apart from the adverse effects of the wars, the later sixteenth century also witnessed a decline in the fishing traffic as the Newfoundland fisheries became popular and the large shoals of herring disappeared from the Irish coast.[12] The Creans continued to trade in a small way, but the wars restricted the movement of shipping. In 1602 when Oliver Lambert arrived in Sligo, he reported that he found nothing in the town but the old ruins of the castle and the abbey. He alleged that the town had been burnt the day before by O'Donnell. Lambert took refuge in the abbey ruins, where he cleared some vaults, presumably as lodgings for himself and his men and to 'laye stones together for a weak defence'.[13] It was the forty years after the war which witnessed the development of Sligo as a town of some importance.

Sligo town 1603–41

The growth of Sligo in the seventeenth century was due to a number of factors. First, from 1603 Sligo became both a garrison and a county town. The strategic value of the town was recognised in the maintenance of a small garrison. The presence of the soldiers, combined with the use of the town as an administrative centre where quarter sessions and the biannual assizes were held, contributed to the increased importance and size of the town. A further boost to the town's status was given in 1612, when it was incorporated and a provost and twelve burghers were appointed. In 1622 it was created a statute staple town.[14]

All these developments helped to attract to Sligo new settlers interested in trading and working in the town. Indeed, one of the most striking features of the history of Sligo town in the years between 1603 and 1641 is the number of new settlers who come to live, work and trade in the town. There are no reliable surveys or rentals from which the population of the town before 1641 can be calculated, but a deponent in the 1640s, Mrs Amy Hawkesworth, who had lived there before the rebellion, claimed that there were at least sixty British protestant families in Sligo town in 1641. An examination of the depositions reveals a total of about forty-three British families resident in the town when the rebellion broke out. If by that time a number of families had already fled the town, then the figure suggested by Mrs Hawkesworth may have been quite accurate.[15]

Some of the new settlers were ex-Elizabethan administrators and soldiers. The most prominent of these was Roger Jones, whose landed possessions have been noted in chapter 6. Jones was the first provost of the town, as well as the first mayor of the staple in 1622. He had a shop in the town and traded in wool and other goods.[16] There were also other new English settlers living in Sligo, such as Edward Carpenter, described as a merchant from London in a Dartmouth port book, and John Hopkins, who like Carpenter was among the first merchants of the staple in 1622. Carpenter was also one of the first burghers of the town in 1612.[17]

Most of the new settlers who came to the town after 1603, however, were of Scottish origin and may have come to Ireland initially with the intention of settling on plantation lands, possibly in Donegal, but subsequently moved to Sligo. The commercial potential of the town presented a more attrative proposition than settling in a remote part of Donegal. As Philip Robinson points out, movement of tenants in the Ulster plantation towards urban centres was quite common.[18]

The depositions list the occupations of many of the settlers who remained in the town until the end of 1641. They included butchers, clothiers, a shoemaker, a cutler and a general merchant. Clearly the occupations of the new inhabitants were closely related to the agricultural economy in which they lived. Butchers, clothiers, shoemakers all required the raw materials produced on the farm for their crafts. Indeed, the depositions indicate that many of the town residents were part-time farmers as well as craftsmen: the property seized from them by the rebels frequently included farm animals and produce. For example, Jane Stewart, wife of the general merchant Thomas Stewart, deposed that the rebels had deprived herself and her husband of goods and wares to the value of £1,200 and included among the items specified were cattle and horses. Similarly, William Walsh (a butcher and resident of the town) included among the goods lost by his father during the rebellion 120 cows, 50 horses, 200 sheep, as well as wheat, malt and other crops. Edward Braxton claimed that he had been robbed of farms

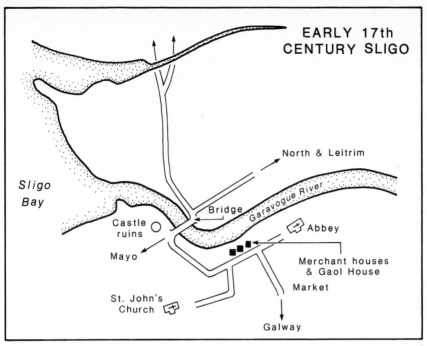

Sligo town in the early 17th century.

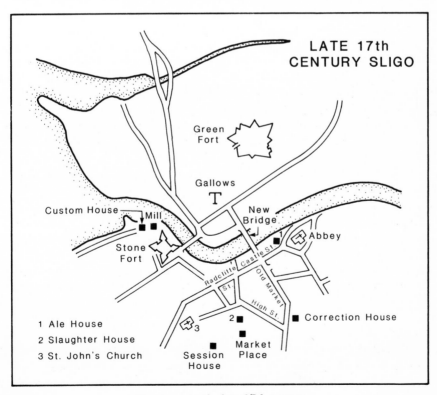

Sligo town in the late 17th century.

and lands to the value of £60 per annum, and Richard Jones listed horses, cattle, corn and hay among the property which had been taken from him. Sligo was therefore still very close to its rural hinterland, and it is likely that most of its inhabitants engaged in some kind of agricultural work, if only to provide food for their own household.[19] The town was unwalled, so it was possible for town residents to cultivate nearby fields, adjacent to their houses. As late as the 1680s many of the residents in the town rented 'parks' in the hinterland where they presumably cultivated crops and grazed stock.[20]

The newcomers not only brought new skills and services to the town; they also played a part in the local government of the town. Apart from Roger Jones, whose role in town government has already been noticed, Edward Braxton was among the first burghers in the corporation and was probably related to John Braxton who described himself as provost of the town in his deposition in 1653. John Braxton was granted the office of customer of the ports of Moyne, Sligo, Ballyshannon, Donegal and Killybegs in 1622 and was licensed to sell wine in Sligo town. The Braxtons were still living in the town in the 1680s. Another family of Scottish origin who also participated in the burgher life of Sligo town were the Gambles. Among the first burghers was Robert Gamble, who later became provost of the town. They too remained in the town throughout the seventeenth century.[21]

Apart from this mixture of English and Scottish tradesmen, the local merchant family of Crean still retained its interest in the commercial life of Sligo. In the sixteenth century the family had co-operated with the new administration, and, as described in chapter 5, by the early seventeenth century, Andrew Crean had established himself as a landlord with an estate and house near the town. Other members of the family were also prominent in the commercial life of the town. The Creans were excluded, for religious reasons, from the corporation in 1612, but three members of the family were listed among the first members of the staple of the town in 1622. The names of the first mayor, constable and society of merchants of the staple in 1622 reflect the mixture of English, Scottish and Irish merchants trading in the town. The list also indicates the growth in importance of the catholic families of Crean and French which has already been noted in the political sphere. In addition to three Creans, the charter also included two Frenches. By 1639 James French had succeeded Roger Jones as mayor and another member of the Crean family, Roebuck, was one of the constables of the staple.[22] The growing importance of these catholic merchants with Old English sympathies in the commercial life of the town complemented the increased influence in county government of other supporters of the Old English interest.

Trade, 1603–41

No detailed analysis of the commercial life of Sligo is possible, but the surviving evidence suggests a small and rather sporadic trade with the continent and with English and Scottish port towns, particularly those of south-west England and occasionally with London. The extent or size of the trade of Sligo is impossible to ascertain, owing to the fact that, as in medieval times, Sligo may have been only one of several ports visited by a trading ship and so may not appear in the records as the destination of the ship.

Customs returns for Sligo as compared with similar statistics for Galway, reflect the small and rather uneven trade pattern of the town (see table 6). The figures suggest a slight decline in the 1620s, but this may be due to inefficient returns rather than being an accurate reflection of the trade of the town.

Table 6: Customs for Sligo and Galway [23]

Year	Sligo			Galway		
1624–5	£167	8s	0d	£790 14s	11½d	
1625–6	£104	9s	0d	£908 8s	1d	
1626–7	£74	10s	3¼d	£705 15s	4½d	
1627–8	£65	7s	7d	£625 14s	4d	
1628–9	£10	12s	3d	£495 3s	8d	
1629–30	£72	5s	2d	£1,247 14s	9½d	
1630–31	£86	15s	3½d	£1,084 13s	5¼d	
1631–32	£116	5s	10d	£658 19s	10d	
1632–33	£123	16s	4d	£1,376 11s	7d	
1641	£144	6s	5d	£636 14s	7d	

Given that the customs paid for goods on any one ship could vary between £1 to £12, it is possible that in most years fewer than a dozen ships came to Sligo to trade.

The surviving English port books indicate only a small amount of direct trading from English ports to Sligo. Early in 1615, for example, Robert Crean is recorded as bringing 150 barrels of beef and pork, eight barrels and one hogshead of tallow, 120 cowhides and one barrel of beef to Dartmouth. He returned to Sligo with ten tons of bay salt and five bags of hops. Crean obviously made use of the salt, because several months later he sent back to Dartmouth 290 salted and dry Irish hides. An English merchant brought from Sligo on the same ship two barrels of tallow and 300 untanned sheepskins.[24] The small quantities of goods exported by Crean and the English merchant reflect the relative unimportance of Sligo's trade by comparison with larger ports such as Galway or Derry. Sligo, however, served a purpose in providing an outlet for local farmers to sell their produce. The most important exports from the town appear to be hides, beef and pork. Wool exports were also significant, as is testified by the granting of the staple charter to the town in 1622, as well as by references to the legal and illegal trading in it.[25]

The high court of admiralty records provide fleeting glimpses of Sligo's trade with English ports. For example, trade with London is evidenced by a case which relates the story of a London ship which came to Sligo in 1640 to collect goods from the merchants there. The ship waited for about three weeks at Sligo to be loaded with 'yarn'. The official report of the case explained that the lading took so long because the merchants could not locate sufficient 'yarn' quickly enough for the waiting ship.[26] The case did not suggest a thriving trade in the town, although the ship involved may have come regularly to Sligo, as six years later it was commissioned by parliament in England to bring guns and ammunition to Sir Charles Coote's regiment, then besieging the town.[27] The sailors aboard the ship in 1640 related that they picked up a passenger in Sligo who brought some goods to London. The passenger was probably a merchant bringing merchandise to sell in London, and this type of small individual trading was probably typical of the town's trade pattern as a whole.

The evidence of trade with Scotland confirms this pattern of individually operating merchants who were often also the masters of the ships.[28] Sligo's trade with continental port towns also continued and probably constituted the most important part of its trade. Again the high court of admiralty records provide the most illuminating, if tantalisingly brief, information. A case before the court related how John Crean, a merchant from Sligo,chartered a ship from St-Malo to bring salt, tobacco and Spanish wine to Sligo. When the ship came to Sligo, Crean laded it with tallow and hides to be delivered to his factor in St-Malo. The ship seems to have been regularly employed on the Sligo–St-Malo route, as its master claimed that he had made the journey three or four times and was planning to return to Sligo when the ship was taken by English privateers.[29] The connections with northern France are corroborated by other references in the port books. For example, a ship from Ushant near St-Malo which came to Dartmouth from Sligo in 1629 with Irish goods of beef, tallow, wool, hides, eels and salmon belonged to Roebuck Crean and Roger Jones. Some years later the same ship is recorded as sailing to Brittany, and on a return journey to Dartmouth its master, Peter Crean, brought back twenty tons of bay-salt. Some months later the same ship visited Bilbao.[30] As in medieval times, therefore, the trade of Sligo could be a triangular affair between Ireland, England, France or Spain.

There was also some indirect trading links between Sligo and Dublin. A Chester port book, for example, records that a Roebuck or Robert Crean imported various types of English cloth into Dublin port which he presumably transported by land to Sligo.[31] A chancery decree issued in the Dublin court concerned a deal between another Crean and a Dublin merchant about a consignment of timber. Such indirect trading which is rarely documented may have been quite common, not just between Dublin and Sligo but also between Galway and Sligo.[32]

It is not possible, therefore, to get much more than an impressionistic picture of the town's trade at this time. The scant evidence suggests a small import trade in agricultural produce in exchange for wine and salt.

Buildings, 1603–41

The expansion of the status and the population of the town inevitably led to the physical growth of the town as well. Apart from the older buildings in the town, such as the abbey, which still functioned as a friary and was used as a burial ground for eminent towns people, and the parish church of St John's (where Roger Jones was buried on his death in 1635), new houses were built in the seventeenth century by the new settlers. The depositions refer to fifteen houses in the town, mostly belonging to the newcomers or members of the Crean or French families, and there were undoubtedly more than this number.[33] The main residential area was along the street now called Castle Street, with the market place (now Old Market Street) of the town to the rear. A market stone known as Bishop Crean's Cross stood in the market place. The new jail house and sessions house were also in Castle Street, and there may have been an ale-house there as well. The town grew in a haphazard fashion in the vicinity of the abbey where the older medieval merchant houses had been built. Crean's castle, which probably dated to the fifteenth century, was next door to Roger Jones's 'castle', which may have been a restored or modernised tower-house. A bridge near the quays where the old castle of O'Connor Sligo had stood connected the town with its northern hinterland and the roadways running north and south through the region. Although the town had no official common land, a chancery case of the 1620s suggests that an attempt was made at that time by the provost and burghers to reserve some land for the use of the town. Lieutenant Hugh Jones, stationed in the garrison in the town, complained that he had leased Abbey Quarter from the Taaffes (who had received a grant of it with their grant of the abbey) in 1616. He had enclosed the property with hedges and ditches, but on 1 August 1628 the provost and burghers of the town had entered the premises and broken down most of his hedges and filled in his ditches.[34] This action seems to have been motivated by a desire to keep the Abbey Quarter for the use of the town. In Ulster the absence of land reserved for the use of the town corporations was a weakness in the urban growth of the plantation.[35] The provost and burghers of Sligo may have tried to ensure the prosperity of their town by reserving Abbey Quarter for corporation use.

Although we do not know how many houses were in Sligo town in 1641, the presence of about sixty British families in addition to the locally born population would indicate that it had more houses and was better populated than many of the towns in the Ulster plantation. Indeed, given that many of the settlers probably came from plantation areas, the success of Sligo may have been at the expense of the growth of town sites in the plantation, particularly in Donegal. There were connections between the Donegal plantation and some of the first burghers in Sligo. Roger Jones was given a grant of Killybegs in 1615 and was instructed to build a town there under the terms of the plantation. A controversy over the title to the land in Killybegs led Jones to abandon his grant of Killybegs some years later, and he seems to have made little impact on the urban development of the site – in strong contrast to his success in Sligo.[36] Another link between Sligo and the plantation was William Wilson, who had a grant of land in Lifford and who was also among the first burghers in Sligo town. Ultimately the development of Sligo town may have proved fatal to the success of the plantation in Donegal as more settlers moved southwards into Connacht.[37] The fact that Sligo was already established as a town with trading links and contacts on the continent and in English ports made it a more attractive prospect for development than Killybegs or Lifford, where no urban settlement had yet been developed. Sligo had a head start in its growth as the main urban centre for the north-west region.

Sligo town after 1641: population

Many of the new settlers who lived in Sligo before 1641 fled the town during that year. After the war some returned to rejoin the small number who had remained in the town during the 1640s. Their numbers were reinforced by the appearance of new British settlers, the majority of whom were of Scottish origin. According to the 1660 poll tax,there were 130 'English' in Sligo town at that time. In a rental of the town in 1682 the number of British tenants was about 106. Both figures probably underestimate the total British population of the town. The 1660 tax seems to have been selective, and the rental only refers to part of the town and to those who rented directly from the landlord: sublessees are not included. The real number of British heads of households may have been at least 200.[38]

If this figure is taken as a conservative estimate for the settler population of the 1660s and 1670s, then it amounts to a possible tripling of the pre-1641 figures. The figures are impressive, although it should be noted that a substantial number of the new settlers were soldiers serving in the fort which was built in the town in the late 1650s. A garrison was maintained in the town throughout the commonwealth and restoration periods. In 1666 it consisted of a major and sixty-six men, which accounts for almost half of the British heads of household in the town (assuming that all the soldiers had separate residences).[39] This was inevitably an usettled population. Comparison of the hearth money roll for 1662 and later rentals suggest that many had left in the intervening period. On the other hand, there is a remarkable continuity of residence between a rental of 1682 and a tripartite agreement concerning the division of the town between its three owners in 1687 which also lists the tenants in the town.[40] By the 1680s the garrison had been reduced and the population had become more stable. Many discharged soldiers obviously chose to remain living in the town. Sligo was therefore very much a garrison town in the second half of the seventeenth century, and most of its British male residents had served or were serving in the army.

Estimates of the locally born population are more difficult to calculate. All of the documentation probably seriously underestimates the number of

Irish people living in the town. A comparison of the 1660 figure and those of the 1680s suggests that there was a substantial decrease in the Irish population of the town in the 1660s and 1670s. Some decline is credible (Sligo town had throughout the eighteenth century a larger proportion of protestants than the rest of the county), but the transformation of the town into a predominantly protestant-occupied centre seems unlikely.[41] The evidence of surviving rentals of 1663, 1682 and 1687 suggests that there were just under 300 households in the town during those years. The proportion of Irish tenants to British was between 23 and 35 per cent, i.e. roughly about one-third, which would imply that there were at least 100 Irish heads of household.

The total population was probably under 2,000. It is not a large population, but it was sufficient for a reasonable sized market town, which was essentially what Sligo was in the late seventeenth century. Its population placed it in the second category of Irish towns: smaller than large and expanding urban centres such as Dublin, Derry or even Galway, but on a par with Armagh, Dundalk or Wexford.

Buildings after 1641

From the existing documents and an illustration by Thomas Phillips of 1685 it is possible to discern the growth and development of the town between the 1660s and 1680s.[42]

Sligo had been badly battered in the late 1640s, although a new fort was built on the hill to the north of the town (known as the Green or Sod Fort). The commonwealth government made a major contribution to the town's development when it authorised the building of a new stone fort on the site of the old O'Connor Sligo castle (where the town hall stands today) to the south of the residential part of the town in the late 1650s.[43]

By the time of the survey in 1663 the town was divided into three different 'quarters' (as they were called): 'the Castle Quarter, now the New Fort'; the Fort Hill quarter, where the Green Fort was; and the Abbey Quarter around the abbey. The Philips map confirms the division of the town between the abbey and the forts, with the main residential parts of the town being depicted around the new fort and the abbey. The 1663 survey listed the occupants and houses of the New Fort Quarter and the Fort Hill Quarter but not the Abbey Quarter. The survey indicates that many soldiers were living in both these quarters. Major Edgeworth, in charge of the new fort garrison, had built a new house in the New Fort Quarter and had many of his officers and men as neighbours. Most of the house occupants in both quarters were British. Out of a total of 144 houses, only about 33 were listed as occupied by Irish people.[44]

Of the 144 residences listed, 92 are described as houses and 52 as cabins. Some of the soldiers were therefore living in cabins, although the difference between a house and a cabin is not clear. Size was one distinguishing factor. The sizes of the houses as provided by the survey varied from 24 to 90 feet in length, but most were between 30 to 45 feet long and 12 to 15 feet wide. Cabins were usually between 18 and 30 feet long and 10 to 15 feet wide. The survey does not provide details about the height of the houses or cabins, but the Phillips drawing does distinguish between low cottage-type houses or cabins with thatched roofs and taller tile-roofed or slated houses. The drawing also suggests that most of the houses around the fort were small, with only a small number of large houses (possibly those of Major Edgeworth or Andrew Lynch, who is noted as having a new stone house in the area). A number of residents, according to the survey, had a house and a cabin which they may have rented out or else possibly used for other purposes such as a shop or business of some kind. Nearly all the occupants had gardens; some had yards, and a few had access to a 'park'. In the Abbey Quarter in the 1680s 'parks' were much more common – a reflection of the greater wealth of the citizens who lived there.

The rentals enable the growth of the town between 1663 and 1687 to be traced. To begin with, by the 1680s the town was divided into streets. There were eight streets listed in the rentals, as well as a number of shorter laneways. Castle Street and Radcliffe Street in the Abbey Quarter were the most fashionable parts of the town, and it was here that the merchants resided and Old English, Irish, English and Scottish families lived side by side. A High Street had also been established. Soldiers or ex-soldiers still dominated the New Fort and Fort Hill Quarters, where Holborn Street, Quay Street and Steven Street (where Edmund Steven, after whom the street had been named, still lived) had been laid out. A new custom house had been built near the new fort, and a new bridge connected the Abbey Quarter with the Fort Hill Quarter. The town also had a 'house of correction'. By 1687 there was also a new market place. The old market had been abandoned, and Old Market Street had already received its name. The new market was to the south of St John's church, alongside the newly created High Street, and a new sessions house had also been built in the same area. The town was therefore expanding southwards. Although most of the tenants listed were of British origin or descendants of older Irish merchant families, there were a small number of Irish tenants of a lower status. Small clusters of Irish tenants are listed as occupying some of the less fashionable streets such as Old Market Street, or lane ways such as Bridge Lane.

Trade after 1641

As the influence of Dublin grew, so too the potential for Sligo's growth beyond that of a market town vanished. In a survey of 1664 the volume of Sligo's export custom was ranked fifteenth out of a total of twenty-one Irish towns, its share of the custom being calculated as 1 per cent. Its import custom was ranked sixteenth and amounted to $\frac{1}{2}$ per cent of the total. The excise figures for Sligo were about the same; and four years later Sligo's rating was similar (with a possible decline in imports).[45]

There was little industry in the town apart from the tanning of hides, slaughter of cattle and sheep and salting of fish. Frieze and linen cloth were exported and may have been woven in the town, but it is more likely that it was produced in the countryside and brought to the town for sale. Sligo's main function continued to be that of a market centre where agricultural produce was sold. An account of the state of Ireland in 1673 described how the market of Sligo was 'resorted to from far and near by very many people to buy cattle and sheep and horses, being one of the famous marts for that purpose of any in that part of the kingdom'.[46] In 1689 there is an account of some protestant settlers from Tireragh bringing their meal, cattle and other commodities to Sligo market to sell.[47] The town thus provided a market outlet for the area, and the importance of the market in the economy of the town is reflected in the creation of the new market place in the restoration period. Sligo was also used as a shopping and service centre providing goods and skills not available in the countryside. The goods included the old favourites of wine and salt, but also increasingly tobacco and new manufactured goods available from trading ships. The O'Hara correspondence suggests that the family occasionally bought such goods in Sligo, although, not surprisingly, Galway and Dublin were considered more attractive shopping centres.[48] Specialised services provided in the town included that of an apothecary, tanner, butcher and smith, as well as access to the assizes and quarter sessions held in the new session house built in the 1660s or 1670s near the new market place.

The small amount of documentation available for an analysis of foreign trade corroborates the role of Sligo as a market centre and outlet for agricultural produce. The English port books reveal a small number of merchants from Sligo exporting small quantities of hides and skins (cow hides and sheep and goat skins), Irish yarn and wool, tallow, butter and oatmeal, as well as some timber.[49] A survey of imports and exports in the early 1680s confirms that Sligo's exports to England consisted mainly of hides and wool, with smaller quantities of timber, tallow, skins, fish, corn, butter, frieze and linen and occasional consignments of beef and mutton and other by-products from stock-raising such as ox-horns and hair of cows and horses. Exports to the continent, in particular to France and Flanders, were similar but less diverse and tended to be in larger quantities. Hides, butter, tallow and corn were the main products exported in the early 1680s, with smaller amounts of frieze, beef and herring. Beef was also sent to the plantations in North America and the West Indies. Imports from England and the continent were dominated by the most important products cultivated in the overseas plantations: tobacco and sugar. Both products reflect the new tastes of society, as do some of the other imports from the continent. Wine (and brandy) and salt continued to be the main imports, but other goods included different types of cloth and manufactured articles such as hats, iron pots, paper and playing-cards. Helling stones (roof tiles) and earthen-ware were also imported into Sligo in the 1670s and 1680s.[50]

Details concerning the business activities of individual Sligo merchants are difficult to locate, but the English port books reveal the operations of a number of merchants trading in or with Sligo. Thomas Powell, who had a house in St John's Lane, traded in tobacco which he brought on English ships from Virginia to Plymouth and then re-exported to Sligo and possibly also to Galway.[51] Another merchant who continued the more traditional trade between Sligo, England (in this case Bristol) and the continent was William Davis, who in 1671 brought three separate cargoes of agricultural produce from Sligo in the *Unity* of Bristol. In between the journeys to Sligo the same ship went to St Martins and brought back wine and salt for Davis. Davis also traded with Greenock in Scotland and may have sent ships to travel along the coast, loading and unloading goods in different ports.[52] Merchants trading in small quantities from Scotland also continued to operate. In 1660, for example, Captain Charles Gore reported some small barques which came to Sligo to buy corn, and Charles O'Hara refers to Scottish pedlars trading in the county.[53] Increasingly, however, overland trade with Sligo must have become more common than trade by sea. O'Hara refers to a Leinster grazier coming to Sligo looking for cattle, and the cattle market in the town must have attracted buyers from other parts of Ireland.[54]

In summary, Sligo's trade was small but typical of the general pattern of Irish trade. Agricultural produce, particularly hides, beef, tallow and butter, dominated its exports, while tobacco, wine and brandy and small amounts of manufactured goods were the most important imports.

The merchant community after 1641

One of the most remarkable aspects of the merchant community in Sligo in the commonwealth and restoration period is its similarities with the pre-1641 community. The Creans, despite the involvement of some members of the family in the wars of the 1640s, continued to live and trade in the town. John Crean occupied the old family tower-house or 'castle' in Castle Street in the 1680s, where he also had a tanyard and obviously still continued to trade in hides. There were also other Creans living in the town at the same time.[55]

Before 1641 Galway merchants had invested large amounts of money in land in County Sligo. They lost most of these landed possessions during the 1650s, but the connection between Galway and Sligo continued. In the restoration period a number of men from Galway merchant families resided and no doubt traded in Sligo town. Prominent among them were members of the French family. Andrew French was noted as having a new house with stone walls in Sligo in 1663; and in the 1682 rental he not only had a house in Radcliffe Street, but also rented property in the hinterland of the town and elsewhere and had a share in the fishery of the town. Another prominent Galway man residing in Sligo was Andrew Lynch, described as an apothecary and merchant in the 1680s. Lynch had several houses in the town and also rented land in hinterland. Other Galway men in Sligo in the 1680s included Peter Darcy, who lived in Castle Street in a rented 'dwelling house' and also held a lease of a 'castle' on the same street (probably the house built or restored by Roger Jones); Walter Lynch, who had a house in Old Market Street and issued tokens inscribed with his name in 1666; and James Darcy, who lived in High Street, as well as members of the Martin and Bodkin families.[56] The presence of these men from old Galway merchant families in Sligo no doubt helped to strengthen the links between the commercial life of the two towns. The 'tribes' families were still trading in Galway in the later seventeenth century and were in the process of expanding and exploiting new outlets for their commercial enterprises. The inclusion of Sligo as a satellite of Galway can be seen as part of this expansion.[57]

Another element of continuity with the pre-1641 urban community was the presence of the Gambles and Braxtons in the rentals of the 1680s. John Gamble was a neighbour of John Crean's and Peter Darcy's in Castle Street, while the widow Gamble lived in Steven Street, and Edward Braxton had a garden in Abbey Quarter near the abbey.[58] The Braxtons and Gambles were prominent in the corporation of the town before 1641, and although they were not so prominent after 1641, they did represent a link and continuity with the remnant of the older settler community.

The new element among the Sligo merchant community was provided by the arrival of new residents in the post-1641 period. The documentation does not permit an analysis of the newcomers in terms of commercial wealth or importance, but nearly all had Scottish surnames and some were undoubtedly substantial merchants, exporting and importing goods and issuing trade tokens. For example, Walter Crawford and John Smith, who lived in Castle Street alongside the Creans, Darcys and Gambles, issued copper trading tokens and were clearly of some importance in the commercial life of the town, as was Philip Cox, who lived in Bridge Street, where he had a slaughterhouse. Cox was included among the burghers approved by James II for the town in 1687. Humphrey Booth was another important official in the town. He was controller of the customs, but also rented land near the town and held leases of several houses in the town.[59] By the 1680s the Scottish community in the town included members of the Delap and Johnston families, who, as L. M. Cullen has noted, had begun to dominate the Dublin wine trade by the beginning of the eighteenth century. There were strong links between the Dublin Scottish families and the north of Ireland and, no doubt, also with Sligo.[60]

Although many of the residents in the town rented lands in the hinterland or elsewhere in the county, few of the landowners in the county had residences in the town. Sligo was not large enough as an urban centre to warrant the building of town houses by the local landlords. There were, however, close family connections and frequent inter-marriages between merchant and landlord families. The marriage alliance of the Gores with the Booths is the best known example of this phenomenon.

Marriage alliances brought protestant merchants and landlords together and militated against a united catholic and protestant merchant community emerging in the town in the 1680s. Irish catholic and British protestant merchants may have lived as neighbours in Sligo town, but their relationship with one another was an uneasy one. As in the countryside, the wars and confiscations of the 1640s and 1650s had left a legacy of bitterness and mistrust. The large number of soldiers who settled in Sligo, combined with the continued presence in the town of catholic merchants whose families had lost a great deal in the 1650s, cannot have contributed to an atmosphere of trust and reconciliation. The catholic presence in the town was strong. The Dominican friars continued to occupy the abbey throughout the seventeenth century. The potential for sectarian conflict emerged in 1688 when the Sligo Association was formed by the protestants of the town and county. It was the only association of its kind outside Ulster. The actions of the catholic merchants Andrew and James French in using 'their endeavours to have some [catholic] companies sent to defend' Sligo was offered as one of the main reasons for the formation of the association.[61]

ABBREVIATIONS

A.F.M.	*Annála ríoghachta Éireann: Annals of the kingdom of Ireland by the Four Masters from the earliest period to the year 1616*, ed. and trans. John O'Donovan (7 vols, Dublin, 1851)
A.L.C.	*The Annals of Loch Cé: a chronicle of Irish affairs, 1014-1590*, ed. W. M. Hennessy (2 vols, London, 1871)
Anal. Hib.	*Analecta Hibernica*
Ann. Conn.	*Annála Connacht: the Annals of Connacht (A.D. 1224–1544)*, ed. A.M. Freeman (Dublin, 1944)
A.U.	*Annála Uladh, Annals of Ulster . . . a chronicle of Irish affairs, 431–1131, 1155–1541*, ed. W. M. Hennessy and Bartholomew MacCarthy (4 vols, Dublin, 1887–1901)
B.L., Add. MSS	British Library, Additional MSS
B.L., Cott. MSS	British Library, Cottonian MSS
B.L., Eg. MSS	British Library, Egerton MSS
B.L., Harl. MSS	British Library, Harleian MSS
Bodl.	Bodleian Library, Oxford
Cal. Carew MSS	*Calendar of the Carew manuscripts preserved in the archiepiscopal library at Lambeth* (6 vols, London, 1867–73)
Cal. pat. rolls Ire., Eliz.	*Calendar of patent and close rolls of chancery in Ireland, Elizabeth, 19 year to end of reign*, ed. James Morrin (Dublin, 1862)
Cal. pat. rolls Ire., Jas I	*Irish patent rolls of James I: facsimile of the Irish record commissioners' calendar prepared prior to 1830*, with foreword by M. C. Griffith (Irish Manuscripts Commission, Dublin, 1966)
Cal. pat. rolls Ire., Chas I	*Calendar of patent and close rolls of chancery in Ireland, Charles I, years 1 to 8*, ed. James Morrin (Dublin, 1864)
Cal. S.P. Ire.	*Calendar of the state papers relating to Ireland* (24 vols, London, 1860–1911)
D.N.B.	*Dictionary of National Biography*

Galway Arch. Soc. Jn.	*Journal of the Galway Archaeological and Historical Society*
Gilbert, *Contemp. hist., 1641–52*	J. T. Gilbert (ed.), *A contemporary history of affairs in Ireland, from A.D. 1641 to 1652* . . . (3 vols, Irish Archaeological Society, Dublin, 1879)
Gilbert, *Ir. confed.*	J. T. Gilbert (ed.), *History of the Irish confederation and the war in Ireland, 1641–9*... (7 vols, Dublin, 1882–91)
I.H.S.	*Irish Historical Studies*
Ir. Econ. & Soc. Hist.	*Irish Economic and Social History: the Journal of the Economic and Social History Society of Ireland*
N.H.I., ii	*A New History of Ireland*, vol. ii: *Medieval Ireland, 1169–1534*, ed. Art Cosgrove (Oxford, 1987)
N.H.I., iii	*A New History of Ireland*, vol. iii: *Early modern Ireland, 1534–1691*, ed. T. W. Moody, F. X. Martin and F. J. Byrne (Oxford, 1976)
N.L.I.	National Library of Ireland
O'Dowd, 'Landownership in the Sligo area'	Mary O'Dowd, 'Landownership in the Sligo area, 1585–1641' (unpublished Ph.D. thesis, University College, Dublin, 1979)
Ormonde MSS, o.s.	*Calendar of the manuscripts of the marquess of Ormonde, preserved at Kilkenny Castle* [original series] (11 vols, Historical Manuscripts Commission, London, 1895–1920)
O'Rorke, *Sligo*	Terence O'Rorke, *The history of Sligo: town and county* (2 vols, Dublin, 1889)
P.R.O.	Public Record Office of England
P.R.O.I.	Public Record Office of Ireland
P.R.O.N.I.	Public Record Office of Northern Ireland
R.I.A.	Royal Irish Academy
R.I.A. Proc.	*Proceedings of the Royal Irish Academy*
R.S.A.I.Jn.	*Journal of the Royal Society of Antiquaries of Ireland*
S.P. Hen. VIII	*State papers, Henry VIII* (11 vols, London, 1830–52)
Stat. Soc. Ire. Jn.	*Journal of the Statistical and Social Inquiry Society of Ireland*
Studia Hib.	*Studia Hibernica*
T.C.D.	Trinity College, Dublin
U.C.D.	University College, Dublin
Wood-Martin, *Sligo*	W.G. Wood-Martin, *History of Sligo, county and town* (3 vols, Dublin, 1882–92)

REFERENCES

Chapter 1: The Sligo area: an introduction (pp 1–11)

1. Capt. C. Plessington to Sir R. Cecil, 17 July 1601 (P.R.O., S.P.63/208, pt iii/81).
2. R. A. S. Macalister (ed.), *Lebor Gabála Érenn* (5 vols, Irish Texts Society, Dublin, 1938–56), iv, 21–3, 80–1, 141–3; Wood-Martin, *Sligo*, i, 12; O'Rorke, *Sligo*, ii, 265n; David Moore (ed.), *The Irish sea province in archaeology and history* (Cambridge Archaeological Association, Cardiff, 1970); Donncha Ó Corráin, *Ireland before the Normans* (Dublin and London, 1972), p. 81; *Leabhar Chlainne Suibhne. An account of the MacSweeney families in Ireland, with pedigrees*, ed. and trans. Paul Walsh (Dublin, 1920), pp 4–7.
3. T. J. Westropp, 'Early Italian maps of Ireland from 1300 to 1600, with notes on foreign settlers and trade' in *R.I.A.Proc.*, xxx, sect. C (1913), p. 366.
4. W. B. Yeats, *Autobiographies* (London, 1966), p. 52.
5. Henry Morris, *Saint Patrick in County Sligo* (Sligo, 1930), pp 23–4. See also p. 41 below.
6. Colm Ó Lochlainn, 'Roadways in ancient Ireland' in *Féil sgríbhinn Eóin Mhic Néill: essays and studies presented to Professor Eóin MacNeill on the occasion of his seventieth birthday*, ed. John Ryan (Dublin, 1940), p. 466.
7. G. A. Hayes-McCoy, 'Ballyshannon: its strategic importance in the wars in Connacht, 1550–1602' in *Galway Arch. Soc. Jnl.*, xv (1933), pp 141–59; G. A. Hayes-McCoy, 'Strategy and tactics in Irish warfare, 1593–1601' in *I.H.S.*, ii (Mar. 1941), p. 265. See also map in *N.H.I.*, iii, 120.
8. I am grateful to Nollaig Ó Muraíle of the Ordnance Survey Office, Dublin, for assistance in the translation of these placenames. For a description, see also O'Rorke, *Sligo*, i, 44–8; ii, 552–4. The roads were first mapped in crude form in 1586 (P.R.O., M.P.F. 71). A more detailed map of the Sligo routes appeared *c.* 1599–1602 (National Maritime Museum, Greenwich, Dartmouth Collection of Irish maps, no. 7).
9. D. Ó Corráin, *Ireland before the Normans*, p. 67.
10. *The Civil Survey, A.D. 1654–56*, ed. R. C. Simington (10 vols, Irish Manuscripts Commission, Dublin, 1931–61), x, 93. The bridges are marked in the maps cited in note 8. See also *Annála Connacht: the Annals of Connacht (A.D. 1224–1544)*, ed., A. M. Freeman (Dublin, 1944), 1533, 5 (hereafter cited as *Ann. Conn.*); *The Annals of Loch Ce: a chronicle of Irish affairs, 1014–1590*, ed. W. M. Hennessy (2 vols, London, 1871), 1586 (hereafter cited as *A.L.C.*); *The life of Aodh Ruadh Ó Domhnaill transcribed from the Book of Lughaidh Ó Cléirigh*, ed. Paul Walsh (2 vols, Irish Texts Society, Dublin, 1948–57).
11. J. H. Andrews, 'Road planning in Ireland before the railway age' in *Irish Geography*, v (1964–8), p. 17.
12. Morris, *Saint Patrick in County Sligo*.

13. Ó Lochlainn, 'Roadways in ancient Ireland'.
14. The most detailed description occurs in 1536 (*Annals of Connacht*). See also ibid, 1476, 11; 1512, 6; *Annála ríoghachta Éireann: Annals of the kingdom of Ireland by the Four Masters from the earliest period to the year 1616*, ed. and trans. John O'Donovan (7 vols, Dublin, 1851), 1595 (hereafter cited as *A.F.M.*), and the numerous references to O'Donnell's journies through Sligo in Ó Cléirigh, *Aodh Ruadh Ó Domhnaill*.
15. See chapter 3 and p. 103 below.
16. See p. 36 below.
17. See Chapter 7.
18. See, e.g., Sir R. Bingham to Lord Deputy Fitzwilliam, 30 Sept. 1593 (P.R.O., S.P. 63/172/2xiii), and chapter 3 below.
19. Sir G. Fenton to Lord Burghley, 28 Oct. 1588 (ibid., S.P. 63/137/49).
20. Bingham to Burghley, 13 Feb. 1588 (ibid., S.P. 63/133/45); see also p. 129 below.
21. R. L. Praeger, *The way that I went* (3rd ed., Dublin, 1947), p. 150.
22. John Colgan's life of St Farannan, cited in Terence O'Rorke, *History, antiquities and present state of the parishes of Ballysadare and Kilvarnet in the county of Sligo* (Dublin, 1878), pp 2–3.
23. *Lr Gabála*, iv, 20–1; O'Rorke, *Sligo*, ii, 260–70; *Ann. Conn.*, 1239, 6; 1261, 8; 1282, 3; 1291, 6; 1308, 4; 1367, 7; 1388, 2; 1495, 3; *A.F.M.*, 1595; Sir R. Bingham to Burghley, 6 Sept. 1595 (P.R.O., S.P. 63/183/5iii); same to same, 25 Dec. 1595 (ibid., S.P. 63/186/4ii); Capt. J. Bingham to Sir R. Bingham, 21 Aug. 1596 (ibid., S.P. 63/192/29ii).
24. See chapter 3 below.
25. See chapter 7 below.
26. J. G. Simms, *War and politics in Ireland, 1649–1730* (London, 1986), pp 168–79.
27. T. W. Freeman, 'Population distribution in County Sligo' in *Stat. Soc. Ire. Jn.*, xvii (1943–44), p. 267.
28. T. W. Freeman, *Ireland a general and regional geography* (2nd ed., London, 1960), pp 423–31; R. L. Praeger, *The way that I went*, pp 141–56; J. B. Whittow, *Geology and scenery in Ireland* (Penguin, 1974), pp 55, 118, 141, 143–6; F. H. A. Aalen, *Man and the landscape in Ireland* (London, 1978).
29. Wood-Martin, *Sligo*, i, 65.
30. Praeger, *The way that I went*, p. 149.
31. See p. 36 below. See also Wood-Martin, *Sligo*, i, 78.
32. Katharine Simms, 'Warfare in the medieval Gaelic lordships' in *Irish Sword*, xii (winter, 1975), pp 98–108.
33. Hugh Allingham (ed.), *Captain Cuellar's adventures in Connacht and Ulster, A.D. 1588* (London, 1897; repr. in *Spanish Armada* (Sligo School of Landscaping Painting, n.d.)), pp 64–6.
34. Ibid., p. 65.
35. Sir R. Bingham to Lord Burghley, 4 Dec. 1588 (P.R.O., S.P. 63/139/3).
36. W. B. Yeats, *Collected works* (8 vols, Stratford on Avon, 1908), v, 39–47; *The bardic poems of Tadhg Dall Ó Huiginn*, ed. E. Knott (2 vols, London, 1922–6), ii, 185–6.
37. John Cowell, *Sligo, land of Yeats' desire* (Dublin, 1989), p. 23. See also W. B. Yeats (ed.), *Fairy and folk tales of Ireland* (Gerrards Cross, Buckinghamshire, 1973); Máire MacNeill, *The festival of Lughnasa* (Oxford, 1962), pp 112–17, 185–88.
38. Morris, *Saint Patrick in County Sligo*, p. 8; Sir H. Sidney to privy council, 27 Jan. 1577 (P.R.O., S.P. 63/57/5); Sir O. Lambert to Sir G. Carey, 18 June 1602 (ibid., S.P. 63/211/61c).
39. Ibid.; *Cal. pat. rolls Ire., Jas I*, p. 391. See also pp 155–6 below.

40. Sir John Fleming to Kean O'Hara, 10 Mar. 1689 (P.R.O.N.I., O'Hara MSS, T.2812/3/15).
41. *Farm and food research*, vii, no. 6 (Nov.–Dec. 1976), pp 128–31.
42. B.L., Harl. MS 2048. (The survey was compiled between 1633 and 1635, but for convenience it is hereafter referred to as the '1635 survey'.) See also chapters 5 and 6 below.
43. *Civil Survey*, x, 93.
44. Eileen McCracken, *The Irish woods since Tudor times* (Plymouth, 1971), pp 37, 42. See also B.L., Harl. MS 2048.
45. McCracken, *Ir. woods*, p. 57.
46. B.L., Harl. MS 2048, ff 197f; see also ff 191d, 196f, 197d.
47. McCracken, *Ir. woods*, pp 92–3, 168; George O'Brien, *Economic history of Ireland in the seventeenth century* (Dublin, 1919), pp 51, 53–4.
48. A. E. J. Went, 'Historical notes on the fisheries of the two County Sligo rivers' in *R.S.A.I. Jn.*, xcix (1969), pp 55–61; John O'Donovan (ed.), *The genealogies, tribes and customs of Hy Fiachrach, commonly called O'Dowda's country* (Irish Archaeological Society, Dublin, 1844), pp 274–5; *Civil Survey*, x, 94; B.L., Harl. MS 2048, ff 176d, 181f.
49. Freeman, 'Population distribution in County Sligo', p. 267.

Chapter 2: The medieval lordships of Lower Connacht (pp 13–23)

1. This account of the Norman settlement of Sligo is based on G. H. Orpen, *Ireland under the Normans, 1169–1333* (4 vols, Oxford, 1911–20), iii, pp 190–224; J. A. Otway-Ruthven, *A history of medieval Ireland* (London, 1968), pp 192–227; H. T. Knox, 'The occupation of Connacht by the Anglo-Normans after 1237', pts iii–v, in *R.S.A.I. Jn.*, xxxiii (1903), pp 58–74, 179–89, 284–94. See also Brendan Ó Bric, 'Galway townsmen as the owners of land in Connacht, 1585–1641' (unpublished M.A. thesis, University College, Galway, 1974), pp 26–35.
2. For O'Donnell involvement in Sligo see Katharine Simms, 'Gaelic lordships in Ulster in the later middle ages' (unpublished Ph.D. thesis, Trinity College, Dublin, 1976).
3. Otway-Ruthven, *Med. Ire.*, p. 255; *Ann. Conn.*, 1338,
4. For a general account of developments in Connacht at this time see Kenneth Nicholls, *Gaelic and gaelicised Ireland in the middle ages* (Dublin, 1972), pp 141–53. See also Knox, 'Occupation of Connacht', and Otway-Ruthven, *Med. Ire.*
5. The history of the O'Connor family can be traced in *Ann. Conn.* See also Mary O'Dowd, 'Landownership in the Sligo area, 1585–1641' (unpublished Ph.D. thesis, University College, Dublin, 1979), pp 38–42.
6. *Ann. Conn.*, 1307, 10; 1362, 9; *Annála Uladh, Annals of Ulster . . . a chronicle of Irish affairs, 431–1131, 1155–1541*, ed. W. M. Hennessy and Bartholomew MacCarthy (4 vols, Dublin, 1887–1901), 1395 (hereafter cited as *A.U.*).
7. O'Dowd, 'Landownership in the Sligo area', pp 42–3.
8. *A.F.M.*, 1386.
9. The position of the O'Garas is uncertain: they appear at this time to be controlled by the Norman family of Costello who took control of Sliabh Lugha, the former territory of the O'Garas (see *Ann. Conn.*, 1330, 3; 1366, 6).
10. O'Dowd, 'Landownership in the Sligo area', pp 44–7.
11. *Ann. Conn.*, 1419, 3; 1420, 4, 6–10; 1416, 10. For marriage alliances see ibid, 1404, 29; 1413, 17; 1436, 7; 'The annals of Ireland from the year 1443–1468 translated by Duald MacFirbis for Sir James Ware, 1666' in *Irish Archaeological Society Miscellany* (Dublin, 1846), i, 238.

12. *A.F.M.*, 1408, 1422; Mac Firbisigh Book of Genealogies (U.C.D.), f. 316. See also H. G. Leask, *Irish castles and castellated houses* (2nd ed., 1941; repr. Dundalk, 1973), p. 75.
13. *Ann. Conn.*, 1420, 3; *A.L.C.*, 1423.
14. *Leabhar Chlainne Suibhne*, pp xxxvii–xxxviii, xl–xli; O'Dowd, 'Landownership in the Sligo area', pp 437–9.
15. O'Dowd, 'Landownership in the Sligo area', pp 229–30.
16. See pp 149–51 below.
17. *Ann. Conn.*, 1464, 20; Chancery pleading, n.d. (P.R.O.I., C.P., x, no. 21).
18. B.L., Harl. MS 2048.
19. See genealogies in O'Dowd, 'Landownership in the Sligo area'.
20. Ruth Dudley-Edwards, 'A study of ecclesiastical appointments in the province of Tuam, 1399–1477' (unpublished M.A. thesis, University College, Dublin, 1968).
21. *Book of Ballymote*, ed. Robert Atkinson (facsimile, R.I.A., Dublin, 1887); *Book of Lecan*, with foreward by Eoin MacNeill (facsimile, Irish Manuscripts Commission, Dublin, 1937).
22. M. J. Blake, *Blake family records, 1300–1600* (London, 1902), pp 12, 17, 18, 33.
23. Simms, 'Gaelic lordships in Ulster in the later middle ages'. For the conflict in Connacht see Nicholls, *Gaelic and gaelicised Ireland*, pp 141–53.
24. O'Dowd, 'Landownership in the Sligo area', pp 53–7; *Ann. Conn.*, 1476, 11.
25. *c.* Aug. 1568 (Bodl., Carte MS 131/76).
26. *Ann. Conn.*, 1512, 66; 1516, 5, 6. See also O'Dowd, 'Landownership in the Sligo area', pp 53–7.
27. 'Agreement between Ó Domhnaill and Tadhg Ó Conchobhair concerning Sligo castle (23 June 1539)', ed. Máire Carney in *I.H.S.*, iii (Mar. 1943), pp 282–96.
28. *Ann. Conn.*, 1526, 5; *A.U.*, 1527; *A.L.C.*, 1528; 1530.
29. *Ann. Conn.*, 1522, 1–8; 1524, 7–9.
30. Ibid., 1533, 2; 1536, 12–21, 23; *A.U.*, 1536.
31. *Ann. Conn.*, 1537, 10, 11; 1538, 5; 1539, 3.
32. *A.L.C.*, 1549, 1551, 1552.

Chapter 3: The lordship of the Tudors (pp 25–44)

1. *S.P. Hen. VIII*, iii, pt 2, pp 359–61, 371–2. 2. Ibid.
3. Richard Bagwell, *Ireland under the Tudors* (3 vols, London, 1885–90), ii, 53–110.
4. In the negotiations with O'Connor the ancestral claim of the earl of Kildare to Sligo was also discussed. See Lord Deputy Sidney, the earl of Kildare, Sir N. Bagenal and F. Agard to Queen Elizabeth, 12 Nov. 1566 (P.R.O., S.P. 63/19/43). For the agreement see Lambeth Palace, Carew MS 614, ff 155–6. It is summarised in *Cal. Carew MSS*, i, 375–6.
5. Lord Deputy Sidney et al to Queen Elizabeth, 12 Nov. 1566 (P.R.O., S.P. 63/19/43). See also Sidney to Sir F. Walsingham, 1 Mar. 1583 (Lambeth Palace, Carew MS 601, ff 89–121).
6. Sidney to Queen Elizabeth, 20 Apr. 1567 (P.R.O., S.P. 63/20/66).
7. Indenture between Queen Elizabeth and Sir Domhnall O'Connor Sligo, 20 Jan. 1568 (ibid., S.P. 63/23/12).
8. Queen Elizabeth to Lord Justices R. Weston and Sir W. Fitzwilliam, 25 Jan. 1568 (ibid., S.P. 63/23/17); minute of a letter to the queen from the lord justices, 23 Mar. 1568 (Bodl., Carte MS 58/166).
9. Hugh O'Donnell to the lord justices, 26 Mar. 1568 (Bodl., Carte MS 131/17); Sir Domhnall O'Connor Sligo to the lord justices, 31 Mar. 1568 (ibid., 58/18); Lord Justice Weston and council to O'Connor Sligo, 13 Apr. 1568 (ibid., 131/38);

Lord Justice Weston and council to O'Donnell, 14 Apr. 1568 (ibid., 131/45); same to Lord Justice Sir W. Fitzwilliam, 14 Apr. 1568 (ibid., 58/446, 213); Lord Justice Weston to Queen Elizabeth, 15 Apr. 1568 (ibid., 58/360, 175); same to same, 18 Apr. 1568 (ibid., 58/70, 39), etc. For arbitration order, 2 Sept. 1568, see ibid., 58/32. See also 'A declaration of O'Donnell's title upon the service due by O'Connor Sligo' (ibid., 131/76). I am grateful to Dr Brian Trainor for permission to use his unpublished calendar of the Carte MSS in the Public Record Office of Northern Ireland.

10. See O'Dowd, 'Landownership in the Sligo area', pp 63–4; Nicholas Canny, *The Elizabethan conquest of Ireland* (Hassocks, Sussex, 1976), pp 93–116.
11. Bagwell, *Tudors*, ii, 321–3; iii, 1–24; O'Dowd, 'Landownership in the Sligo area', pp 64–71.
12. 'A discourse of Sir N. Malby's service . . ., 8 Apr. 1580' (P.R.O., S.P. 63/72/39); Orders to be observed by Sir N. Malby, 31 Mar. 1579 (*Cal. pat., rolls Ire., Eliz.*, 18–20); draft of orders (B. L., Cott. MS Titus B xii, ff 206–14); Malby to Lord Burghley, 4 Jan. 1580 (P.R.O., S.P. 63/71/4); same to same, 8 Apr. 1580 (ibid., S.P. 63/72/38).
13. Ibid.
14. Bagwell, *Tudors*, iii, 116–37; privy council to Lord Justice Drury, 8 Apr. 1579 (*The Walsingham letter-book or register of Ireland, May 1578 to December 1579*, ed., James Hogan and N. McNeill O'Farrell (Irish Manuscripts Commission, Dublin, 1959), pp 64–5); Malby to Burghley, 11 June 1580 (P.R.O., S.P. 63/73/52); 'Calendar of the Irish council book, 1 March 1581 to 1 July 1586, made by John P. Prendergast between 1867 and 1869', ed., D. B. Quinn, in *Anal. Hib.*, xxiv (1967), p. 121; Sir G. Fenton to Burghley, 14 Sept. 1581 (P.R.O., S.P. 63/85/41); Malby and Fenton to privy council, 3 Oct. 1581 (ibid., S.P. 63/86/7).
15. Sir R. Bingham to Burghley, 7 Aug. 1584 (P.R.O., 63/111/52); same to Walsingham, 30 Aug. 1584 (ibid., S.P. 63/111/81); same to same, 21 Dec. 1584 (ibid., S.P. 63/113/31).
16. Bingham to Walsingham, 21 Dec. 1584 (ibid., S.P. 63/113/31); Sir J. Perrot to Walsingham, 11 Jan. 1585 (ibid., S.P. 63/114/19); indenture between Perrot and Sir Domhnall O'Connor Sligo, 23 Dec. 1584 (ibid., S.P. 63/113/34).
17. *The compossicion booke of Conought*, ed., A.M. Freeman (Irish Manuscripts Commission, Dublin, 1936). See also Bernadette Cunningham, 'The composition book of Connacht in the lordships of Clanricard and Thomond, 1577–1641' in *I.H.S.*, xxiv (1984), pp 1–14.
18. See pp 89–91 below.
19. Bagwell, *Tudors*, iii, 138–71. See also Ciarán Brady, 'Sixteenth-century Ulster and the failure of Tudor reform' in Ciarán Brady, Mary O'Dowd and Brian Walker (eds), *Ulster: an illustrated history* (London, 1989), pp 77–103.
20. Wood-Martin, *Sligo*, i, pp 381–3, 384–7, 393–4; Donogh O'Connor Sligo to the earl of Leicester, 17 Feb. 1588 (P.R.O., S.P. 63/133/64); Sir R. Bingham to Burghley, 13 Feb. 1588 (ibid., S.P. 63/133/45); same to same, 24 Feb. 1588 (ibid., S.P. 63/133/79); G. Bingham to acting Lord Deputy Perrot, 6 Mar. 1588 (ibid., S.P. 63/134/5); same to Lord Justice Gardiner, 7 Mar. 1588 (ibid., S.P. 63/134/9). See also B.L., Cott. MS Titus B xiii, ff 420–9.
21. O'Dowd, 'Landownership in the Sligo area', pp 87–91; Sir R. Bingham to Walsingham, 26 Aug. 1588 (*Cal. S.P. Ire. 1588–92*, pp 9–10); same to Burghley, 26 Aug. 1588 (P.R.O., S.P. 63/136/13); Lord Deputy Perrot and council to privy council, 12 Oct. 1588, and enclosures (ibid., S.P. 63/137/10i–xix).
22. 'A note of such allowances as Bingham hath . . .' (P.R.O., S.P. 63/127/77); 'Account of rents of Sligo received by Sir G. Bingham', 1588–91 (ibid., S.P. 63/

157/52); 'Account of rents received . . . in . . . Ballymote', c. May 1591 (ibid., S.P. 63/158/14).

23. Ibid.; see also chapter 6 below. For more detailed analysis see O'Dowd, 'Land-ownership in the Sligo area'.

24. See complaints of David O'Dowd and Ambrose Carew against Sir G. Bingham, *c.* June 1589 (P.R.O., S.P. 63/147/3); complaints of Rory O'Hart, Ferdoragh McEdmound McDonagh doe, etc., *c.* Oct. 1589 (ibid., S.P. 63/147/6); Bingham's answers, 2 Oct. 1589 (ibid., S.P. 63/147/2, 2i, 4, 5, 7, 8).

25. See note 22 above.

26. T. O. Ranger, 'Richard Boyle and the making of an Irish fortune, 1588–1614' in *I.H.S.*, x (1957), pp 257–97.

27. See note 24 above.

28. 'A discourse of services done by Sir R. Bingham in the county of Mayo . . .', July–Sept. 1586 (P.R.O., S.P. 63/126/53i); see also *Cal. Carew MSS*, ii, 429–34.

29. See G. Bingham's answers to O'Dowd's complaints, 2 Oct. 1589 (P.R.O., S.P. 63/147/4). See also comments of Capt. J. Merbury, 1 Aug. 1589 (ibid., S.P. 63/146/2); Sir R. Bingham to Burghley, 14 Apr. 1594 (ibid., S.P. 63/174/15); O'Dowd, 'Landownership in the Sligo area', pp 471–5.

30. Lord Deputy Perrot and council to privy council, 12 Oct. 1588 and enclosures (P.R.O., S.P. 63/137/10i–xix); 'Discourse of overthrow and shipwreck of Spaniards', *c.* Sept. 1588 (ibid., S.P. 63/136/57i, 58).

31. Ibid.; see note 24 above; commission by Sir R. Bingham to John Browne, 13 Jan. 1589 (P.R.O., S.P. 63/140/20); H. T. Knox, *The history of the county of Mayo* (Dublin, 1908), pp 220–45.

32. Commission by Sir R. Bingham to John Browne, 13 Jan. 1589 (P.R.O., S.P. 63/140/20); Knox, *Mayo*, pp 220–45; 'Discourse of overthrow and shipwreck of Spaniards', *c.* Sept. 1588 (P.R.O., S.P. 63/136/57i, 58); Lord Deputy Fitzwilliam to Burghley, 9 Apr. 1589, and enclosures (ibid., S.P. 63/143/12i–xiv).

33. Lord Deputy Fitzwilliam and council to privy council, 29 Apr. 1589 (P.R.O., S.P. 63/143/47i–iii); Lord Deputy Fitzwilliam to Burghley, 30 Apr. 1589 (ibid., S.P. 63/143/48i–vi); Sir R. Bingham to Walsingham, 23 May 1589 (ibid., S.P. 63/144/55); summary by Capt. J. Merbury of rebellion in Connacht, 1 Aug. 1589 (ibid., S.P. 63/146/2); mixed collections by Capt. J. Merbury, 27 Sept. 1589 (ibid., S.P. 63/146/57).

34. For the complaints and George Bingham's response see note 24 above. For the activities of the commissioners in Sligo see O'Dowd, 'Landownership in the Sligo area', pp 92–4.

35. Bingham to Burghley, 17 Nov. 1589 (P.R.O., S.P. 63/148/12); Queen Elizabeth to Lord Deputy Fitzwilliam, 19 Nov. 1589 (ibid., Entry Books, Ire., ff 12, 296); resolution of council of Ireland acquitting Sir R. Bingham, 4 Dec. 1589 (ibid., S.P. 63/149/10).

36. Capt. R. Fowle to Queen Elizabeth, 23 May 1592 (ibid., S.P. 63/164/40).

37. Sir R. Bingham to Burghley, 23 Apr. 1590 (ibid., S.P. 63/151/84); same to same, 26 May 1590 (S.P. 63/152/42).

38. Same to same, 13 Sept. 1590 (ibid., S.P. 63/144/24).

39. R. Lane to Burghley, 28 Sept. 1592 (ibid., S.P. 63/166/70); Lane to Burghley, 26 Dec. 1592 (ibid., S.P. 63/167/42); 'Plot for erecting certain wards in Connacht', *c.* Dec. 1592 (ibid., S.P. 63/169/17). For Lane see *D.N.B.*. See also O'Dowd, 'Landownership in the Sligo area', pp 94–6.

40. List of sheriffs and sub-sheriffs of Connacht, compiled by Sir R. Bingham in Sept. 1589 (P.R.O., S.P. 63/146/35ii); 'Account of rents of Sligo received by Sir

G. Bingham', 1588–91 (ibid., S.P. 63/157/52); 'Account of rents received . . . in . . . Ballymote', *c.* May 1591 (ibid., S.P. 63/158/14).

41. Sir R. Bingham to [Sir R. Cecil], 7 June 1595 (ibid., S.P. 63/180/16); Lord Deputy Russell and council to privy council, 27 June 1595 (ibid., S.P. 63/180/53); State of Ireland, *c.* July 1595 (ibid., S.P. 63/181/7i).
42. Bagwell, *Tudors*, iii, 196–241.
43. Ibid.
44. Bingham to [Cecil], 7 June 1595 (P.R.O., S.P. 63/180/16); *A.F.M.*, 1595; Bingham to Lord Deputy Russell, 15 July 1595 (P.R.O., S.P. 63/181/48i); same to Burghley, 30 Sept. 1595 (P.R.O., S.P. 63/183/65).
45. Entry for 23 Oct. 1594 in journal of Lord Deputy Russell (Lambeth Palace, Carew MS 612, f. 8a).
46. Summary of state of Ireland, *c.* Apr. 1597 (Lambeth Palace, Carew MS 632, ff 158–62).
47. Bingham to Lord Deputy Russell, 6 Sept. 1595 (P.R.O., S.P. 63/183/5iii); same to Burghley, 10 Oct. 1595 (ibid., S.P. 63/183/82); Capt. J. Price to same, 20 Oct. 1595 (ibid., S.P. 63/183/97); Sir G. Fenton to same, 9 Jan. 1596 (ibid., S.P. 63/186/10); Bingham to same, 22 Apr. 1596 (ibid., S.P. 63/188/50); *A.F.M.*, 1595.
48. Articles propounded by the commissioners to Hugh O'Donnell and answers of O'Donnell, 28–30 Jan. 1596 (*Cal. Carew MSS*, iv, 153–4, 161–2). See also B.L., Add. MS 37536, ff 48–53.
49. O'Dowd, 'Landownership in the Sligo area', pp 110–2; Sir F. Shane to Sir R. Cecil, 8 April 1600 (P.R.O., S.P. 63/207, pt ii/96); instructions for Mountjoy [Jan. 1600] (*Cal.S.P.Ire., 1599–1600*, pp 445–6).
50. O'Dowd, 'Landownership in the Sligo area', pp 112–3; Sir O. Lambert to Mountjoy, 26 June 1602 (ibid., S.P. 62/211/61c).
51. C.F. Brady, 'The O'Reillys of East Breifne and the problem of surrender and regrant' in *Breifne*, vi (1985), pp 233–62.

Chapter 4: The county of Sligo (pp 45–62)

1. See p. 39 above.
2. See pp 54–56 below.
3. For an analysis of the establishment of the assizes and a list of the judges see John McCavitt, 'The lord deputyship of Sir Arthur Chichester in Ireland, 1605–16' (unpublished Ph.D. thesis, Queen's University, Belfast, 1988), pp 146–214.
4. Observations made by Sir John Davies [4 May 1606] (*Cal. S.P. Ire., 1603–6*, pp 463–77). See also Sir A. Chichester and council to privy council, 7 Mar. 1606 (P.R.O., S.P. 63/218/23); Sir R. Jacob to Salisbury, 18 Oct. 1609 (ibid., S.P. 63/227/141).
5. See proclamation of general pardon, 11 Mar. 1604 (P.R.O.I., R.C., 2/2, ff 93–7); Sir A. Chichester to Sir John Davies, 3 May 1611 (Bodl., Carte MS 62, ff 95–6); same to same, 15 Feb. 1612 (ibid., ff 57–8).
6. T. G. Barnes (ed.), *Introduction to Somerset assize orders, 1629–1640* (Somerset Record Society, vol. lxv, Frome, 1959), p. xx.
7. Chancery pleadings (P.R.O.I., C.P., A–Z, AA–BB); chancery decrees (ibid., R.C. 6/1, 2); exchequer records transcribed by James Ferguson (ibid., Ferguson MSS).
8. The Taaffe and other legal disputes concerning Sligo land are documented in O'Dowd, 'Landownership in the Sligo area'.
9. For the Sligo inquisitions see Wood-Martin, *Sligo*, i, 194–209; P.R.O.I., R.C. 9/15; N.L.I., MS 2163.

10. Ibid. See, e.g., Co. Sligo exchequer inquisitions, James I, no. 28, 6 June 1610 (P.R.O.I., R.C. 9/15); Co. Sligo chancery inquisitions, James I, nos 5–8, 5–9 June 1610 (N.L.I., MS 2163). See also O'Dowd, 'Landownership in the Sligo area', pp 125–7.

11. *Report on the manuscripts of the earl of Egmont* (2 vols, Historical Manuscripts Commission, London, 1905–9), i, pt i, pp 50–1.

12. T.C.D., MS 643, ff 31, 59d, 84f, 122d–123d, 173d; MS 644, ff 192–4; MS 645, ff 94d, 103f–104d, 137f–139f, 202d, 241f–243f; P.R.O.I., R.C. 9/15; H. F. Kearney, 'The court of wards and liveries in Ireland 1622–41' in *R.I.A. Proc.*, lvii, sect. C (1955), pp 39–40.

13. See Mary O'Dowd, ' "Irish concealed lands papers" in the Hastings Manuscripts in the Huntington Library' in *Anal. Hib.*, xxi (1984), pp 71–80.

14. Information concerning surrenders in Connacht [Sept. 1607] (P.R.O., S.P. 63/222/145A); Co. Sligo chancery inquisitions, James I, no. 4, 26 Apr. 1609 (N.L.I., MS 2163).

15. Sir A. Chichester and council to privy council, 22 May 1605 (P.R.O., S.P. 63/217/32); same to Salisbury, 29 Sept. 1607 (ibid., S.P. 63/222/146); undated note on the composition (ibid., S.P. 63/222/135a); grant to Tadhg O'Hara, 28 Oct. 1613 (*Cal. pat. rolls Ire., Jas I,* pp 258–9).

16. Sir G. Carew to Salisbury, 28 July 1611 (Hatfield House, Salisbury MS 196/45); Sir O. St John to same, 6 Oct. 1611 (Lambeth Palace, Carew MS 629/154); questions and instructions concerning the composition book of Connacht (Lambeth Palace, Carew MS 629/158–64); Sir A. Chichester to Sir J. Davies, 4 Oct. 1611 (Bodl., Carte MS 62/3).

17. Based on P.R.O., S.P. 63/226/262A; S.P. 63/230; N.L.I., MS 8013(2).

18. *The earl of Strafforde's letters and despatches,* ed. William Knowler (2 vols, London, 1739), i, 454–8; Sheffield Central Library, Wentworth-Woodhouse MS 24–25; *The compossicion booke of Conought,* ed., A.M. Freeman (Irish Manuscripts Commission, Dublin, 1936), pp 120–39.

19. See J. McCavitt, 'The lord deputyship of Sir Arthur Chichester', p. 50; *Cal. S.P. Ire., 1615–25,* pp 85–6. For reference to horses, mares and garrons being seized by the Co. Sligo collector of the subsidy see P.R.O.I., Ferguson MS xi, p. 217.

20. Aidan Clarke, *The Old English in Ireland, 1625–42* (Worcester and London, 1966), pp 28–89; *Cal. S.P. Ire., 1625–32,* p. 462; list of commissioners to the counties of Ireland (P.R.O., S.P. 63/245/729); Lord Deputy Wentworth to Sir Edward Coke, 7 Apr. 1635 (Sheffield Central Library, Wentworth-Woodhouse MS 9, ff 1–17).

21. *Cal. pat. rolls Ire., Jas I,* pp 222, 258–60, 266, 294.

22. Philadelphia papers (P.R.O., S.P. 31/2/334); Acta Regia (P.R.O.I., R.C. 2/5, f. 177). See also Lambeth Palace, Carew MS 613/75–6; B.L., Add., MS 36775, f. 181.

23. Bernadette Cunningham, 'The composition book of Connacht in the lordships of Clanricard and Thomond, 1577–1641' in *I.H.S.*, xxiv (1984), pp 1–14.

24. Acta Regia (P.R.O.I., R.C. 2/5, ff 177–84). T.C.D., MS 570 contains seventeenth-century transcripts of all the inquisitions held by the commissioners with the exception of Co. Leitrim. See also N.L.I., MS 2163 for Sligo inquisitions. Grants were enrolled 20 Mar. 1617, 2 July 1617 (*Cal. pat. rolls Ire., Jas I,* pp 321–2, 331–2).

25. *N.H.I.*, iii, 222; Clarke, *Old English,* pp 64–5. See also B.L., Add., MS 3827, f. 45; Add. MS 11,033, ff 45–7; *Cal. S.P. Ire., 1625–32,* pp 639–40, 665–6; *Strafforde's letters,* i, 401–2.

26. *Strafforde's letters,* i, 457.

27. H. F. Kearney, *Strafford in Ireland, 1633–41: a study in absolutism* (Manchester, 1959), pp 85–103. See also Sheffield Central Library, Wentworth-Woodhouse MS 8, f.

269; MS 9, ff 52–59, 66–77, 79–86, 121–8, 251–7, 305; MS 15, ff 227, 236; MS 21, f. 138; MS 24–5, ff 280, 297, 314.

28. De Freyne papers (N.L.I.,unsorted).
29. See *Cal. S.P. Ire., 1633–47*, p. 236; Sheffield Central Library, Wentworth-Woodhouse MS 9, ff 91–7; MS 10, ff 6a, 182a; MS 15, ff. 94b; MS 17, ff 78b, 87b, 103b, 273e; MS 21, f. 190.
30. Brendan Ó Bric, 'Galway townsmen as the owners of land in Connacht, 1585–1641' (unpublished M.A. thesis, University College, Galway, 1974), chapters 3 and 4; Bernadette Cunningham, 'Political and social change in the lordships of Clanricard and Thomond, 1569–1641' (unpublished M.A. thesis, University College, Galway, 1979); O'Dowd, 'Landownership in the Sligo area', pp 117–22.
31. Privy council to Sir A. Chichester, 27 July 1609 (Philadelphia Papers, P.R.O., S.P. 31/199/196); Sir O. St John to Sir R. Winwood, 3 Mar. 1615 (P.R.O., S.P. 63/233/9).
32. *Cal. pat. rolls Ire., Chas I*, p. 70. See chancery pleadings cited in note 7 above.
33. *Patentee officers in Ireland, 1173–1876*, ed. J. L. J. Hughes (Irish Manuscripts Commission, Dublin, 1960).
34. Equity exchequer orders (P.R.O.I., Ferguson MS xi, p. 217).
35. List of sheriffs printed in Wood-Martin, *Sligo*, iii, 496–9.
36. Sir N. Malby to Walsingham, 10 Nov. 1577 (P.R.O., S.P. 63/59/43); same to same, 17 Aug. 1580 (ibid., S.P. 63/75/53); same to same, 4 Jan. 1580 (ibid., S.P. 63/71/5); same to same, 3 Dec. 1582 (ibid., S.P. 63/98/10); W. Burke to same, 7 Apr. 1583 (ibid., S.P. 63/101/17).
37. See pp 35–39 above.
38. A. Hassell-Smith, *County and court. government and politics in Norfolk, 1558–1603* (Oxford, 1974), p. 49.
39. Abstract of revenue exchequer orders, 1609–11 (P.R.O.I., Ferguson MS ix, ff 76; 1613–18 (ibid., ff 27–59); N.L.I., MS 8013 (iv).
40. Wood-Martin, *Sligo*, iii, 496–9. For landed possessions of sheriffs see O'Dowd, 'Landownership in the Sligo area', and entries in *Cal. pat. rolls Ire., Jas I* (computer index available in Queen's University, Belfast).
41. Lord Deputy Falkland to Lord Conway, 23 Aug. 1625, and enclosure (P.R.O., S.P. 63/241/111i); Ó Bric, 'Galway townsmen as the owners of land in Connacht', pp 161–3.
42. Clarke, *Old English*, pp 28–74; Wood-Martin, *Sligo*, iii, 496–9.
43. See pp 74–75, 124 below and O'Dowd, 'Landownership in the Sligo area', pp 475–7.
44. O'Dowd, 'Landownership in the Sligo area', p. 335; B. L., Harl., MS 2048, ff 178d, 179f, 185d, 193d.
45. See pp 124, 126 below.
46. T.C.D., MS 672, f. 180d.
47. See deposition of Jane Stewart, 23 Apr. 1644, printed in Wood-Martin, *Sligo*, ii, 212. See also p. 76 and chapter 7 below.
48. Abstract of equity exchequer orders (P.R.O.I., Ferguson MS xi, p. 217); abstract of equity exchequer orders (ibid., Ferguson MS xii, p. 355).
49. See p. 154 below.
50. Genealogical Office, Dublin, MS 172; Raymond Gillespie, *Colonial Ulster* (Cork, 1987), p. 145.
51. See lists in T. W. Moody, 'The Irish parliament under Elizabeth and James I' in *R.I.A. Proc.*, xlv, sect. C, (1939), pp 41–81; Clarke, *Old English*, pp 256–61; Kearney, *Strafford in Ireland*, pp 247–9.
52. See chapter 3 above.

53. *Cal. S.P. Ire., 1603–6*, pp 523–5; 'Money desired to be spent in reparation of forts ...' (P.R.O., S.P. 63/225/259A); Irish treasurer's account, Oct. 1609 – 30 Sept. 1611 (P.R.O., E351/270).
54. See J. L. J. Hughes, *Irish patentee officers*, and chapter 6 below.
55. Charles I to Lord Deputy Wentworth, 10 July 1634 (P.R.O., T/1/6535C, f. 387–8).
56. Document dated 7 May 1636 (Sheffield Central Library, Wentworth–Woodhouse MS 16 (23)).
57. *Cal. pat. rolls Ire., Jas I*, pp 99, 238; *Cal. S.P. Ire., 1615–25*, p. 343. See also note 53 above.

Chapter 5: Gaelic economy and society, *c.*1585–1641 (pp 63–87)

1. *A census of Ireland circa 1659, with supplementary material from the poll money ordinances (1660–1661)*, ed. Séamus Pender (Irish Manuscripts Commission, Dublin, 1939).
2. *Cal. pat. rolls Ire., Jas I*, pp 20–4. See also Gearóid MacNiocaill, *Irish population before Petty* (Dublin, 1981), pp 1–5.
3. *The compossicion booke of Conought*, ed. A. M. Freeman (Irish Manuscripts Commission, Dublin, 1936); N.L.I., MS 8013 (2); B. L., Harl. MS 2048.
4. B. L., Harl. MS 2048, ff 136f–d, 144f, 262d.
5. Katharine Simms, *From kings to warlords* (Woodbridge, Suffolk, 1987), p. 133.
6. See pp 140, 158–9 below.
7. T.C.D., MS 570, ff 34–70; *Cal. pat. rolls Ire Jas I*, pp 321–2, 331–2.
8. This analysis of native landholding customs in the Sligo area is based on Mary O'Dowd, 'Land inheritance in early modern County Sligo' in *Ir. Econ. & Soc. Hist.*, x (1983), pp 5–18.
9. Ibid.; O'Dowd, 'Landownership in the Sligo area', p. 406.
10. O'Dowd, 'Landownership in the Sligo area', pp 235–46. See also Brendan O Bric, 'Galway townsmen as the owners of land in Connacht, 1585–1641' (unpublished M.A. thesis, University College, Galway, 1974), pp 357–97; O'Rorke, *Sligo*, i, 135–45. For the sale to Radcliffe and Wentworth, see De Freyne papers (N.L.I., unsorted).
11. O'Dowd, 'Landownership in the Sligo area', pp 499–512; Simms, *From kings to warlords*, pp 49–59.
12. O'Dowd, 'Land inheritance in early modern County Sligo', p. 11; O'Dowd, 'Landownership in the Sligo area', pp 431, 474–6.
13. Mac Firbisigh Book of Genealogies (U.C.D.); R.I.A., MS D i 3 (539). Both genealogical lists provide the names of the males in the family in the seventeenth century. I excluded those families where only one man is listed in the genealogy, as is often the case with less important families. For more genealogical information on Sligo families see O'Dowd, 'Landownership in the Sligo area'. See also Mac Niocaill, *Irish population before Petty*, p. 9.
14. O'Dowd, 'Landownership in the Sligo area', pp 364–6, 495A–496.
15. O'Dowd, 'Land inheritance in early modern County Sligo', pp 11–15, 18; O'Dowd, 'Landownership in the Sligo area', pp 332–5, 480–1; Mary O'Dowd, 'Gaelic economy and society' in Ciarán Brady and Raymond Gillespie (eds), *Native and newcomers* (Dublin, 1986), pp 126–7.
16. O'Dowd, 'Land inheritance in early modern County Sligo', pp 12–13.
17. See, e.g., B.L., Harl. MS 2048, ff 180f–d, 191d.
18. The Lodge MSS in P.R.O.I. contain many examples of this type of transfer. See, in particular, Records of the rolls: wardships, liveries and alienations, vol. ii, pp 33–4.

19. Margaret Spufford, 'Peasant inheritance customs and land distribution in Cambridgeshire from the sixteenth to the eighteenth centuries' in Jack Goody, Joan Thirsk and E. P. Thompson (eds), *Family and inheritance* (Cambridge, 1976), p. 157.

20. R. A. Dodgshon, *Land and society in early Scotland* (Oxford, 1981), p. 114.

21. L. K. Berkner, 'Inheritance, land tenure and peasant family structure: a German regional comparison' in *Family and inheritance*, op. cit., pp 73–4.

22. See, e.g., B.L., Harl. MS 2048, ff 149f, 157f, 163d, 180f–d, 181f, 183d, 186f, 187d, 189d, 191d.

23. O'Dowd, 'Landownership in the Sligo area' p. 245; O'Rorke, *Sligo*, i, 142.

24. B.L., Harl. MS 2048, ff 178f, 194f–d, 195f.

25. Ibid., ff 143d, 181f, 194d; N.L.I., Report on private papers, no. 493 (O'Hara MSS), pp 277–9.

26. B.L., Harl. MS 2048, ff 195f, 267f.

27. O'Dowd, 'Landownership in the Sligo area', pp 480–1; see also pp 99–101 below.

28. O'Dowd, 'Landownership in the Sligo area', pp 441, 471, 477–8; P.R.O.I., Lodge MSS: Records of the rolls: wardships, liveries and alienations, vol. i, pp 11, 16, 18, 20, 21, 23, 24, 28; B.L., Harl. MS 2048, ff 154d, 158f. For a dispute over the O'Gara inheritance see Co. Sligo exchequer inquisitions, James I, nos 17 and 19, 12 Apr. 1614 and 28 Oct. 1615 (P.R.O.I., R.C. 9/15).

29. See B.L., Harl. MS 2048, ff 183f–d, 184d.

30. *Cal. pat. rolls Ire., Jas I*, p. 475; O'Dowd, 'Landownership in the Sligo area', pp 499–512.

31. O'Dowd, 'Landownership in the Sligo area', pp 321–6.

32. Ibid., pp 239–40. See pp 92–4 below.

33. O'Dowd, 'Landownership in the Sligo area', pp 253–6.

34. See, e.g., agreements in *Compossicion booke of Conought*. See also p. 51 above.

35. See also pp 80, 81–3 below.

36. De Freyne papers (N.L.I., unsorted).

37. E.g., pp 35–6, 50 above.

38. B.L., Harl. MS 2048, ff 130f, 134f, 146d, 149d, 165f, and section on Coolavin.

39. O'Hara MSS (N.L.I., unsorted).

40. Kenneth Nicholls, *Land, law and society in sixteenth-century Ireland* (Dublin, 1976).

41. Complaints of Ambrose Carew and George Bingham's answers, Sept. 1589 (P.R.O., S.P. 63/147/2i, 4).

42. B.L., Harl. MS 2048, ff 155f, 180f.

43. See pp 38–9 above, 96, 98 below,

44. For decline in woollen industry in the 1620s see Peter Bowden, 'Agriculture prices, farm profits, and rents' in Joan Thirsk (ed.), *The agrarian history of England and Wales*, vol. iv: *1500–1640* (Cambridge, 1967), pp 640–2.

45. Hugh Allingham (ed.), *Captain Cuellar's adventures in Connacht and Ulster, A.D. 1588* (London, 1897; repr. in *Spanish Armada* (Sligo School of Landscape Painting, n.d.)), pp 59–60.

46. B.L., Harl. MS 2048, ff 132d, 133f,d, 144d, 146d, 149d, 150f. On different types of mills see A. T. Lucas, 'The horizontal mill in Ireland' in *R.S.A.I.Jn.*, lxxxiii (1953), pp 1–36; W. A. McCutcheon, 'The corn mill in Ulster' in Desmond McCourt and Alan Gailey (eds), *Studies in folklife presented to Emyr Estyn Evans* (Belfast, 1970), pp 72–97; Gavin Bowie, 'Corn drying kilns, meal milling and flour in Ireland' in *Folk Life*, 17 (1979), pp 5–13. I am grateful to Dr Anne O'Dowd for these references.

47. See chapter 6. See also A. T. Lucas, 'Cloth finishing in Ireland' in *Folk Life*, 6 (1968), pp 18–67.

48. For family genealogies see O'Dowd, 'Landownership in the Sligo area'.

49. O'Rorke, *Sligo*, ii, 134–6; Co. Sligo chancery inquisition, James I, no. 4, 26 Apr. 1609 (N.L.I., MS 2163); B.L., Harl. MS 2048, f. 149d).

50. *The Book of O'Hara*, ed., Lambert McKenna (Dublin, 1951); *A.F.M.*, i, pp lv–lxiv.

51. See O'Dowd, 'Landownership in the Sligo area', chapters 6–11.

52. O'Hara MSS (N.L.I., unsorted). See also p. 88.

53. O Bric, 'Galway townsmen as owners of land in Connacht, 1585–1641', pp 247–8.

54. O'Cunnegan's tenancy can be traced through an examination of the Tirerrill section of the survey.

55. De Freyne papers (N.L.I., unsorted).

56. P.R.O., S.P. 63/158/14.

57. See pp 50–53 above.

58. Book of matters against Sir Richard Bingham, 29 Aug. 1589 (P.R.O., S.P. 63/147/18i); matters of complaint exhibited at Sligo against Sir George Bingham *c.* Aug. 1589 (P.R.O., S.P. 63/147/6).

59. Allingham, *Captain Cuellar*, p. 58.

60. Ibid., p. 60; *Another extract of several letters from Ireland intimating their present state* . . . (London, 1643), pp 20–1, 36–7, 38.

61. 'Answers of George Bingham to the . . . articles . . . against him . . .', *c.* Aug. 1589 (P.R.O., S.P. 63/147/2i, 4). See also *Cal. S.P. Ire., 1586–8*, p. 189 for reference to Ballymote market in 1586.

62. See list in *Report of the commissioners appointed to inquire into the state of the fairs and markets in Ireland*, H.C. 1852–3 (1674), xli, appx, pp 106–7.

63. *Cal. pat. rolls Ire., Jas I*, pp 20–4. See also B.L., Harl. MS 2048, f. 170d for the grant of land by the O'Dowds to a MacDonnell to 'be their usual carpenter or mason about their works'.

64. Allingham, *Captain Cuellar*, p. 64.

65. See chapter 7.

Chapter 6: New landlords in County Sligo, *c.* 1585–1641 (pp 89–104)

1. P.R.O., S.P. 63/195/22; T.C.D., MS 570, ff 34–70; B.L., Harl. MS 2048.

2. O'Dowd, 'Landownership in the Sligo area', pp 147–50.

3. Ibid., pp 154–6.

4. Ibid., p. 164; Co.Sligo exchequer inquisition, Eliz., no. 4, 17 Mar. 1585 (P.R.O.I., R.C. 9/15).

5. O'Dowd, 'Landownership in the Sligo area', pp 147–50; H. T. Crofton, *Crofton memoirs* (York, 1911), pp 43–77.

6. Forfeiture of land can be traced through the inquisitions (see pp 47–8 above and O'Dowd, 'Landownership in the Sligo area', pp 125–7, 145–52).

7. Ibid., pp 160–2, 251–3.

8. T. O. Ranger, 'Richard Boyle and the making of an Irish fortune 1588–1614' in *I.H.S.*, x (1957), pp 257–97.

9. Ibid. and O'Dowd, 'Landownership in the Sligo area', pp 145–68, for a more detailed analysis.

10. B.L., Harl. MS 2048. For examples of Cork's mortgages see ff 130f, 157d.

11. De Freyne papers (N.L.I., unsorted).

12. Brendan Ó Bric, 'Galway townsmen as owners of land in Connacht, 1585–1641' (unpublished M.A. thesis, University College, Galway, 1974), pp 367–8.

13. De Freyne papers (N.L.I., unsorted).

14. Ibid. and pp 115–16, 162 below.

15. The figures are calculated from B.L., Harl. MS 2048. See O'Dowd, 'Landownership in the Sligo area', chapters 6–11, for a more detailed analysis.

16. B.L., Harl. MS 2048, f. 181d. See also pp 122, 123, 127 below.
17. See O'Dowd, 'Landownership in the Sligo area', pp 239–40.
18. P.R.O., S.P. 63/145/12v; S.P. 63/147/3,6; S.P. 63/195/22.
19. O'Dowd, 'Landownership in the Sligo area', p. 432; salved chancery pleadings (P.R.O.I., C.P. BB, 78).
20. B.L., Harl MS 2048, ff 183f,d, 184d. See p. 75 above. See also Kenneth Nicholls, *Gaelic and gaelicised Ireland in the middle ages* (Dublin, 1972), p. 58, for the occupation of waste land.
21. *Cal. S.P. Ire., 1615–25*, p. 285.
22. See pp 74–5 above.
23. O'Dowd, 'Landownership in the Sligo area', pp 239–40, 317–28, 331, 397–8, 401–4.
24. Ibid., pp 396–7; rental of lands of Ballymote, 1585–91 (P.R.O., S.P. 63/158/14); answer of George Bingham to complaints of David O'Dowd, *c.* Aug. 1589 (ibid., S.P. 63/147/21).
25. See B.L., Harl. MS 2048, ff 252f–268f.
26. Ibid., ff 196d–198d; O'Dowd, 'Landownership in the Sligo area', pp 321–6.
27. O'Dowd, 'Landownership in the Sligo area', pp 404–5; B.L., Harl. MS 2048, ff 253f,d.
28. B.L., Harl. MS 2048, ff 252f–268f; Joyce Youings, *Sixteenth-century England* (Penguin, 1984), pp 54–5; G. E. Mingay, *The gentry: the rise and fall of a ruling class* (London, 1976), pp 12–13.
29. B.L., Harl. MS 2048, ff 183f, 184d, 256d, 257d, 258f,d, 265d.
30. *Memoirs of the family of Taaffe* (privately published, Vienna, 1856), pp 6–12.
31. Genealogical Office, Dublin, MS 172.
32. O'Dowd, 'Landownership in the Sligo area', pp 321–6; George Boyle to Richard Boyle, 2 Aug. 1617 (N.L.I., MS 13236 (11)); William Taaffe to George Boyle, 11 Dec. 1614 (calendared in N.L.I., MS 12813); George Boyle to Richard Boyle, 6 Nov. 1617 (ibid.); *Memoirs of the family of Taaffe*, pp 6–12.
33. T.C.D., MS 672f, 180d. See pp 59–60 above.
34. *Crofton memoirs* provides information on all the branches of the family in the west of Ireland.
35. B.L., Harl. MS. 2048, f. 153d. See also ff 152f,d.
36. Ibid., ff 152d, 161d.
37. Ibid., ff 152f–153d; O'Dowd, 'Landownership in the Sligo area', pp 469–70; *Cal. pat. rolls Ire., Jas I*, p. 391.
38. *Crofton memoirs*, pp 271–6.
39. Ibid., p. 275.
40. O'Dowd, 'Landownership in the Sligo area', pp 164–6, 247–50, 480–1; section on Carbury and Leyny in B.L., Harl. MS 2048, ff 129f–159d; Genealogical Office, Dublin, MS 69, p. 310.; O'Rorke, *Sligo*, i, 461.
41. B.L., Harl. MS 2048, f. 133f.
42. See pp 151–4, 157–8 below
43. Genealogical Office, Dublin, MS 69, p. 310 (both Jones's children were illegitimate); O'Dowd, 'Landownership in the Sligo area', pp 480–1; O'Rorke, *Sligo*, i, 253–4.
44. Deposition of John Ridge, 11 Mar. 1643 (T.C.D., MS 830, ff 14–15).
45. See pp 154–8 below.
46. O'Rorke, *Sligo*, i, 301–4.
47. *An extract of several letters from Ireland, intimating their present state* . . . (London, 1643), pp 22–3. See also *The information of Sir Frederick Hamilton . . . concerning Sir William Cole* (London, 1645).

48. B.L., Harl. MS 2048, f. 181f. See also pp 107–8 below.
49. Deposition of William Brown, 8 Jan. 1644 (Wood–Martin, *Sligo*, ii, 198–202).
50. Deposition of Henry Dodwell, 25 Feb. 1642 (ibid., pp 194–7).
51. See Books of Survey and Distribution for Co. Sligo (Annesley set, P.R.O.N.I., D1854/1/19).
52. B.L., Harl. MS 2048, ff 142d–151f, 160f–172f.
53. Depositions of Henry Langford, Robert and James Brown, 18 July 1643 (T.C.D., MS 830, ff 36–7); deposition of Richard O'Crean, 24 May 1653 (Wood-Martin, *Sligo*, ii, 252–3).
54. Deposition of Henry Langford and Robert Brown (loc. cit.); deposition of Amy Hawkesworth, 16 Oct. 1644 (T.C.D., MS 830, ff 39–41).
55. Raymond Gillespie, *Colonial Ulster* (Cork, 1985), p. 39.
56. T.C.D., MSS 830–1.
57. Wood-Martin, *Sligo*, ii, 205–9, 212–14.
58. Gordon Batho, 'Landlords in England' in Joan Thirsk (ed.), *The agrarian history of England and Wales*, vol. iv: *1500–1640* (Cambridge, 1967), p. 291; J. T. Cliffe, *The Yorkshire gentry from the reformation to the civil war* (London, 1969), pp 51–3.

Chapter 7: Rebellion and war, 1641–52 (pp 105–130)

1. This account is based on deposition evidence. The Sligo depositions were printed in Wood-Martin, *Sligo*, ii, 194–260. See also ibid., pp 33–59.
2. See pp 52–4 above.
3. See p. 53 above, and Aidan Clarke, *The Old English in Ireland, 1625–42* (Worcester and London, 1966), pp 91–110.
4. For Darcy's landholdings see B.L., Harl. MS·2048, ff 168d, 171f. For Westmeath's see p. 102 above.
5. Clarke, *Old English*, pp 33, 36, 38, 41–3, 83–4, 91–110. Patrick Darcy leased some of his Sligo land to James French, a resident of Sligo town. See also Brendan Ó Bric, 'Galway townsmen as owners of land in Connacht, 1685–1641' (unpublished M.A. thesis, University College, Galway, 1974).
6. O'Rorke, *Sligo*, ii, 105–7; H. T. Knox, *Notes on the early history of the dioceses of Tuam, Killala and Achonry* (Dublin, 1904), pp 328–9, 365–6.
7. See Robert Wyse Jackson, *Archbishop Magrath – the scoundrel of Cashel* (Cork, 1974).
8. Alan Ford, *The protestant reformation in Ireland, 1590–1641* (Frankfurt am Mein, 1985), p. 129; see also p. 81.
9. Ibid., pp 81, 135–7; T.C.D., MS 1066.
10. Ford, *Protestant reformation in Ireland*, p. 137. See also T.C.D., MS 1067, and *Cal. pat. rolls Ire., Chas I*, pp 26, 111, 316, 436, 511, 585.
11. *Cal. S.P. Ire., 1633–47*, p. 221; Richard Mant, *History of the Church of Ireland* (London, 1841), pp 542–3.
12. Ford, *Protestant reformation in Ireland*, pp 136–7; *Cal. S.P., Ire., 1633–47*, pp 189–90; petition of Randolph Barlow, archbishop of Tuam, Edward King, bishop of Elphin et al. to Lord Deputy Wentworth, n.d. (Sheffield Central Library, Wentworth–Woodhouse MS 20 (144)).
13. K. W. Nicholls, 'Rectory, vicarage and parish in the western Irish dioceses' in *R.S.A.I. Jn.*, ci (1971), pp 53–70.
14. Orders for the ecclesiastical commissioners in Ireland (B.L., Harl. MS 4297, f. 70). See also other Sligo examples in the same volume (ff 31, 41, 47, 65, 69, 73, 88, 89, 104–5).
15. For a summary of eighteenth-century agrarian agitation against changes in the tithe system see David Dickson, *New foundations: Ireland, 1660–1800* (Dublin, 1987), pp 132–4.

16. See p. 119 below.

17. *Memoirs and letters of Ulick, marquis of Clanricarde* (London, 1657), p. 59.

18. O'Rorke, *Sligo*, i, 259–64; P. F. Moran (ed.), *Spicilegium Ossoriense* (1st series, Dublin, 1874), pp 158–9; Brendan Jennings, 'Brussels MS 3947: Donatus Moneyus de provincia Hiberniae S. Francisci, c. 1616–18' in *Anal. Hib.*, vi (1934), pp 27, 48–9, 104.

19. Donal Cregan, 'The social and cultural background of a counter-reformation episcopate, 1618–60' in Art Cosgrove and Donal McCartney (eds), *Studies in Irish history presented to R. Dudley Edwards* (Dublin, 1979), pp 85–117.

20. E. A. D'Alton, *History of the archdiocese of Tuam* (2 vols, Dublin, 1928), i, 249–55; O. J. Burke, *The history of the catholic archbishops of Tuam* (Dublin, 1882), p. 121; *Cal. S.P. Ire., 1633–47*, pp 308–9.

21. D'Alton, *Tuam*, pp 254–5.

22. See, e.g., order of Tadhg O'Connor Sligo printed in *Another extract of several letters from Ireland intimating their present state* (London, 1643), p. 51.

23. Aidan Clarke, 'The breakdown of authority, 1640–41' in *N.H.I.*, iii, 270–6.

24. List of new army, endorsed 23 Apr. 1640 (Bodl., Carte MS 1, f. 183).

25. 'Heads of what has been done . . . by the council of war . . . April 1640' (ibid., ff 179–80); Charles Coote to Ormond, 1 Sept. 1640 (ibid., f. 243).

26. Strafford to Ormond, [1640] (ibid., ff 307–8). For fear of army in England see *The journal of Sir Simond D'Ewes*, ed. Wallace Notestein (New Haven and London, 1923), pp 14, 346–7, 229–31.

27. Charles I to Ormond, 8 May 1641 (Bodl., Carte MS 1, f. 381).

28. Ibid.

29. Clarke, *Old English*, pp 154–5.

30. Ibid., pp 155–6; *Clanricarde memoirs*, pp 1, 4–5, 17.

31. See pp 115, 117–8 below.

32. Clarke, *Old English*, p. 156. See also Aidan Clarke, 'The genesis of the Ulster rising of 1641' in Peter Roebuck (ed.), *Plantation to partition* (Belfast, 1981), pp 29–45; Jerrold Casway, *Owen Roe O'Neill and the struggle for catholic Ireland* (Philadelphia, 1984), pp 42–50.

33. J. T. Gilbert, *Ir. confed.*, i, 217–9; *Report on the manuscripts of the earl of Egmont* (Historical Manuscripts Commission, London, 1905), i, 141. See also T.C.D., MS 809, ff 122ff.

34. Deposition of Patrick Dowd, 25 Nov. 1652 (Wood-Martin, *Sligo*, ii, 219–20); deposition of Oliver Albanagh, 18 May 1653 (ibid., pp 220–2).

35. Ibid.

36. The poor pay and conditions for the soldiers in the new army must also have contributed to their frustration (See Ormond to Sir Henry Vane, 10 June 1641 (Bodl., Carte MS 1, f. 426); Charles Coote to Ormond, n.d (ibid., f. 278); Edward Chichester to Ormond, 4 May 1641 (ibid., f. 379); Sergeant Pleisley to Ormond, 10 May 1641 (ibid., f. 385). See also Michael Perceval-Maxwell, 'The Ulster rising of 1641, and the depositions' in *I.H.S.*, xxi (1978), p. 155.)

37. See note 34 above.

38. Cited in James Touchet, earl of Castlehaven, *Memoirs of James, Lord Audley, earl of Castlehaven* (Dublin, 1815), pp 17–18.

39. De Freyne papers (N.L.I., unsorted).

40. Ibid.

41. Ibid. *Cal. S.P. Ire., 1633–47*, p. 312; H. F. Kearney, *Strafford in Ireland, 1633–41: a study in absolutism* (Manchester), pp 225–6; Clarke, *Old English*, p. 138; Thomas Carte, *An history of the life of James, first duke of Ormonde* (6 vols, Oxford, 1851), v, 516–17; De Freyne papers (N.L.I., unsorted).

42. See p. 60 above.
43. Deposition of Oliver Albanagh (Wood-Martin, *Sligo*, ii, 220–1.
44. *Another extract of several letters from Ireland . . .*, p. 18.
45. Depositions of Patrick Dowd and Oliver Albanagh (Wood-Martin, *Sligo*, ii, 219–22).
46. See note 30 above.
47. *Clanricarde memoirs*, pp 12–14, 17.
48. Deposition of Oliver Albanagh (Wood-Martin, *Sligo*, ii, 221).
49. Deposition of William Walsh, 28 Feb. 1644 (ibid., pp 205–9); deposition of John Harrison, 14 Jan. 1644 (ibid., pp 210–11); deposition of John Crean, 14 May 1653 (ibid., pp 244–6); deposition of Jane Boswell, 16 Apr. 1653 (ibid., pp 232–4); deposition of Mrs Christian Oliphant, 3 Feb. 1646 (ibid., pp 217–18).
50. Clarke, *Old English*, pp 193–4.
51. See depositions of John and Peter Crean, 14, 18 May 1653 (Wood-Martin, *Sligo*, ii, pp 244–6).
52. Depositions of John Crean and Owen O'Rourke, 17 May 1653 (ibid., pp 249–51); *Another extract of several letters from Ireland . . .*, pp 45–6.
53. Carte, *Ormonde*, v, 269–70.
54. Deposition of Mrs Christopher Oliphant (Wood-Martin, *Sligo*, ii, 217); deposition of Jane Boswell (ibid., pp 232–4).
55. Ibid.; deposition of Ann Loftus, 16 Apr. 1653 (ibid., pp 239–40); deposition of Rose Ennis, 16 Apr. 1653 (ibid., pp 240–1); deposition of Jane Brown, 8 Jan. 1644 (ibid., pp 204–5). See also Ciarán Ó Murchadha, 'Land and society in seventeenth-century Clare' (unpublished Ph.D. thesis, University College, Galway, 1982), pp 50–6.
56. This account is based on depositions printed in Wood-Martin, *Sligo*, ii, 194–260.
57. *Another extract of several letters from Ireland . . .*, pp 16–24.
58. *Clanricarde memoirs*, pp 10–11, 32, 37, 52; Carte, *Ormonde*, v, 270–1, 283–5.
59. *Another extract of several letters from Ireland . . .*, p. 23.
60. Mary Hickson, *Ireland in the seventeenth century* (2 vols, London, 1884), i, 376.
61. Viscount Ranelagh to Ormond, 20 Feb. 1643 (Bodl., Carte MS 4, f. 400).
62. Bodl., Carte MS 5, f. 145; Carte, *Ormonde*, v, 447–8; deposition of William Walsh, 28 Feb. 1644 (Wood-Martin, *Sligo*, ii, 207–9); deposition of Edward Braxton, 8 Jan. 1644 (ibid., pp 197–8).
63. *Clanricarde memoirs*, pp 6–7.
64. Gilbert, *Contemporary hist., 1641–52*, i, 379–80.
65. Hickson, *Ireland in the seventeenth century*, i, 377–8. See also pp 127–8 below.
66. See p. 116 above.
67. Letter dated 13 Dec. 1641 (printed in *Another extract of several letters from Ireland . . .*, p. 51.
68. See pp 76, 90, 95–7 above.
69. Gilbert, *Ir. confed.*, i, 94–5; deposition of Walter Burke, 11 Dec. 1642 (T.C.D., MS 831, ff 171–3). See also letter from assembly at Ballinrobe, 15 Sept. 1642 (*Another extract of several letters from Ireland . . .*, pp 257–8).
70. For Taaffe see *D.N.B.*; see also Timothy Crist (ed.), *Charles II to Lord Taaffe: letters in exile* (Cambridge, 1974). For O'Hara see pp 58, 74–5 above.
71. Deposition of William Brown, 8 Jan. 1632 (Wood-Martin, *Sligo*, ii, 201–2); deposition of Walter Burke (T.C.D., MS 831, ff 171–3).
72. *Another extract of several letters from Ireland . . .*, pp 52–3.
73. *Clanricarde memoirs* , p. 75.
74. See, e.g., Hickson, *Ireland in the seventeenth century*, ii, 4.
75. Depositon of Andrew Adair, 9 Jan. 1643 (T.C.D., MS 831, ff 177d–178f).

76. Hickson, *Ireland in the seventeenth century*, ii, 5.
77. In Connacht it was only in Leitrim that the rebels, who had supported the northern rebellion from the beginning, claimed that they had the king's warrant to dispossess Englishmen (County Leitrim depositions in T.C.D., MS 831).
78. Deposition of Walter Burke (T.C.D., MS 831, f. 171).
79. See order, 12 Mar. 1643 (printed in *Another extract of several letters from Ireland . . .*, pp 48–9).
80. *Clanricarde memoirs*, pp 161–2; John Lowe (ed.), *Letter-book of the earl of Clanricarde, 1643–47* (Irish Manuscripts Commission, Dublin, 1983), pp 56–7.
81. Carte, *Ormonde*, vi, 239–41; Gilbert, *Ir. confed.*, ii, 122–4; iv, 152–3; *Clanricarde letter-book*, p. 146.
82. *Another extract of several letters from Ireland . . .*, pp 21–55; deposition of Ann Frere (T.C.D., MS 830, f. 32); deposition of Tomultagh Murry McDonogh (ibid., f. 60f).
83. Gilbert, *Irish confed.*, ii, 372–3; iii, 92–4, 125–6, 162–5, 196–8; *Clanricarde letter-book*, pp 22, 26, 49–50, 70–2, 74–5, 84, 120–1, 128–34; Carte, *Ormonde*, vi, 92–4, 135–6. For the general background see Richard Bagwell, *Ireland under the Stuarts* (3 vols, London, 1909–16), ii, 56–9, and Casway, *Owen Roe O'Neill*, pp 98–100.
84. Gilbert, *Ir. confed.*, iii, 139–42.
85. Petition of Theobald, Viscount Taaffe [Feb. 1644] (Bodl., Carte MS 14, f. 67); *Clanricarde letter-book*, pp 46, 48–51, 66–7; Gilbert, *Ir. confed.*, ii, liii; Casway, *Owen Roe O'Neill*, pp 84–5, 120, 136.
86. *Clanricarde letter-book*, pp 138, 145.
87. *Castlehaven memoirs*, pp 85–6; Gilbert, *Ir. confed.*, iii, 149–50; iv, 152–3; *Clanricarde letter-book*, pp 76–7, 145–9; Carte, *Ormonde*, vi, 127–9, 239–41.
88. Wood-Martin, *Sligo*, ii, 75–84; Bagwell, *Stuarts*, ii, 95–6; Gilbert, *Ir. confed.*, iv, 353–6; Sir James Dillon to Ormond, 5 July 1645 (Bodl., Carte MS 15, ff 209–10); same to same, 11 July 1645 (ibid., f. 224); Gerald Dillon to Ulick Burke, 9 July 1645 (ibid., f. 238); Robert Ward to [ ], 17 July 1645 (ibid., f. 268).
89. Charles I to Viscount Taaffe, 24 June 1645 (Bodl., Carte MS 15, f. 114); see also other correspondence ibid., 324–578; Gilbert, *Ir. confed.*, iv, 16–18; *Clanricarde letter-book*, pp 168–71, 182–6, 188–90.
90. Gilbert, *Ir. confed*, vi, 446.
91. See *Clanricarde letter-book*, pp 170–1.
92. Gilbert, *Ir. confed.*, vi, 289–91.
93. Edmund Hogan (ed.), *The history of the warr of Ireland from 1641 to 1653. By a British officer of the regiment of Sir John Clotworthy* (Dublin, 1873), p. 58; see also Casway, *Owen Roe O'Neill*, pp 184–7.
94. O'Rorke, *Sligo*, i, 172–3; Gilbert, *Ir. confed.*, vii, 120; Gilbert, *Contemp. hist., 1641–52*, iii, 222–3.
95. Wood-Martin, *Sligo*, ii, 83–85; Robert Dunlop (ed.), *Ireland under the commonwealth* (Manchester, 1913), pp 173–4, 222, 232–3, 236–9; Gilbert, *Contemp. hist., 1641–52*, iii, 120, 307–9, 322, 330–3.

Chapter 8: Land and society, 1652–88 (pp 131–42)

1. P. J. Corish, 'The Cromwellian conquest, 1649–53' in *N.H.I.*, iii, 336–86; J. P. Prendergast, *The Cromwellian settlement of Ireland* (Dublin, 1922), pp 101–2.
2. Dunlop, *Ireland under the commonwealth*, pp 375–6, 410, 524, 616; *Cal. S.P. Ire., 1647–60*, pp 687–9.
3. Ibid.; N.L.I., MS 758, ff 72–3, 88, 103; B.L., Add. MS 33589, f. 87.
4. Dunlop, *Ireland under the commonwealth*, pp 380–3, 507–8, 559.

5. Ibid., 397–8; Wood-Martin, *Sligo*, iii, 3–6; Gilbert, *Contemp. hist., 1641–52*, iii, 350–5.

6. T. A. Larcom, *History of the survey of Ireland* (Dublin, 1851), pp 66, 71–75.

7. *Cal. S.P. Ire., 1633–47*, p. 596 (19 Jan. 1647).

8. Dunlop, *Ireland under the commonwealth*, pp 363–5.

9. Ibid., pp 355–9, 427.

10. Gilbert, *Contemp. hist., 1641–52*, iii, 350–5.

11. Larcom, *History of the survey of Ireland*, pp 66, 71–5; R. C. Simington (ed.), *The transplantation to Connacht, 1654–58* (Irish Manuscripts Commission, Dublin, 1970), pp xii–xiii, xxi; Bagwell, *Ireland under the Stuarts* (3 vols, London, 1909–16), ii, 338; *Cal. S.P. Ire., 1647–60*, p. 622; De Freyne papers (N.L.I., unsorted).

12. For Coote's career see *D.N.B.* See also P. A. Morris, 'Ormond's army: the Irish standing army, 1640–1669, with special reference to personnel and administration after the restoration' (unpublished Ph.D. thesis, Vanderbilt University, Tennessee, 1980).

13. Simington, *Transplantation to Connacht*, pp 86, 102, 112, 154, 194, 195, 202, 210, 217, 261.

14. See, e.g., Dunlop, *Ireland under the commonwealth*, pp 569–70; Prendergast, *Cromwellian settlement of Ireland*, pp 569–70.

15. Most of the documents in the De Freyne papers (N.L.I., unsorted) relate to the legal argument in the 1660s concerning the ownership of the O'Connor Sligo estate. See also pp 115–7 above.

16. Ibid.; T. C. Barnard, *Cromwellian Ireland: English government and reform in Ireland, 1649–1660* (Oxford, 1975), p. 70n. Browne never took his seat, as a new election was called and he was defeated. I am grateful to Dr Jane Olhmeyer for discussing Browne's career with me.

17. See, e.g., B.L., Eg. MS 212, f. 9d, for payment to transport Lord Taaffe's regiment to Spain. See also Dunlop, *Ireland under the commonwealth*, p. 198.

18. Eva Butler to Kean O'Hara, 22 Apr. 1671 (P.R.O.N.I., O'Hara MS T2812/2); Wood-Martin, *Sligo*, ii, 94–140; O'Rorke, *Sligo*, i, 209–21.

19. De Freyne papers (N.L.I., unsorted); *Cal. S.P. Ire., 1660– 62*, p. 259; *Cal. S.P. Ire., 1663–5*, pp 613–14; O'Rorke, *Sligo*, i, 201–2.

20. *Cal. S.P. Ire., 1660–62*, pp 125–6, 246, 282–3, 453, 552–3; B.L., Eg. MS 789, ff 28, 32, 34, 37, 47, 63, 68. For Theophilus Jones see *D.N.B.*

21. Books of Survey and Distribution for Co. Sligo (Annesley set, P.R.O.N.I., D1854/1/19); Wood-Martin, *Sligo*, ii, 271–86.

22. Details of family histories can be found in O'Rorke, *Sligo* and Wood-Martin, *Sligo*, and relevant manuscripts in the Geneaological Office, Dublin (see R. J. Hayes (ed.), *Manuscript sources for the history of Irish civilisation* (14 vols, Boston, 1965–75)).

23. Based on analysis of 1662 hearth money roll (N.L.I., MS 2165; edited by Edward MacLysaght in *Anal. Hib.*, xxiv (1967), pp 1–89).

24. O'Rorke, *Sligo*, ii 14–15.

25. T. C. Barnard, 'Planters and policies in Cromwellian Ireland' in *Past and Present*, lxi (1973), pp 31–69.

26. Thomas Bartlett, 'The O'Haras of Annaghmore *c.* 1600–*c.* 1800: survival and revival' in *Ir. Econ. & Soc. Hist.*, ix (1982), pp 34–52.

27. Viscount Ranelagh to Ormond, 20 Feb. 1643 (Bodl., Carte MS 4, f. 400); James Dillon to Ormond, 24 May 1645 (ibid., MS 14, f. 583); *Clanricarde letter-book*, pp 241–2; *Cal. S. P. Ire., 1660–62*, pp 125–6; *Crofton memoirs*, pp 134–6, 271–3, 362–3; *Memoirs of the Taaffe family*, pp 14–15.

28. O'Rorke, *Sligo*, i, 461–2.

29. *Ormonde MSS*, o.s., i, 240–1, 244–5, 261, 266, 274–6, 348–51, 351–4.
30. F. J. Riegler, 'Anglo-Irish catholics, the army of Ireland, and the Jacobite war' (unpublished Ph.D. thesis, Temple University, 1983), pp 31–9; J. C. Beckett, 'The Irish armed forces, 1660–1685' in John Bossy and Peter Jupp (eds), *Essays presented to Michael Roberts* (Belfast, 1976), pp 41–53.
31. P. A. Morris, 'Ormond's army', pp 98ff; *Cal. S. P. Ire., 1660–62*, pp 3, 18–19, 232, 265–6,; *Cal. S. P. Ire., 1666–9*, p. 32; Wood-Martin, *Sligo*, iii, 430, 434; N.L.I., MS 758, f. 69; *Ormonde MSS*, o.s., ii, 337–8, 352–4.
32. Wood-Martin, *Sligo*, ii, 102; W. G. Wood-Martin, *Sligo and the Enniskilleners from 1688–1691* (Dublin, 1880), pp 31–3; O'Rorke, *Sligo*, i, 212.
33. Riegler, 'Anglo-Irish catholics, the army of Ireland, and the Jacobite war', pp 82, 84, 113–14, 115, 150–1, 252, 303.
34. See note 23 above; *A census of Ireland circa 1659, with supplementary material from the poll money ordinances (1660–61)*, ed. Séamus Pender (Irish Manuscripts Commission, Dublin, 1939), pp 597–607.
35. J. G. Simms, *War and politics in Ireland, 1649–1730* (London, 1986), p. 310.
36. D. M. Waterman, 'Some Irish seventeenth-century houses and their architectural ancestry' in E. M. Jope (ed.), *Studies in building history* (London, 1961), pp 251–74.
37. P.R.O.N.I., T2812/10, p. 6.
38. N.L.I., Report on private papers, no. 493 (O'Hara MSS), pp 288, 292.
39. P.R.O.N.I., T2812/10.
40. Ibid.

Chapter 9: Conclusion (pp 143–48)

1. Wood-Martin, *Sligo*, iii, 13; see also pp 7–12, 14.
2. J. C. McTernan, *Here's to their memory* (Dublin and Cork, 1977), pp 161–4.
3. Wood-Martin, *Sligo*, iii, 51; see also pp 37–62; H. D. Inglis, *A journey through Ireland, during the spring, summer and autumn of 1834* (4th ed., London, 1836), pp 269–77.
4. W. B. Yeats, *Autobiographies* (London, 1966), p. 14; W. M. Murphy, *The Yeats family and the Pollexfens of Sligo* (Dublin, 1971), p. 87.

Appendix: Urban growth and development: Sligo town (pp 149–64)

1. Geoffrey Martin, 'Plantation boroughs in medieval Ireland, with a handlist of boroughs to *c.* 1500' in D. W. Harkness and Mary O'Dowd (eds), *The town in Ireland* (Belfast, 1981), p. 50; O'Rorke, *Sligo*, i, 68–81; Wood-Martin, *Sligo*, i, 191–5.
2. T. J. Westropp, 'Early Italian maps of Ireland from 1300 to 1600, with notes on foreign settlers and trade' in *R.I.A. Proc.*, xxx, sect. C (1913), pp 366, 412; Timothy O'Neill, *Merchants and mariners in medieval Ireland* (Dublin, 1987), p. 114; E. M. Carus-Wilson, 'The overseas trade of Bristol' in Eileen Power and M. M. Postan (eds), *Studies in English trade in the fifteenth century* (London, 1933), p. 196; Wendy Childs and Timothy O'Neill, 'Overseas trade' in *N.H.I.*, ii, 505; Wendy Childs, 'Ireland's trade with England in the later middle ages' in *Ir. Econ. & Soc. Hist. Jn.*, ix (1982), p. 11.
3. O'Neill, *Merchants and mariners*, pp 30, 71.
4. Ibid., p. 39.
5. Ibid., pp 48, 86.
6. Ibid., pp 36, 41; O'Rorke, *Sligo*, i, 241–52; Gearóid Mac Niocaill, *Na Manaigh Liatha in Éirinn, 1142 – c. 1600* (Dublin, 1959), pp 67–70, 73–4.

7. O'Dowd, 'Landownership in the Sligo area', pp 49–50.

8. See pp 20–25 above.

9. See, e.g., James Hardiman, *History of the town and county of the town of Galway* (Dublin, 1820), p. 68.

10. Sir N. Malby to Sir F. Walsingham, 10 Nov. 1577 (P.R.O., S.P. 63/59/43; Sir R. Bingham to Walsingham, 21 Dec. 1584 (ibid., S.P. 63/113/31).

11. Sir Henry Sidney and others to Queen Elizabeth, 12 Nov. 1566 (ibid., S.P. 63/19/43).

12. O'Neill, *Merchants and mariners.*

13. Sir O. Lambert to Sir G. Carey, 26 June 1602 (P.R.O., S.P. 63/211/61c).

14. *Cal. S.P. Ire., 1603–6*, pp 435–7; *Cal. S.P. Ire., 1611–14*, pp 293–4; *Cal. Pat. rolls Ire., Jas I*, p. 518.

15. Wood-Martin, *Sligo*, ii, 194–260.

16. See pp 99–101 above; O'Rorke, *Sligo*, i, 301–4.

17. P.R.O., E190/941/7, f. 10d. I am grateful to Mr R. J. Hunter for this and other references to Sligo in the port books. For burghers and merchants of the staple of Sligo see O'Rorke, *Sligo*, i, 320.

18. Philip Robinson, *The plantation of Ulster* (Dublin, 1984), pp 95–6, 118–19.

19. Wood-Martin, *Sligo*, ii, 197–8, 205–6, 209, 212.

20. R.I.A., MS 14 D 13; N.L.I., MS 10223.

21. *Cal. pat. rolls Ire., Jas I*, pp 481, 518; O'Rorke, *Sligo*, i, 320; Wood-Martin, *Sligo*, ii, 244.

22. *Cal. pat. rolls Ire., Jas I*, pp 260, 518; B.L., Add. MS 19843.

23. Based on Sheffield Central Library, Wentworth–Woodhouse MS 24–5 (174); B.L., Harl. MS 2048, f. 42; P.R.O., S.P. 63/259, ff 215–24; H. F. Kearney, 'The Irish wine trade, 1614–15' in *I.H.S.*, ix (1955), pp 400–42.

24. P.R.O., E190/942/12, ff 6d, 23f,d, 27f,d. See also J. J. Bourhis, *Le trafic du port de Dartmouth, 1599–1641* (2 vols, Brest, 1972).

25. E.g. pardons granted to Sir Roger Jones and others, 27 June, 26 Oct. 1634 (P.R.O., T/1/6535c).

26. P.R.O., H.C.A. 13/56, ff 64–6. I am grateful to Dr John C. Appleby for this and other references to Sligo in the records of the high court of admiralty.

27. Examination dated 9 Aug. 1646 (P.R.O., H.C.A. 13/60); *Another extract of several letters from Ireland intimating their present state* (London, 1643), p. 37.

28. See, e.g., Kearney, 'The Irish wine trade, 1614–15', p. 417.

29. Examination dated 25 July 1644 (P.R.O., H.C.A. 13/59, ff 399d–400d, 402d, 407f.

30. Ibid., E190/945/10; E190/949/1, ff 5f, 12d.

31. Ibid., E190/1330/11, f. 17.

32. P.R.O.I., R.C. 12/1, f. 49.

33. See depositions printed in Wood-Martin, *Sligo*, ii, 194–260.

34. P.R.O.I., C.P., G, no. 35.

35. R. J. Hunter, 'Towns in the Ulster plantation' in *Studia Hib.*, xi (1971), pp 54–5.

36. R. J. Hunter, 'Ulster plantation towns, 1609–41' in Harkness and O'Dowd, *The town in Ireland*, p. 61.

37. *Cal. pat. rolls Ire., Jas I*, p. 164.

38. *A census of Ireland circa 1659, with supplementary material from the poll money ordinances (1660–1661)*, ed. Séamus Pender (Irish Manuscripts Commission, Dublin, 1939), pp 597–607; N.L.I., MS 10223.

39. See pp 131, 139–40 and references above.

40. N.L.I., MS 10223; R.I.A., MS 14 D 13.

41. J. G. Simms, *War and politics in Ireland, 1649–1730* (London, 1986), pp 307–16.

42. See note 40 above and W. G. Wood-Martin, *Sligo and the Enniskilleners froom 1688–1691* (2nd ed., Dublin, 1882), pp 189–208; N.L.İ., MS 3137, pt 3.
43. For a description of the building of the fort see B.L., Add. MS 33589, f. 87.
44. Wood-Martin, *Sligo and the Enniskilleners* (2nd ed.), pp 189–208.
45. *Cal. S.P. Ire., 1663–5*, pp 460–1, 693–8; *Cal. S.P. Ire., 1666–9*, pp 672–3; *Cal. S.P. Ire., 1669–70*, p. 683.
46. Wood-Martin, *Sligo*, ii, 99.
47. John Mackenzie, *A narrative of the siege of Londonderry* (London, 1690), p. 16.
48. P.R.O.N.I., T2812/10.
49. See, e.g., P.R.O., E190/959, f. 6; E190/1137/3, ff 12f,d, 43f, 66f.
50. B.L., Add. MS 4759.
51. P.R.O., E190/953/6, f. 11d; E190/954/4, f. 11d; E190/1038/8 (11 July 1668); E190/1038/12 (8, 14, 22 Aug. 1668); E190/1041/14. For Powell's house in Sligo see N.L.I., MS 10223, f. 10.
52. P.R.O., E190/1137/3, ff 12f,d, 27d, 29d, 35d, 43f, 66f, 102d.
53. *Cal. S.P. Ire., 1660–62*, pp 128–30; P.R.O.N.I., T2812/10, p. 6.
54. P.R.O.N.I., T2812/10, p. 6.
55. N.L.I., MS 10223, ff 1–2.
56. Wood-Martin, *Sligo and the Enniskilleners* (2nd ed.), p. 205; N.L.I., MS 10223.
57. L. M. Cullen, 'Galway merchants in the outside world, 1650–1800' in Diarmuid Ó Cearbhaill (ed.), *Galway: town and gown, 1484–1984* (Dublin, 1984), pp 63–89.
58. N.L.I., MS 10223; R.I.A., MS 14 D 13.
59. Ibid. For tokens see Wood-Martin, *Sligo*, ii, 95–6; iii, 172–3 and p. 147 above.
60. L. M. Cullen, 'The Dublin merchant community in the eighteenth century' in Paul Butel and L. M. Cullen (eds), *Cities and merchants: French and Irish perspectives on urban development, 1500–1900* (Dublin, 1986), pp 199–200.
61. M. Ó Duigeanáin, 'Three seventeenth-century Connacht documents', in *Galway Arch. Soc. Jn.*, xvii (1937), p. 154. I am grateful to Mr John Bradley for permission to consult his report on Sligo for the Urban Archaeology Survey.

INDEX